LB
41
H663

Current printing (last digit):
10 9 8 7 6 5 4 3 2 1

ISBN: 0-87620-320-9 (C)
ISBN: 0-87620-319-5 (P)

Library of Congress Catalog Card Number: 73-88184

Y-3209-7 (C)
Y-3195-8 (P)

Book design: Jill Casty

Printed in the United States of America

preface

Each year literally hundreds, perhaps even thousands, of books about education are published. Each one of them carries the same dream, the same conviction of author and publisher that *these* are words worth reading; indeed, that they *must* be read, or at least ought to, if the world is to improve. This preface is our opportunity as editor and publisher to explain briefly why we feel that way about THE FUTURE OF EDUCATION 1975–2000.

The idea for the book was rather straightforward: why not ask leading people in the field of education to write an essay about the future of education as they think it will be, or as they think it ought to be, or both. The response was gratifying; the result is the book you now hold.

Their work is, we think, compelling reading, fascinating reading, so much so that one of us, Ted Hipple, succumbed to his own challenge, briefly stepped out of his role as editor, and added his own thoughts to the collection. The essays contain general thoughts and specific thoughts; agreements and disagreements. Moreover, they are about the present as well as the future, for none of these men wrote in a vacuum, inventing futures out of thin air. Rather, they extrapolated from the observable present so that implicit in each essay is a vision of what's right and wrong with education right now as well as a vision of the possibilities and pitfalls waiting in the future. As you read these visions—Illich's call for the abolition of schools as we know them, Hentoff's dark view of the place unions may occupy in education's future, Weingartner's speculations on the possibilities of transcendental meditation in the curriculum—we feel certain that you will be engaged and stimulated. And concerned.

There is, after all, some urgency in this business of speculating about the future of education. Our current ecological/energy crisis has shown us that simple acts may have quite unexpected consequences and that some of those consequences can be very difficult, if not impossible, to undo. Unless we learn to anticipate such difficulties through creative speculation about the future, we may find ourselves in an educational future we did not want and do not like but cannot reasonably escape.

Alfred W. Goodyear
President, Goodyear Publishing Company

Theodore W. Hipple
editor

acknowledgements

Throughout the process of doing this book—the initial correspondence, the many telephone calls, the revision—the authors were wonderfully cooperative. I thank them for that cooperation. I thank them, too, for their exciting contributions, most of which were prepared especially for this volume.

Also richly deserving my thanks are three members of the staff of Goodyear Publishing Company: Vice President Jim Levy, who helped with the design of the project and with the selection of the contributors; Education Editor David Grady, who kept track of the contracts, the requests for permission to reprint, etc.; Production Editor Sue MacLaurin, who met a tight editing and printing schedule with grace, tact, and efficiency. Finally, I should like to thank my wife Marjorie, herself a professor of education, for her assistance and support throughout the entire project.

T.W.H.

Contents

Dwight
Allen

Dwight Allen

Dean of the College of Education at the University of Massachusetts, Dr. Allen has had an industrious career in education. Among his many contributions to the field is his book A New Design for High School Education, *which established the framework and implementation for the increasingly widespread use of flexible scheduling in secondary education. He has written widely on this and other topics and has been an active consultant with schools interested in improving their instructional practices.*

what the future of education might be

There is an old Army song about a fat little fellow who makes sausages. His name is Johnny Robeck, and he builds a sausage machine so he can make sausages more easily. Unfortunately, one day while he is inside making repairs, Johnny is accidentally ground into sausage himself. If the song contained nothing else, its only moral would be that each of us sows his own destiny—but there is more to the song. Against great protest, Johnny had been grinding into sausages all of the neighbors' cats and dogs, and it is Johnny's own wife who walks in her sleep and turns the crank while he is inside the machine. If we can learn a lesson from this more complex version of Johnny's tragedy, it is that while we do make our own destinies, it is not without getting mixed up with other people.

Likewise, shaping a future for education is impossible without acknowledging the social context of education. We can work for educational change, but we must consider that our society is already changing. Our attempts to achieve a synthesis between education and society will be fruitless if we allow the two to run off in opposite directions. As educators, we cannot run away to build our sausage machines and expect to grind up and grind out whatever suits our tastes. We must consider the cats and dogs and neighbors and wives, the economics, the politics, and the social world around us.

The greatest single problem in education today is the pervasive attitude that any interaction between education and society must be avoided. This attitude stems from the myth that education should not deal with values. Education is supposed to be objective, to take neither side of any issue, to ignore any question to which there is no single, factual, right answer. Of course, this immediately precludes education from considering any societal issues and automatically condemns education to perpetual isolation from the real world. This myth that education should not deal with values condemns education to failure for two reasons.

First, the ultimate function of education is to prepare students to be members of our society. Attempting to do this without structuring in societal interaction is as foolish as it would be for a parent to raise a child without ever exhibiting any personal desires or emotions. Children need to be brought up by parents who have definite feelings and opinions in response to themselves and to others. The child does become shaped by his parents, but also he learns to define his personal needs and to respond to the personal needs of others. Similarly, education based on values may influence students, but it also enables them to define their own beliefs about society and to respond to the beliefs of others.

Second, education—even in pretending to be value free—necessarily takes value-laden positions. The decision not to have values is a value! For example: Education values a focus which is confined to cognitive achievement. We reward a small range of abstractive, cognitive skills and ignore all other attributes—thus implicitly labeling them as inferior. These values that are built into our present educational system are dangerous, not because they are values but because they are covert. If values within education were placed on the table, they would be less insidious—perhaps they might even be examined and changed.

The greatest problem in education is the highly artificial separation between education and society that is caused by this myth about education and values. Future studies—studies of alternative futures and of the variables that determine which of these futures will occur—have revealed several alarming crises which will soon have a major impact on our already chaotic world. Forecasts such as *The Limits to Growth* (Dennis Meadows) and *An Alternative Future for America II* (Robert Theobald) sketch major world problems which we must face in the next ten to twenty years if we are to survive. The causes of these problems are inherent in the fundamental structures of our society, and so we must use education—and every other means at our disposal—to reorient society. This can only be done if the educational system is an integral part of society; as long as education remains artificially isolated, our society will be without one of its most potent tools for shaping its future.

Many of the future societal problems coming in the next thirty years can be solved *only* through education. Three examples: The population explosion will be controlled only when we decide to stop having so many children. The collapse of hierarchical techniques for administration (which will take place as our society moves to an information-based economy) will be disastrous if we do not develop and disseminate new, nonhierarchical administrative models. Adaptation to our new biological technologies can only take place through the evolution of new value systems with new ways of defining the nature of man. Clearly, education must be at the forefront of any solution to these and other major future problems.

The most frightening aspect of these problems is that by the time they are most evident, it will be too late to solve them. In fact, some less optimistic futurists compare our world to a brakeless train heading pell-mell for a missing section in the track. They say our only hope is to slow its speed, to delay the inevitable crash—they believe it is already too late to repair the break. I do not believe that we are headed for disaster no matter what we do, but I do believe that our societal values have to change quickly if we are to survive. I believe that only by moving education *immediately* from its present position outside of society to a position as a significant part of society acting for social change can we give ourselves the power to solve these future problems. Five or ten years from now may well be too late. If we want to maintain the benefits man has achieved so far, we should not gamble on holocaust. We have the power to think about tomorrow, and we still have the power to change it. We must not be indecisive while our future is being decided for us.

My model for making education a significant contributor to our civilization's dynamics looks like this: First, we need to implement new educational structures which will move the educational system back to its proper place as the hub of society. Specifically, we need to make education cross-generational, diversify and expand our nonformal educational resources, increase the number of sites where education takes place, and add a social service component to education. Second, we need to reorient educational content to a new concept of information and a new psychology of man that will be relevant to tomorrow's world. Let me expand on each of these ideas in turn.

Education must become cross-generational—a focus for interaction among all ages in society. If we seriously believed that young people could be educated only when cloistered off from persons of other ages, we would shut children away from their parents. The fact is, more learning takes place when all ages learn together than when young, middle-aged, and old are isolated. Further, we can no longer give a "forty year warranty" on the educational concepts we teach—the world is changing too quickly. Older people need to continue their education, and what better way than in conjunction with the young! I believe that education would become a much more integral part of society if youth tutored youth, young and old learned together, family units participated in common educational experiences, and nonstudents and students periodically changed places.

Clearly linked with this concept of cross-generational education is the idea of diversifying and expanding our nonformal educational resources. If children (and adults) spend more time watching television than attending school, let's make the media part of education by developing enjoyable educational programs for all ages. Newspapers, movies, and television all are major sources of societal information—we need to make them deliberate sources of diverse educational experiences as well. The major barrier to this is our system of rigid prerequisites and lockstep credentialing. Students are not allowed to learn about World War II until they've "had" the American Revolution, the Civil War, and the Depression, and if June rolls around before we get to page 842 and the year 1940, too bad. This is a strange way to prepare children for the future!

To get past this rigidity, we need to implement nonlinearity, simultaneity, and random access to education. Only by allowing students to learn what they want, when they want it, can we hope to make education self-directed, continuing, and enjoyable. Prerequisites and credentialing have always been scrapped whenever a military emergency has arisen, and no major losses in quality have ever occurred. If we can bypass credentials without harm in emergencies, we can certainly implement nonlinearity now, when we have more time to plan and control the results. As soon as we do so, our educational resources will double or triple, and will diversify as well.

A related change is to increase the number of sites where we conduct education. Schools resemble prisons and hospitals in being physically confining and crowded—and therefore unenjoyable—but education can take place anywhere in the community. An important factor in the present heavy focus of education on abstraction is the fact that our schools are physically abstract from the world. We need to base education on experience, not abstraction. We must move our education out into industries, homes, public meetings, and all the other places where society is working. This in turn may change our conceptions of educational interactions. For example, instead of courses, we might implement short-term apprenticeships between students and people in the community. Also, we can use simulated environments to enhance learning. The military and space program use extensive environmental simulation in their educational programs—why don't we?

The best vehicle for combining these three interrelated changes—cross-generational, nonformal, and location-free education—is to add a social service component to education. We need to give students a chance for participation as well as preparation. Future studies have made it abundantly clear that we need *more* than purely cognitive competence to solve tomorrow's problems—and we cannot create this transcognitive competence without building mechanisms of social involvement and service into education.

A social service component of education would be both a force for change today and a valuable preparation for students who wish to lead change in the future. Further, all students would feel less alienated from our society, and they would feel a greater sense of self-definition and self-worth if they were given a chance to make a *present* contribution to society. Requiring students to abstain from societal participation until they graduate is as foolish as training a prospective football player solely by having him listen to games on the radio.

A very important aspect of this cross-generational, nonformal, location-free social service would be that it would not be defined or judged in terms of academic equivalency. These mechanisms for involving education in society are not intended as substitutes for intellectual skills, to be judged by the same criteria as we judge courses. Rather, this would be a whole new area of education, designed to convey transcognitive skills and judged only in terms of its contributions to society. By implementing this new area, we can take the first step toward making education a significant force in shaping the future—we can move education to the hub of societal interaction.

The second step is to reorient educational content to a new concept of information and a new psychology of man. In the past, the professional was the person with the most information. However, recent technological developments (such as the computer) have destroyed forever the conception of the educated man as a Talmudic scholar or a Homeric bard who can quote any line of his knowledge on request. Professionalism as information storage is obsolete, and many other traditional functions of the professional are being taken over by machines or technicians as the professions become more routinized. In the medical profession, for example, diagnosis was once the exclusive province of the doctor—now computers and technicians are assuming many diagnostic functions. These computer-based changes in data retrieval and information access make it imperative that we find new ways of defining professionalism and that we reevaluate two things dear to almost every educator: specialization and competition.

Specialization can be a positive sign of individualization and the freedom to be different, at least at the adult level. Competition serves as a valid and healthy incentive. But too much importance is placed on these methods of accomplishing things. They have been all but deified, too often at the expense of cooperation and wholeness, both of which are indispensable to any movement for social change.

Untempered specialization can cause the wasteful isolation of good minds and the neglect of social responsibilities. The ecological destruction we have wreaked upon the world is a fine example of specialized selfishness and an inability to see an interconnectedness in life. With industries and individuals freely using up what they consider their God-given pieces of the world, we have ignored entirely the impact of our actions on the complex ecostructure that we have all but destroyed. Even today we are reluctant to meet our obvious ecological responsibilities when it means an economic loss, or even just inconvenience. We simply have not achieved a feeling of the vital interdependence in the world.

There is a universal nodding of heads when mention is made of the well-rounded individual in our colleges, and yet there is great pressure for him to choose a major and specialize! Our future society will be one of high mobility, great exchange of ideas, and faster changes than any society before it. It is essential that students understand life as the truly complex system of facts and ideas that it is. They must come to value not only specifics but the unity and interrelatedness of those specifics. In establishing priorities and weighing alternatives, they will need an acute awareness of the complexity with which they are dealing and of the repercussions that even a small change can have.

Transdisciplinary curricula are rare in our schools today. They are, in fact, usually accidental. If you ask a child what he learned in school today, you should not be surprised if he asks back, "Which subject do you mean?" As the complexity of our world grows even greater, so will our need for organizing it and understanding its interconnected parts, for seeing it as a whole.

Wholeness also demands an emphasis on cooperation rather than competition. As long as grading takes place on a "normal curve" so that for each student who receives a high grade, another must receive a low grade, our students will take a winners-implies-losers attitude with them into the communities. We must encourage group experiences and problem solving, and explain that competition is worthless and even dangerous when it is at the expense of any of the persons participating. A classroom cannot function on cooperation alone; but competition should be carefully checked, if we are to prepare our students for community problem solving that will last into the future.

Transdisciplinary education and cooperation are giant steps towards the realization of individualized education and student participation in social change. Recognizing the value of diversity, students will be freed from compartmentalized stagnation. Research activities and group interaction will flourish as students realize the broadness of the category *life*. Generalizing education does not mean eliminating specialization; it means increasing awareness of and appreciation for the way diversity becomes a whole. Once those levels of awareness are reached, individual differences and specialization can be actively utilized in cooperative efforts to solve social problems.

By changing our conception of professionalism and reassessing specialization and competition, we can begin to revise our ideas about what information a person needs to be truly educated. I would go a step further and suggest, if not doing away with "subjects" altogether, at least replacing presently required disciplines with new ones. History, English, science, and math will become electives; esthetics, communication, technology, and human relations will be requirements for all. A new perspective is needed, and the subjects I propose are more directly relevent to day-to-day life than those now required. Esthetics combines beautifully with physics and math for a student interested in architecture. Human relations are the keys to any historical event, no matter how political that event may have been. Technology and communications combine with English to make up visual and verbal journalism, not to mention the all-encompassing field of cybernetics. If we make today's "basics" optional and elevate to "first class" the subjects normally considered elective when they are offered at all, students will learn first of all that education is to be used. Once they understand the facts, they will look for theories on their own as they need them. Making education applicable will increase the crossover of information, and students will get a feel for the wholeness of knowledge instead of for the rigidity of school subjects.

Along with these new conceptions of information, we need to reorient education to a new psychology of man. A Skinnerian psychology of punishment and reward may have been educationally acceptable when our society was predominantly industrial; but now that we are moving to a postindustrial, information-based society, we need to move

to a Maslovian psychology of individual self-expression. In addition
to the six psychological areas that Maslow has delineated, I feel that
diversity must be an essential component of this new psychology.

Diversity is important for many scientific reasons, as Kenneth
Watt has documented: Diversity insures against risks—the more different alternative conceptions of *human* we have, the less likely it is
that the obsolescence of one conception (by some invention such as
the computer) will produce profound alienation. Human diversity also
promotes stability—a single dangerous philosophy (such as Hitler's) will
not easily take root in a truly diverse society. Finally, diversity seems
necessary for mental well-being; going off to a stimulus-rich area like
the wilderness often provides a profound mental release after working
for a long time in a stimulus-poor, "civilized" environment. In fact,
when rats are given levers with which to control their environment,
they deliberately choose a nonoptimal environment occasionally—
diversity is more important to health than comfort!

By moving education to a Maslovian psychology of man and
a new conception of information, we can revise educational content
to reflect the challenges we will face in the future. These changes,
coupled with the ideas I have already described for moving education
into the mainstream of society, represent my conception of the ideal
education system for America for the next thirty years. To implement
this conception, we must revise three of the pervasive educational values: our fear of educational change, our myth of educational *sameness*,
and our glorification of educational *objectivity*.

We value educational stability more than educational change.
America is a mobile, science oriented, highly literate society. We spend
our days in search of better medicine, constant economic growth, new
transportation, more efficient communication, and exciting entertainment; but when confronted with the prospect of educational or personal change, we balk. We may don airs of open-mindedness to mirror
a fast-stepping world, but they are glittering coats that come off in
the privacy of our homes. We accept scientific changes with a "what
will they think of next" attitude, and we absorb technological hardware
without prompting, but we do not tamper with our philosophies. We
flare up at challenges to our values, we hem and haw about legislation
long overdue, and we accept showpiece alterations in our social gar-
ment when we really need a whole new suit. As long as we relegate
change to the laboratory, we will remain socially immovable. We must
realize the value of changing socially, personally, and scientifically all
at once. Change, as an on-going social process, shapes a truly progressive society. Recognizing change as a life style, not a threat, can give

us the confidence and freedom we need to complement our physical and mental mobility.

Change-as-process demands perpetual social adjustment, not only to new technology and scientific discoveries but also to social, political, and economic issues. It demands a society on its toes and open-minded enough to weigh fairly the advantages and the disadvantages of the alternatives given it. And it requires a voluntary social commitment from every citizen. But once we catch up to change and keep up with its demands for our time, change will no longer be a threat to us—change itself will be our status quo.

Traditionally, our educational system has been the slowest evolver in society. As a public institution it is vulnerable to endless myths, which shackle it even tighter to people's frightened hearts. But precisely because education is such a bulwark of American faith, educators must accept the change-as-process commitment of our society. The relationship between education and society is reciprocal: to change our society, we will have to change our schools, for obviously any social ills will be proportionately evident in the educational system.

If education begins to change rapidly, I expect to see educators leading society for a while. But the important thing is to get the two systems running, not walking, hand in hand toward change. I have a theory that says "Change Big," and I expect the schools to do just that. If we change small, we will be open to comparisons with the old system. If we change big, no one will know what to compare us to. Education needs to change big—then society can begin to do the same.

Another value about education that we will need to change is our myth of educational sameness. It is a paradox of our culture that the world's most pluralistic nation is as afraid of differences as it is of change. Despite the positive nature of true diversity, fear of difference penetrates every American institution and is most grossly and harmfully manifested in our schools. We pass our paranoia from generation to generation by teaching our children to fear nonconformity in themselves and in their friends. And we teach it well, with public marks of failure for those who do not or cannot comply.

Racism is the most obvious example. In our zeal for sameness, we strive to make things relevant only to a White, middle-class culture. Our schools are laden with Anglo-Saxon ideologies which simply do not make sense to most Black, Oriental, American-Indian, Chicano, or immigrant children. We rate people's intelligence as it corresponds to Anglo-Saxon language and customs, and we ignore the millions of people who live with different values or systems of logic. How many

White suburban children would score well on a ghetto IQ test? Yet we permanently brand as unfit the non-White, non-middle-class children who perform poorly on the tests we give today.

Once we have labeled everyone, we perpetuate the racial differences in a class division of those who perform and those who do not. Take homework, for example: How many children, besides White children, have homes conducive to study? What kind of homework is done in a ghetto or in a culture which simply frowns on schools? Teachers who assign work to be done at home are making an assumption which is terrifying when one considers the confusion which an inability to conform may create in the child.

When we use textbooks, we again aim our education at some shadowy concept of child called "average student" who lives somewhere in White, middle-class America. Textbooks are overtly racist in the single-minded stories they pass off as objective description. For example, imagine the history of American westward expansion as seen through the eyes of the Indians, or the Mexicans of the Southwest, or even the buffalo. We have neglected 50 percent of every battle, every American contest ever waged: the other side. As long as we neglect the more unfortunate results of our exploits both at home and abroad, our children will continue to be indoctrinated with racist, bigoted values.

Textbooks also perpetuate the division between the performers and nonperformers. For years we have been labeling as *good* anyone who manages to survive the questions at the back of the book. And, of course, any failure to be intellectually stimulated is the fault of the student and he is promptly, and often permanently, labeled *bad.* Anyone who watches beauty pageants knows that when they total up all the contestants' heights and divide for the average, there is usually not one who is exactly that height. In beauty pageants, deviation from the numerical middle is tolerated, even rewarded; but in our schools it is punished. Textbook education assumes that every student adjusts to all material in the same way. For example, it supposes that all ten-year-old fifth graders are equally interested in Guatemala. It assumes that each child is slightly interested in Guatemala's imports and exports, social customs, and geography. But it has no answers for Susan, who is interested in the kinds of bugs they have in Guatemala; or for Jimmy, who wants to know a lot, not a little, about the music there. And it especially has no answers for Janet, who is just plain bored and who never understood the unit on Panama. Textbook teaching fails because it is boring. It simply cannot make knowledge applicable to a child's emotional or intellectual needs, because it cannot acknowledge his individual interests, his background, or his level of development.

A less concrete but very real manifestation of our quest for sameness is the equation we make between knowledge and time. We break learning into units of hours per day and years per lifetime and expect our children to imbibe prescribed amounts of information in equal amounts of time. At nine o'clock we study spelling; at ten o'clock we study math because spelling is "over." Never mind that Jimmy still cannot spell the last word on the list, or even "math" for that matter. It is time to move on.

By assuming that people learn at equivalent rates, we have based our advancement criteria on time. Our basis for judging a child's achievements is the amount of time he puts in instead of the skills or knowledge he acquires. The correlate is that once Janet has put in her time with the rest of the group, she is ready to move on. She may have failed the test, but that only explains the statistics that say that in a group of thirty students, someone has to fail. So Janet moves on to the next unit with the rest of the class, and later goes on to the next grade. And chances are she never will appreciate Guatemala or Panama.

It is so very simple to believe that people are different, but we find it impossible to act on that belief. Janet's bad luck is that she is statistically handy. Her failures can be explained away as easily as Susan's successes can be glorified. We could not run our schools as easily if we admitted that some six-year-olds should be third graders and some eight-year-olds first graders. It is especially messy to suggest that grades as units of time be done away with altogether. It upsets our middle-American sense of order, and it admits officially that people are different and have a right to remain so. And yet, isn't this admission just what America should be all about?

Students are not the only victims of sameness. Teachers, too, are subject to generalized expectations. They are allowed to do nothing more than teach. Their involvement in social reform is often ignored; their involvement in political activities is frowned upon. Witness the recent surge of firings and court cases surrounding teacher activism on college campuses. In many cases, administrations have openly stated that a college is a neutral institution and that professors must remain publicly neutral on all political issues.

We consider it a teacher's job to teach: he is to present the facts and step aside. Seldom does he get a chance to explain what he knows best or to teach an extra class in something he happens to be curious about. Teaching assignments are based solely on the number of teaching bodies available rather than on the specific abilities of the individual teachers.

Advancement criteria for teachers are also time-oriented. Once he puts his time in, a teacher gets his tenure—but there is no professionalism in that. It denies any and all chance for individual recognition. And it makes it impossible to get rid of poor teachers.

The move to individualize education must be applied to all areas of the spectrum. Teachers and students are people, and people have powerful and beneficial differences. We will only accept change as a life style when we realize that our world of plurality should not be roped in and pigeonholed, that it should be allowed to flower and cross-fertilize itself. Variance in our abilities makes for variance in our interests and experiences which can and absolutely must be shared. We cannot accept constant change without first accepting and utilizing the differences among ourselves.

The third educational value we must change is our glorification of *objectivity*. Our science-minded culture has ridiculed the teaching of subjective opinions and values and has made student evaluation a matter of percentages and numbers. We have glorified the unbiased teacher and the objective grading curve, but we have never really had either one.

What teacher lacks an opinion about anything? None, I should hope. Each one of us is biased about everything. It is a lie for any teacher to maintain that he can objectively summarize anything. In our pluralistic society values should be reflected honestly, not covered up in fruitless attempts to fool students. Forcing teachers to spend their professional and even private lives straddling fences of feigned objectivity damages students, teachers, and the profession alike. My ideal school would teach everything that is legal; teachers would teach what they believe in and do a good job because of their convictions. School would be an intellectual marketplace in which students do their own squeezing and picking and choosing of real ideas.

For future studies, eliminating the myths about objectivity will mean a shift from literal prediction to value-oriented decisions. This is an important shift and one that may well carry over to other areas of study. Open education on values is seriously lacking both in our schools and in our society at large. Values are inculcated in us without our awareness. It is necessary to teach students what values are, where they come from, and how they are developed. It is equally important to help them adopt values of their own. Objectivity cannot be feigned in value education. Honest, subjective appreciation of people's biases and backgrounds is imperative.

Faith in the objectivity of evaluation and grading extends the myth that our teachers are nonopinionated machines. It is commonly assumed that a grade must be uncluttered by such subjective factors as student-teacher relationships. We fear the teacher's subjective judgment. But what else is a grade? Not even percentages are assigned without some tinge of opinion. We also assume that only a teacher can dispense a grade, because we believe that only he can be objective in the evaluation. Students' understandings or explanations of the circumstances surrounding an exam or even an entire semester are seldom considered at grading time. This is especially a problem in our large colleges, where professors often have no personal contact at all with their students. Take, for example, an English professor who tells his students the first day of class: "When it comes to grading time I'm as cold as steel. I just add up the numbers." A student who does poorly on the exam may complain that he was ill or depressed that day, but that professor's comment would be, "Better luck next time." He does not care about what the student has learned. He is objective.

Of course, even such professors are biased in their evaluations. Being people, they will react favorably to a writing style or to an opinion that they especially like, and more negatively to one that bores them. It is a different subjectivity than the very personal one possible with the grade school or high school teacher, but it is subjectivity nonetheless. To assume the reality of objective grading is to fool ourselves, for to assume the need for objectivity is to assume that an understanding of individual personalities or circumstances confounds a teacher who is evaluating students. It is essential that the biases in any evaluation be exposed; we have to admit the subjective nature of evaluation and turn it to our advantage.

Teaching the new types of content I described earlier also necessarily ties into making education subjective, for there are no "right" answers. The myth of objectivity can be eliminated by the teacher who is committed, dedicated, and honest. Such honesty is imperative if we are to establish in our schools an atmosphere of trust and respect for people's backgrounds and ideas. A commitment to eliminate the myth of and desire for objectivity is thus a solid commitment to social tasks. By exposing and eliminating under-the-table prejudice and grade D objective teaching, we only express our need for honesty.

This commitment is made when we realize that subjective education means 100 percent fair play. A teacher who teaches a controversial subject may come under some fire, but that possibility is recognized by all sides before he begins. Likewise, he is free to tackle any issue he chooses, with the understanding that he makes it clear that he has opinions to share, not just facts to teach. Subjective teaching keeps things on the table top. People know where other people stand, and from there education skyrockets.

Subjective evaluation, when evaluation is necessary, also means honesty on both sides of the desk. Fair evaluation uses and reflects every relevant aspect of a person's achievement. Fair judgment by the teacher and self-grading by the student combine in discussion to make evaluation a useful part of the learning spiral.

Subjectivity denies the games we play in school today. Teachers no longer have to feign disconcern when they are excited over a subject; neither do students have to labor under the belief that the only value in school is its irrelevant facts. Threats disappear at every level, as they are no longer necessary to effect action. Real education is finally a possibility once the lines of honesty are opened up. Opinions and values can be accepted stigma-free once we admit their intrinsic worth to education. By keeping our pluralistic values before us, we will have taken the first step toward cooperative social reform. Only when we can trust one another's sincerity will we get anywhere inside or outside of our schools.

Once we have altered our educational values about change, sameness, and objectivity, once we have begun to move toward a cross-generational, location-free, nonformal educational system, once we have revised educational content within a new conception of information and a new psychology of man, what should we do with our schools? I am sure that any future educational system will make some use of schools; for some types of learning, they are very effective. There are two basic changes in structure, however, that every school in our future educational system should implement.

The first structural change is *flexible scheduling*. We must acknowledge that children learn at different rates and that they have enough curiosity to keep them going for a double lifetime if that curiosity is properly tapped. Flexible scheduling means contracting or expanding class time to fit the amount of subject material, eliminating the padded minutes wasted in waiting for that omnipotent bell to ring. Of course, if they must, the bells will still ring, but at smaller intervals. For example, the day can be divided into eighteen 20-minute modules. A class might last for one module or eighteen, depending on its content and its importance to the student.

This brings us to a crucial element of flexible scheduling: independent study. This does not mean a free-for-all. It means realizing that students are people, not puppets, and that a most important part of growing up is learning to direct oneself through a specific task or through one entire day. Flexible scheduling does not eliminate all boundaries; it merely trusts a percentage of the student's day to the student. It assumes, of course, that as educators we can handle that trust. I have no qualms about the students handling it.

Flexible scheduling is great for teachers who use it well. It means more creative lessons and more creative students. Experimentation is increased at all levels as fear of failure and pressure of the clock are diminished. Teachers are free to teach experimental courses in experimental ways; students are free to tell them what flops and what soars. People are honest and people care, because the responsibility for at least part of the learning process is at the grass roots.

Twenty years ago, organizing flexible scheduling would have been impossible. Keeping track of two thousand students was difficult enough even when each was in an assigned place at an assigned time. But with computers at our disposal, there is no need to fear that flexible scheduling is messy or disorganized. Computers work quickly and compactly. They are accurate; they know all the possible combinations. And computers free teachers of the dirty work required to organize an entire semester or to set up independent scheduling for thirty or sixty or ninety students.

Of course, as our knowledge increases, the uses to which we put our computers will also grow. Flexible scheduling will benefit from new computer techniques or languages. In fact, as society becomes more and more information-oriented, the computer will be relied on to keep track of what we know and what we need to know, not only about scheduling but also about the students, the administration, the teachers, and mounds of other related data needed to keep a school running.

The second structural change which all schools should implement is *differentiated staffing*. There is no ladder of recognition or advancement within the profession today. Teaching is teaching. Lacking concrete differentiation among our teachers, we reward them all with tenure. Differentiating a staff involves putting teachers in the positions for which they are best qualified. And that involves public knowledge of both their abilities and their disabilities as professional men and women. Following differentiated staffing assignments, we should compensate our teachers with salaries proportional to their positions, abilities, and performances. It would be possible then, to move up within the profession and to be paid accordingly. This sets a premium on creativity, and teachers will have to produce to advance. The teachers who produced even under the tenure system will be at last recognized and rewarded. Teachers who have been unsure of their abilities can find confidence and explore new avenues once they are placed where they really belong. In short, differentiated staffing individualizes education for the educators.

Our future feasibly holds much transience in careers as well as in residence, and that would make differentiated staffing imperative. Tenure will become an anachronism. We will hire teachers not only for their teaching talents but also for their experiences in other fields.

Transience, when turned to our benefit, will be powerful indeed in providing more experienced educators and better criteria on which to hire them.

To summarize: I believe that changing our educational system to make it an integral part of society is crucial to solving the future societal problems inexorably appearing on the horizon. I propose the following model for making these changes:

1. Education should move to the center of societal interaction by implementing cross-generational, nonformal, location-free social service programs.

2. Education should reorient itself to a new conception of information based on interdependence and cooperation, and on a new psychology of man based on Maslovian principles and diversity.

3. Our present values about educational change—sameness and objectivity—must be radically altered.

4. In the schools that remain after we have transposed to education for social service, flexible scheduling and differentiated staffing should be implemented.

Overall, then, I believe that education—for all ages—involves three nonnegotiable kinds of experiences. At the base of all education is the first: personal enrichment. Personal enrichment will be an activity in which the entire society engages on a conscious and deliberate level. It will be respected and expected of everyone. It will be a way of life.

The second type of experiences around which education is based is competence and credentials—publicly establishing one's abilities in a profession. Testing and evaluating are essential in this type of education, but formal school work is not always required. Experience itself is viewed with enough respect so that it equals or even outweighs what might be learned in books. Of course, the circumstances of one's profession will determine the prerequisites for credentialing; it is surely more justifiable to expect a doctor to go to school than it is a plumber.

Social tasks form the third group of experiences and complete my educational triad. Under this label are included the furthering of the intellectual disciplines, social welfare work, and scientific investigation—in short, our social task is to teach one another. Everyone is teacher and everyone is a learner. There is an interchanging of roles and tasks at every level, for teaching is informal. Aunt Jane's trip to Canada is an experience she is expected to share as much as a professor is expected to share his understanding of nuclear physics. Teaching is a social responsibility that everyone shares and everyone accepts.

What I visualize as the ideal school system is not a school system at all but an attitude and a life style. It is a deschooled society, but very much an intellectual one. It will, of course, have an educational core: a community educational resource center. Here our children will have highly skilled teachers, both professional and paraprofessional. Here people will go for education in the disciplines and for certification in the professions. Industries will use the center as a training center for any and all who want to learn an industrial trade, regardless of whether or not the students will work for a particular organization later on. A combination of federal, state, and local funding will make the center the locus of social enrichment activities.

Aside from the resource center itself, it is important to remember that in this ideal system education is an attitude. Everything that happens is regarded as a potentially educational event; all things and all people are respected for their educational value. What necessarily evolves in such a society is an appreciation of differences and a willingness to change. A perpetually learning society will be one that accepts plurality and teaches its young to deal with ambiguous futures as well as past certainties. And such a society will relate on a person-to-person level of interdependence and cooperation.

Future studies work on the assumption that there are many alternative futures and that the future which emerges will arise from forces and beliefs acting in the present. There are many present forces which combine to constrain what education might be: lack of funding, racism, and disparate values in our society. But I believe that the greatest single obstacle to implementing better education is made up of our beliefs about education and society. If we can change education in the ways I have described, we will have taken the most important step needed to create a better future for our society. Let us work together to take that step.

Harry S.
Broudy

Harry S. Broudy

In 1957 Dr. Broudy assumed his present position as professor of philosophy of education at the University of Illinois. Prior to that time he had taught at North Adams State College and Framington State College, both in Massachusetts. Among his many books are the commonly used text, Building A Philosophy of Education, *and the recent and very favorably reviewed* Real World of the Public Schools. *He also served as editor of* The Educational Forum *from 1964–1973.*

education:
1975-2000

It is not especially difficult to make predictions or to give reasons for their plausibility. The real difficulty is to make accurate predictions. This would be simply a truism, except that predictions of affairs that involve human responses, as distinguished from predictions of the movements of the planets, are liable to a peculiar sort of fallibility.

PERILS OF PREDICTION

Human behavior cannot be extrapolated in any simple linear fashion. We can extrapolate the increasing need for energy by using the current rates of use as a base. But we cannot predict that the demand for energy, as measured by the demand for air conditioning, electrical heating, and household appliances, will increase at the same rate as it has in the last decade. It may increase at an even more rapid rate if, for example, people are prevented from fleeing hot apartments during the summer. But people may get sick and tired of the trouble of maintaining these contrivances, and so the popularity of electrical appliances may decline. In other words, a human desire can become satiated; people become bored with things that at one time entranced them. This is the dynamic on which fashion depends. One can predict that fashions will change, but every so often they are revived. Why? There may be hidden laws that would enable us to predict these tides of favor and disfavor, but so far they seem to be less laws of nature than the results of advertising.

For these reasons I am hesitant about predicting by simple extrapolation a linear increase in the uses of technology in education, the growth of the open university, the deschooling of America, the three-day work week, and a half dozen other movements that are now agitating the educational scene. Within a decade the fashion in schooling shifted from intellectual excellence in the early sixties to redemption of the poor in the late sixties. Where are the educational innovations of yesteryear? The colleges during the 1960s were overflowing, but by 1971 enrollments were decreasing.

I am also hesitant about making predictions by matching the characteristics of a culture with a corresponding set of characteristics in a school system. For example, does an explosion of knowledge or information give grounds for predicting that every individual will have to know more and more, and that the schools will have to teach more and more? Plausible as an affirmative answer may sound, it may well be that after the information load exceeds a certain point, the most efficient way of handling it is by simplifying the cognitive apparatus required of the individual rather than by making it more complex.

We have some reasons for believing that human beings operate on the principle of least cognitive strain. This may be an explanation for the alleged failure of the schools to make their teachings relevant to a wide spectrum of pupils' interests. According to this hypothesis, pupils are bored with school, not because what is taught is irrelevant to their problems, but because they have much simpler ways of coping with life predicaments than by trying to understand them in the manner of educated men and women. For example, as the law becomes more complex, the notion of negotiating that procedural jungle by understanding the law becomes wholly unrealistic—although one of my academic colleagues, when forced to spend a weekend in jail, did ask that appropriate lawbooks be brought so that he could study his own case. Such behavior is not only rare—for most of us it is futile. It is safer to hire a lawyer and rely on his expertise to lead us through the jungle. Knowledge explosions have to be absorbed by the culture, but they do not have to be absorbed uniformly by everyone.

Take the simple equating of the role of science in technology with the amount of scientific understanding needed by the citizen in a mature technological society. The user of the products of technology does not have to understand the theory that went into the technology; indeed the best product is customer proof. The best refrigerator is one the user has to know the least about. Hence a scientifically literate public is not necessary in a mature technological society, albeit a competent scientific elite is indispensable. We cannot predict the future shape of schooling by simply matching the structure or the content of what is to be known with isomorphic arrangements for everybody to learn them.

PARAMETERS OF PREDICTION

For these and kindred reasons, I find it necessary to make some stipulations, not only about the general nature of the culture that we can expect to dominate the scene in the future, but also about human nature that will respond to that culture.[1] I am assuming that our society will continue to develop technologically; the alternative would seem to be severe population limitations that I cannot envision. As consequences of technological maturation one might expect: increased specialization in the field of work; increased bureaucratization in social organization; and even greater reliance on mass production techniques for material goods and also for intellectual ones.

Is this assumption too glib, too easy? Are there not those who say that technology already has been launched on a course from which there is no escape save complete destruction of the environment itself? Dennis Meadows has led a group at Massachusetts Institute of Technology that used computers to estimate the consequences of continued exponential growth of population, food production, pollution, industrialization, and consumption of nonrenewable natural resources. He found that within fifty years there will be catastrophe.[2]

The comment on this finding by one science writer illustrates two points. The first is that if we understand a trend of events, we can by a change of attitude change the trend itself:

The computer is unaware of changing human behavior. Concern about the population explosion and such matters as pollution has already had profound effects . . . the rate of growth of population in this country has been slowing. The rate of increase of important polluting chemicals has been slowed, stopped, or is even decreasing.[3]

The second point is that the dangers of technology can be countered only by technology:

The study also does not adequately take into account ingenuity with respect to natural resources. Current technology is based on the availability of certain raw materials, such as copper and natural gas. As these resources become scarce, technology will change and, for example, aluminum will be used as a conductor, while methane will be obtained from coal.[4]

As many have pointed out, if sufficient energy is available, there are few problems involving the physical environment that cannot be solved. It takes energy to produce energy, and it takes more energy to remove the pollutants that accompany the production and use of energy. If we are ever able to utilize the energy of the sun or from fusion or the heat of the earth, it will be by the application of science to technology. Glenn T. Seaborg notes that:

The heat of the earth's crust is sufficient to satisfy much of our energy requirements for hundreds of years if it can be extracted efficiently. For some of the near-surface geothermal sources, the present state of technology may suffice; for deeper-lying sources of hot rock, new technologies will be required.[5]

Indeed, even in such a problem as overpopulation, where human will and intelligence count so heavily, a cheap, reliable, simple contraceptive (a product of technology) will do more than a thousand conferences on the subject.

Technological maturity entrains interdependence, large-scale collective enterprises, and a high degree of uniformity in the clothes we wear, the automobiles we drive, and the news and opinion that we absorb from a variety of media. Moreover, these developments put a premium on the elite: a governing elite, an industrial, military, taste-making elite. The many will live—presumably quite well—on the brains of the few.

These assumptions conjure up an Orwellian world, a Walden II society, and robotism in various forms. These fears are not unfounded, for these are the usual accompaniments of a mass technological society. Education that does not keep these possibilities in mind is as mindless as education that considers only these possibilities. An example of the first sort of myopia is the uncritical use of a school to accommodate its clientele to an Orwellian world, by devoting its energies almost exclusively to specific vocational preparation and training for predetermined social roles. The latter kind of shortsightedness is exemplified by a school that fosters illusions that we can enjoy the benefits of a technologically mature society without paying a price for it—that we are at liberty to pick from countless alternatives in every domain of experience and do what we please as the mood moves us.

I have in mind the frenetic pleas for alternatives and individual freedom in the schools, as uttered or written by Jonathan Kozol, John Holt, and others, including the champions of cultural autonomy for ethnic minorities and the advocates of voucher systems as means for providing alternatives to the public schools.

As to human nature, I am assuming first of all that there is one. This, I realize, will turn off all those who have been told repeatedly that there is no constancy in human nature, and that only old Aristotelians and Thomists stubbornly refuse to be disillusioned. I argue here that we can speak of a constant and unchanging human nature in at least two senses.

One sense is exemplified by history. Has the psychological structure of those creatures we call human changed as history has been recording the doings of men? There is an almost boring sameness in the motives that inspire work, love, revenge, the drive for power and esteem. There are differences, but are they essential differences or accidental ones?

The second sense is harder to explicate. Humanness is a self-sealing concept. By this I mean that we exclude from the human species entities that do not display specific features. Of these necessary and sufficient features, perhaps the most important are imagination and a sense of morality. I have not cited intelligence, because formal reasoning can be simulated by a robot computer. But a creature that could not imagine things to be otherwise than they happen to be could probably not be included in the human family. Imagination and a sense of morality go together—if we could not imagine things being otherwise, we could hardly regret anything that happened. We could not formulate ideals, and the pangs of conscience would be stilled. We could not speak of praise or blame.

Furthermore, the sense of morality is remarkably stable as regards its basic forms. Self-mastery or temperance, courage, loyalty, truthfulness, integrity, and prudence are virtues that define goodness of character in any culture. They evoke admiration when present and censure when absent. To be sure, the behaviors that exemplify these virtues or human excellences vary from culture to culture, from epoch to epoch. One might not regard Spartan behavior as the exemplar of courage in our time; willingness to face loss of job and approval of friends in behalf of what one believes to be a just cause might be more exemplary of courage. Nevertheless, both Spartans and Americans would agree that self-control in the face of clear and present danger is admirable, and that loss of self-control, panic, and flight are cowardly and reprehensible.

The virtues, therefore, seem to act as parameters for defining the human essence. Should we encounter on another planet live beings, and should they fail to display imagination and a sense of morality, we would refuse to classify them as human, however remarkable they might be in every other way. They might, for example, have to be classified as angelic, behaving perfectly without effort and having no alternatives before them; but human they would not then be.

Because men have the twin gifts of imagination and moral reflection and can entertain visions of what they might be, men will always desire and value the freedom to determine their lives. They will always desire self-realization because they can sense a discrepancy between their achievements and their potentialities. They will always desire self-integration because they can envision incompatible roles that will rob them of coherence, effectiveness, and peace of mind.

What has this disquisition about human nature to do with the future shape of education? Simply that these are the constants of human response that we can anticipate in 2000 and beyond—if there is to be a beyond. We can be more sure of this than we can that 2000 will find our culture still in the grip of technological development, although I am assuming that this also will be true.

I have not made a universal yearning for a free society an assumption for the future because one can be far less sure of such a yearning than of a desire for individual freedom—a desire that no amount of repression can stifle completely. Nonetheless, the need to maintain some form of democratic society makes a great difference in the demands on schooling and in the ways the demands are met. I shall assume that the press for democracy will still be a feature of our own society in 2000.

Within these parameters, what can we expect the demands on schooling to be? And what can we expect the response of the schools to be?

DEMANDS ON SCHOOLING—VOCATION

On the face of it, a mature, technologically-dominated society should demand of its participants increased sophistication about science and technology, both for vocational competence and for understanding of the culture as a whole. It is expected that service jobs will increase relative to those involved in industrial operations. However, the myriad of symbolic operations that now attend every phase of economic activity, including industrial production, presages a high level of linguistic and conceptual competence on the part of workers in all fields. It has been said that it takes a ton of paper to make a ton of steel. All power today involves idea power.

On the basis of considerations of this sort, we have heard predictions from high sources that in the future the minimum formal schooling required for a viable economy would go as high as sixteen years. It was this sort of argument that in part—how much one can only guess—sparked the enthusiasm for college education during the sixties.

But as the sixties drew to a close, a reverse trend set in. Instead of complaints about scholastic underqualification in the labor pool, we began to hear about overqualification in terms of formal schooling.[6] Schooling was found to be unnecessary—beyond a minimal amount—not only for jobs on the lower end of the occupational scale, but even on loftier levels. It was contended that achievement in the Harvard Business School did not correlate well with success in management.[7] Medical schools and law schools also began to scrutinize their curricula for nonfunctional theory and sought ways to substitute clinical experience for it. In 1972 the U.S. Office of Education, under the aegis of Commissioner Sidney P. Marland, Jr., announced its top priority to be career education, a genteel term for vocational training. Presumably, the more specific the training the better. In the same vein, the deschooling arguments of Ivan Illich found great favor with the avant-garde educational reformers—greater than with the prospective beneficiaries. While Illich's followers were hurling bricks at the public school system because allegedly it was no longer the vehicle for social upward mobility for the poor, the poor were vociferously demanding more of what their "betters" thought was not good for them.[8]

However, there need be no contradiction between forecasts that a technological society requires more schooling and forecasts that it requires less. They can both be right, albeit not for the same personnel. Let us leave out for the moment the nonvocational uses of schooling—for example, as preparation for civic competence, leisure time, or self-development—and confine the argument to vocational uses. Two alternative prospects are possible. One is that the system requires everybody or nearly everybody to acquire a fairly high level of general education—of conceptual and symbolic competence. The other is that only a small cadre in each vocational field needs to do so. The first alternative would give the individual more flexibility to cope with job obsolescence, but it might lower the tolerance for highly routinized, assembly line operations. If automation fulfills the promises made earlier for it, the number of highly routinized jobs could be decreased to the point where only those who could tolerate them would be consigned to them. However, we are now hearing less optimistic predictions about automation.

The counterargument holds that job fractioning goes hand in hand with technological progress. It is more profitable to chop complex jobs up into routinized component operations that cheaper help can perform. If this is true, then the second alternative is the more likely pattern for the future. Only the top professionals will need large amounts of formal schooling for their jobs; the much larger cadres of paraprofessionals, technicians, and aides will require progressively less schooling for their vocational assignments.

I have no basis for predicting which of these two developments will dominate the scene in decades to come, but what does seem probable is that there will be a wider range of vocational levels at which the individual can choose to operate. This may come about for two sorts of reasons. The first is that, as the different grades of work within a field exfoliate, there is a better chance of matching up the goals of the individual with something in the vocational inventory. Thus in the field of health services, there will be dozens of jobs that vary in the cognitive strain they exert on the individual—from the neurosurgeon to the sweeper of hospital corridors. Presumably the different levels of occupation will require different amounts of formal preparation.

The second factor militating for greater choice of careers is that in the future, for large numbers of people, the role of work may be deemphasized. Traditionally, the so-called work ethic tended to make vocation the nucleus of life. All other activities revolved around it: social life, political activity, diversions. The second question that we ask about a new acquaintance—after ascertaining his name—is "What do you do?" Men have identified with their jobs much more than working women. "Mary Jones is a secretary" tells us much less about Mary Jones than "Bob Jones is a certified public accountant" tells us about Mr. Jones. Women's liberation may change that, of course, but for both men and women the job may no longer be the identifying role. It may be that routinized jobs employing one's hands only for thirty to thirty-five hours a week may provide sufficiently attractive incomes to make such jobs worth working in but not worth identifying with. One might in such cases identify oneself with a hobby, a social cause, political activity, art, or weekend fishing trips.[9]

For others the job may become everything, and this is more likely to occur at the higher rungs of the occupational ladder—higher not only in terms of economic returns but also in intellectual challenge. Once the close ties between money, status, and the job are loosened, there will be less pressure to qualify for a job on the higher levels of the occupational ladder.

This opportunity for occupational choice is not an unmixed blessing. Options force upon us the necessity of choosing or at least of deciding whether to choose. This is but one of the paradoxical results of technology: it may rob of us many kinds of freedom, but it is just as likely to bestow upon us far more freedom than we want. The soul-searching that adolescents undergo in trying to decide on a career is too familiar to need elaboration.

Nevertheless, it would be foolish to believe that even a much greater variety of job opportunities will permit the kind of occupational flexibility that Karl Marx envisioned in his classless society. Workers will be allowed only such freedom of choice as the interdependence of the whole system permits. If the system needs more high-level workers, it has means for steering people into such jobs. Thus, when our country needed aerospace workers and battalions of physicists and mathematicians, it got them by pouring research funds into the universities; it could, if it wished, get larger numbers of practical nurses or potato peelers by using similar inducements.

Having noted these reservations, it nevertheless remains probable that by 2000 most of our population will need much more general education than it now evades. We tend to underestimate the degree to which the technological mentality pervades our perception and thought until we try to introduce technology to a population that perceives its world via a nonscientific mentality. Giving machines—the product of technology—to these people often produces anomalous results, such as the use of the machines in magical rituals. Providing people who are ignorant of the germ theory of disease with modern medical technology also can produce odd responses—for example, the washing of a thermometer in water teeming with harmful bacteria. Even relatively uneducated people in a technologically mature culture think scientifically about natural phenomena, the current craze for the occult notwithstanding.

How much of this general intellectual sophistication will be provided by formal schooling and how much by the informal massage of the mind by the mass media is hard to say, but the odds are in favor of a greater role for media. Indeed, some predict that the home television set will become the standard vehicle for instruction. Although video cassettes for this purpose are not yet ready to fulfill this promise, there is no a priori reason why they should not help to do so, if only because it will be easier to study at home than to travel to school. It is more difficult to solve the transport problem in a megalopolis than to bring information into homes or into numerous neighborhood centers via electronic media. The projections of architects like Paolo Soleri, who are planning for whole communities to live out their lives in one vast building (archology), may provide one solution to the transportation problem. Long before pollution or waste of our natural resources destroys our civilization, the time and effort needed to move the urban population to and from their work, stores, and schools may exceed the time and energy needed to do whatever it is they are traveling for. Because improvement of transportation merely augments the demands for transportation, we may consider it a candidate for election to the class of insoluble problems.

Before ending this digression, it is tempting to speculate that the failure to solve the transport problem may indirectly return us to combining factory and residence into one unit—a new version of home industry—and to restoring the extended family in urban residential complexes replete with facilities for care of children by senior citizens.

DEMAND ON SCHOOLING—CIVIC COMPETENCE

In a technologically mature society, there are no simple problems. Interdependence sees to that. The face-to-face deliberations of citizens in the small New England town meeting are a type of democracy that is hard to find—even in the small New England village. Once citizens could decide about local school issues and about the construction of streets and sewers without worrying about what Washington would say. Now virtually any problem that is not completely trivial depends on cooperation or collaboration with the state or federal government. The erection of a dam involves hundreds of communities, as does the building of an interstate highway. Farmers in the Midwest worry about international trade, and sleepy backwaters fear invasions by hoodlums and hopheads who may do anything from robbing the bank to kidnapping the minister. Not only is no man an island, no community is even a peninsula.

What does this mean for civic competence? Karl Mannheim spoke of the need for "correlational thinking" as distinguished from linear thinking. Today we are more likely to talk about the need for systems analysis. But thinking in terms of many variables taxes the brain of even agile computers; what is the plain citizen to do?

For one thing, he may wish to renounce the role of a plain citizen and become knowledgeable about taxation, foreign trade, international finance, the effects of roads and strip mining on ecology, the alternatives to the exploitation of fossil fuels, and similar problems. If so, then the level of his general education will have to be raised to something beyond graduation from high school. This will certainly have to be done if he takes seriously the notion that, as a citizen in a democracy, he ought to participate in government and make decisions on the basis of his best knowledge, or even if he just wishes to pay more than lip service to thinking for himself.

However, he can choose to remain a plain citizen. He need not think for himself. Ideas and opinions can be mass distributed as well as automobiles and aspirin tablets; this is the genius of a technological society. Television filters and reports the news and employs pundits to interpret it. Newspapers hire columnists to do the same thing for those who still have the time to read them. Opinion polls are the most efficient thought-savers of all—although a pundit or columnist may on occasion be wrong, the majority opinion as reported by the polls in a sense cannot be wrong, at least not in a democratic society.

Another method for evading the need to become educated enough to think and decide for oneself is membership in some organization that takes positions on public policy. A labor union, a medical association, a taxpayers' league helps its members to get straight about relevant social problems. Political parties are becoming less useful for this purpose, because they harbor too broad a spectrum of prejudices. Because of this diversity, the party tells one how to vote but not what to think. This means, I suppose, that one can vote right without thinking right, a feat even more remarkable than voting right without thinking at all.

DEMAND ON SCHOOLING—HUMANNESS

Any future culture will have to contend with the inveterate demands for individuality, personhood, and freedom. What does this mean for the schooling of the future? Briefly, the problem is this: a technologically developed society involves a finely graduated division of labor. This, in turn, necessitates a complex system for coordinating the numerous and diverse component functions. The coordinating apparatus must ignore the idiosyncrasies of individuals and thereby depersonalizes them. Individuals are treated not as persons but as consumers, taxpayers, automobile owners, theatergoers; for computerization it is convenient to designate them by a number—for example, a social security number. Although men and women can be so regarded and often are so regarded, they resent being deprived of their idiosyncrasies. Individuality is a nuisance to those who have to classify, but it is dear to the hearts of individuals. The search for identity is not the search for one's social security number but rather for some evidence that one is somebody, not just anybody.

How can I be sure that I am a particular somebody? Only if I can recognize myself as a center of influence or choice or, as Kant would have it, as a moral law giver, as a rational will. A person and only a person can have a conscience, act from a sense of duty, and justify his action—on occasion—as being "the right thing to do."

To play this role as a genuine human being in a technologically mature society will require a high order of imagination, thought, and determination. If schooling is a doubtful source of determination and commitment, it can be a source for the development of disciplined thought and imagination. Indeed, it is hard to imagine a better reason for the establishment of schools. The sciences and the humanities represent the appraised residue of centuries of reflection on experience. The educated man interiorizes these resources for his own imagination, thought, and commitment. The commitments of educated men may be called enlightened cherishing.[10] To be sure, formal schooling is not the only source of enlightenment for cherishing, but it is the only source designed to serve this end.

By and large we rely on general or liberal studies for this purpose, but we have a strong tradition in our own country that this sort of schooling is a luxury that only the elite can afford. The elite, for reasons that they cannot always elucidate and do not feel that they have to explain, have put a high value on liberal studies. At one time this marked the end of formal schooling for the elite, because the vocations their young were to enter did not require much formal preparation. Business, finance, industrial leadership did not require it. Law, medicine, and the clergy did, but they were studied as addenda to liberal education rather than as a substitute for it. Today, all or nearly all, the offspring of the elite find it advisable to get some formal vocational training for business, finance, and the like, and the future will not change this trend. Whether the elite will continue to value liberal studies as a prelude to professional education is not so certain.

Much depends on whether the liberal arts college can make a case for the formal study of general education; the gut feeling that liberal studies do function well in adult life is hard to support with the kind of evidence that persuades either skeptical students or anti-intellectual legislators. Perhaps the solution will lie in substituting informal cultivation of the liberal studies through the media, as hobbies in adult life, intermittently on the campus of some open university, or for three or four years of concentrated study at some college or university.

The masses, historically, were supposed to make do with training for some trade or low-skill occupation, a modicum of literacy, and large doses of piety and social docility. What would they do with general or liberal studies? They would have neither the time nor the money to make use of it, and it could only make them dissatisfied with their lot.

This distinction between schooling for the elite and for the masses is still with us, despite the endless rhetoric to the contrary. Many of the most articulate champions of the poor, reformers who live for no other reason than to redeem the masses from their poverty and misery, are the loudest advocates for a kind of schooling that is suspiciously like the schooling the masses have always had—a modicum of literacy and some job training. The old requirements of piety and social docility have been dropped. The other requisites for personhood and humanness are to come through avenues other than the school or the church—presumably through participation in some form of community action.

What about the future? Will the masses be satisfied with this pattern of schooling? They will not if the leisure available to them is substantially increased. Can we invent distractions fast enough to dispel the boredom that leisure creates for the uncultivated person? What are the alternatives to a losing race with distraction? Participation in community action is one; self-cultivation in the arts or the sciences is another. But both will require much more general education than has been thought appropriate for the masses. Paradoxically, it may be the worker at the ordinary job, not the elite, who will be able to afford the luxury of a really liberal education in the Aristotelian sense—that is, an education undertaken solely for the development of human excellence.

SOME PARADOXES OF A TECHNOLOGICAL SOCIETY

In every area of experience—vocational, civic, personal development—a technologically mature society offers the individual some important options. The most significant, as far as education is concerned, is the choice of the level of self-cultivation. I use the word choice advisedly, because I believe educational opportunity will become far more widespread than it is now. This means that for those who want it and are willing to invest the effort and ability to get it, there will be fewer arbitrary obstacles—such as lack of money. With the promise of electronic dissemination on a large scale, schooling at every level will be increasingly accessible. It will be less demanding of residence at an institution and of fixed scholastic requirements.

But there will be a genuine alternative to self-cultivation that requires considerable effort, because there will be no drastic penalties if one decides to remain uncultivated or very modestly cultivated. Indeed the more radical reformers are already denouncing all compulsory schooling. More and more of the good things of life will be free or cheap because of the beneficent economies attending mass production. The economies, moreover, are cognitive as well as monetary. Prepackaged ideas and opinions will be readily available, and they will embody very good thought indeed, because experts will design the packages. Just as the very best engineering brains go into designing an automobile, the principles of which the driver need not understand, so the best minds will design ideologies that the citizen can parrot without understanding. And if reading proves too taxing, then visual media can present these ideas in nonlinear "discourse" so that the desired mood is created instantly.

Why is ready-made culture repugnant, especially to intellectuals? Is it the low quality of the prepackaged culture? I am not so sure that the quality of the mass-produced thing—object or idea—is inferior to the custom-made article, even in the domain of ideas. I doubt, for example, that a man mindlessly repeating James Reston's views on politics as they appear in the *New York Times* is mouthing something inferior to what the professor of political science is saying in his class or in some coffeehouse.

No, the revulsion we feel toward parroting has nothing to do with the substantive merit of the ideas being uttered. If true or highly probable, they are so regardless of the speaker. The revulsion is occasioned by the low quality of intellect being exhibited by the parroter. The truth is not *in* him, so to speak, unless he has contributed something to the inquiry that makes it true or unless he can supply the context which makes it true. Unlike an automobile, a view, a commitment, a judgment is not something external to the utterer; it is not authentic judgment if the speaker does not dwell in it. Hence it is no reflection on a man if he does not make his own automobile or even understand what went into the making of it on an assembly line. But it is an indictment of a man if he does not in some sense form his own mind.

Yet because it is so much easier to be carried than to walk, the technologically mature society is the great tempter; it will carry us, and fairly well, if we are too lazy to walk. The greatest temptation of all is the notion that in such an interdependent, bureaucratic, impersonal society there is really no choice but to be carried along; that there is no room for individuality, for freedom, for choice, for decision, for authenticity.

The import of this discussion may be brought out more concretely by three brief scenarios that clarify the potentialities and constraints on the quality of individual life.

(a) The moral obligation of Moses, Socrates, and St. Francis with regard to cancer was zero, for the impossible is never the object of moral obligation. For us the possibility—created by science and technology—to do something about cancer research and treatment in turn creates a possible source of obligation. Whether to devote one's time or resources to promoting this possibility could become a theme for moral reflection. Because the reasons one does or does not fulfill what he regards to be his obligation in this sphere are likely to remain unknown to others, the inner quality of the moral situation is deepened. Is it possible that technology moralizes the culture by creating power to do what could not be done before? This runs counter to the commonly accepted dogma that science and technology are confined to means and are themselves either value-free or value-indifferent.

(b) Improvements in contraceptive technology have been charged with the demoralization and depersonalization of sex partners. The morality of sex has been largely institutional, with the family at its core. Morality in sex meant loyalty to marriage vows and restriction of sex activity to marital partners. This activity, in turn, was validated by the facts of reproduction and the need to nurture the young, provide for inheritance, and the like. Ergo, if reproduction can be made a nonsequitur of sex, the moral imperatives will be destroyed and promiscuity will ensue. Perhaps it will, but why should persons be willing to let themselves be used as sex objects merely? And can persons so use each other without psychic damage? Is it possible that affection is harder to separate from sex than babies? If so, then freedom resulting from contraceptive technology may be the very factor in remoralizing and repersonalizing sex. In other words, the source of moral relationships would be the respect for persons rather than respect for the marriage laws.

(c) If we solve the problems of pollution and social injustice, mature technology conceivably could approach the ideal of providing an adequate level of mass-produced goods, services, entertainment, information, and the like for the vast majority of the population. Suppose this were to come to pass. We now afford the individual with fairly easy access to what by all historical standards would be a very adequate level of standardized life. The price for such comfort would be a willingness to use mass-produced products and to conform to a fairly uniform life style. Suppose, however, that the human spirit rebels at such uniformity. Does a mass culture permit anything more individualized? One answer might be an outright no; another might be a loud yes; and a third might be a very qualified yes. For example, individuality might be possible but only at fairly high cost in efforts at self-cultivation. Whether to pay the price might be an agonizing choice—especially if a much lower cost in effort yields a life that is good enough. Here again a technologically mature society might, paradoxically, offer a very real opportunity for moral strenuousness.

These paradoxes, for which we must credit the vagaries of the human mind, can make a shambles of linear extrapolation when it comes to predicting the future. They also may help bring about the realization that science, although it expands the volume of value possibilities, does not create the patterns of life that will utilize these potentialities. Thus science, and the technology attendant on it, has freed women from the inevitability of motherhood, but it has not suggested the appropriate life style for the liberated woman. Science has opened possibilities for a moral relationship between the sexes, but it has not given us an image of the kind of life that would actualize that relationship. And one could make the same point for the other freedoms that man might extort from a bureaucratic, interdependent society.

For these life forms we shall have to look to the artist, because it is in his domain that images are created. Although artists may not create images for this purpose, their creations serve as trial balloons that may capture the imagination of a generation or even of an epoch. I would anticipate that it is in the novel, the play, the film, the poetry, and the painting of the future that the new life forms will first be adumbrated. Which of these will catch on cannot be predicted—that is why art is not science.

For schooling this has more import than merely confirming our allegiance to study of the humanities or the arts—an allegiance, by the way, that has wavered with every budgetary crisis. What some of us have called "esthetic education" may in the future move much further toward the center of the curriculum than it ever has been, because such education may become more crucial to our survival than it has hitherto been—if wresting individuality and freedom from a technological society is what we mean by *human* survival.

Disharmony in the world is produced by neglect, not only of moral principles but also of esthetic ones. Our esthetic sensibilities react to foul air, ugly buildings, the dehumanizing effects of poverty and disease, unsightly swellings induced by greed, and the ugly lesions produced by hatred and envy long before the scientific causes of these phenomena are explicated. That we can no longer afford to ignore these warnings of the spirit, which somehow find their way into art, needs no further elaboration here. We know—as Lewis Mumford,[11] Horatio Greenough[12] and others have long argued—that in a benign technological society, esthetic form and efficient function do not clash but converge toward identity.[13]

In a technologically mature society such as I am assuming we shall have in the decades to come, there is a real possibility of reinstating the sharp cleavage between the elite and the masses, but the basis for the distinction may not be primarily economic. Class difference could be based on the amount and degree of self-cultivation that people were willing to undertake. One cannot foreclose the possibility that people may arrange themselves on a continuum of self-cultivation, so that there would not be a sharp division between the self-cultivated and the noncultivated. Yet there lurks in my mind the hunch that the number who will exert the effort needed for an authentic, self-determined life will be small compared to the population at large. Opportunity will be there for all; in that, the future may differ radically from the past. But it is by no means obvious that a much larger proportion of the population will prefer to walk than to be carried.[14]

THE FUTURE SHAPE OF SCHOOLING

An essay on the future of education ought to say something about the way educational services will be delivered and to whom. It would seem that two broad conclusions can be drawn. First, the amount and depth of general education will have to be increased for the bulk of the population—for the entire educable spectrum between the ages of three or four to eighteen or twenty. Second, the high degree of vocational specialization will make highly differentiated vocational education in the postsecondary years routine for virtually everyone. In this I differ from the majority prognosis that specialized vocational training should be initiated in secondary school or even in the later years of the elementary school. I shall not defend my view at length, but several factors militate against such early training in job specifics: the relative ease with which many jobs can be learned on-the-job; the obsolescence of some categories of employment; and the youth themselves. That highly job specific training will have to be done sometime by somebody goes without saying, but it would be a mistake for the schools to do it at the expense of general education. I would defend this view, not on the ground that more general education is needed for vocational purposes—because for most jobs this may not be true—but because general education will be needed by all the citizens for the civic and personal dimensions of experience, and above all to lay the groundwork for self-cultivation should the individual choose to make that commitment.

I do not anticipate any radical change in the content of general education. This may betoken an infirmity of imagination, but I prefer to blame the lack of novelty on the belief that the most generalizable education—that is, the simplest package adequate to a great diversity of life situations—has no better source than a mix of the humanities and the sciences. If this strikes anyone as an apologia for tradition, let me note that the tradition of sciences and the humanities does not preserve everything that has been thought and wrought, but only that which continuous critical activity has judged to be the best that has been thought and wrought. If it is asked, "What is 'best'?" I offer a simple answer, but one to which I know of no genuinely viable alternative: The best is what the consensus of the learned and the wise in the various intellectual domains at any given time says it is.

What may well change in the future is the method of delivering educational services. I would anticipate that technology and the mass production techniques made possible by technology will influence education. Given the kind of technical improvements that we have every reason to expect in computer-aided instruction, television instruction, and video cassettes, there is at least one kind of teaching that might become almost the exclusive province of educational technology. This province is that of didactics. It includes all instruction in which the outcomes and the means thereto can be made explicit—can be programmed. In principle I do not see why anything that can be stated and analyzed unambiguously in terms of some logical language cannot be programmed.

So far as schooling consists of didactics—and much of it at all levels of instruction does—one can foresee it being carried on by machines. The staff necessary to implement this would be composed of: (a) developers of strategies, materials, and programs; and (b) personnel to tend the machines. I do not share the apprehensions of many school people about such a development, because as far as didactics are concerned, the ordinary live teacher functions as an inefficient machine.

Two consequences of this development can be anticipated. One is the change in the instructional staff, from one made up of "professional" teachers expected to do didactics and the two other types of teaching (about which something will be said shortly) to a staff made up largely—perhaps as much as 85 percent—of teachers who do nothing but didactics at the level of the paraprofessional technician. The other development is that didactics may be greatly decentralized, inasmuch as the appropriate electronic equipment could be set up in neighborhood libraries, in small study centers, or even—as with cassettes—in the home. Gathering large numbers of pupils on one site for didactics would be unnecessary.

Unfortunately, schooling is usually taken to include at least two other types of interaction between pupils and teachers—heuristics and philetics. By heuristics I mean the sort of interchange, between pupils and teachers, in which problems of one kind or another are discussed and structured by teacher and learners. Here the goals and the materials are not wholly explicit; process rather than product is both the outcome and the means. It is achieved in relatively small groups, and no attempt is made to cover a given number of topics or a specific amount of material.

Philetics is merely a Greek word meaning love. It stands for the type of teacher-pupil relationship currently expressed by the term *relating.* Searching for identity, fighting the stresses of adolescence, "doing one's thing," giving the elders their comeuppance. All of these amorphous but to the pupil very pressing concerns—commonly referred to as humanistic—can be covered by the term *philetics.*

Heuristic teaching should be experienced by every pupil some time in his career, but by its very nature it does not lend itself to mass methods. If didactics could be done efficiently by machines, there might be some time and money left to hire the sort of personnel who can do heuristics and to provide the time and conditions for it. A beginning could be made through problems courses in the high school, but the full development of heuristics should come in higher education where, alas, most of the time and resources are still spent on didactics that should have been completed by the end of the secondary years. The final quarter of the century may see the end of the long quest for a clear distinction between the secondary school and higher education, and I expect that that will result in a decrease of didactics in higher education and a greater emphasis on heuristics.

As for philetics, I doubt that they can be done well in school at all. The affective relationships implied by philetics do not comport well with the role of the teacher who serves *in loco parentis, in loco communitatis,* and *in loco humanitatis.* The teacher who tries to do didactics stands in the role of judge; even the heuristic teacher is the superior partner; the philetic teacher cannot take this role; teacher and pupil are just human beings trying to get along with each other. The philetic teacher is more a counselor than a teacher, and even something of a therapist in an unobtrusive way.

Perhaps an institution that is not really a school but rather something of an adjustatorium for middle and late adolescents is in the cards. I can see such an institution staffed by counselors and therapists who help adolescents know themselves, get rid of some of their hangups, kick the drug and other nasty habits, get some notion of an adult future, and gain acceptance by their peers. I doubt that this sort of interaction can be carried on as an incidental accompaniment to what is ordinarily known as study, whether didactic or heuristic. Certainly the number of Messrs. Chips who can combine these functions in one person are rare. The attempts by schools to integrate didactics and philetics have never been successful. The aim of the first is to ignore the demands of the affective and impulsive life, whereas the goal of the second is to cope with it. Only private schools can give equal attention to both, but even they don't try to do it all in the classroom. And they are most successful when they are boarding schools, so that learning and living can both be supervised, although not necessarily simultaneously.

The merit of an adjustatorium lies in the relative simplicity of its organization; it could be decentralized, because perforce it deals with small groups. Its ministrations need not cover a fixed period of time. It can be an adjunct to some school building, but it need not be. It might just as well be under the jurisdiction of the health department as under that of the school authorities.

This I know. The formal school is not an ideal place in which to cope with adolescent problems. Neither the high school nor the modern university is equipped for this. Both traditionally are devoted to intellectual development and not to the conditioning of the autonomous nervous system. Modern institutions of higher education recruit their staff from academic professionals. The professors belong to a guild that values scholarship in some well-defined domain, the narrower the better. Even the tutorial relationship that undergraduates at the Oxbridge institutions enjoy are denied to most American undergraduates, although good graduate students get it from the advisors whose apprentices they are. American undergraduates—at least until they declare a major—are nobody's apprentices, and the masters have eyes primarily for those who will become apprentices, disciples, and ultimately colleagues.

Before leaving the effects of technology on schooling, I must speculate on the role of drugs, neurosurgery, and genetic manipulation. While electronics nourish hope for doing didactics more efficiently, drugs and surgery may help repair conditions that give rise to antilearning syndromes. Drugs are already used to quiet hyperkinetic children, and one can hardly resist the speculation that some day drugs or surgery can make all learning easy and automatic. Perhaps they can even solve the problem of philetics. As for genetic manipulation, we are told that is a long way into the future and may create as many problems as it solves. Still, one cannot omit it from the inventory of possibilities for the future.

If I am skeptical of these last three methods for insuring learning or conditioning, it is not for technical reasons. One can conceive the discovery of learning pathways analogous to the nerve pathways that acupuncture is supposed to exploit so successfully. One can also conceive of a society that closely controls the genetic pool. No, the skepticism comes from the human qualities of people. Suppose that we could achieve perfect control of learning—that we could teach anybody anything we chose to have them learn. Suppose we could vote secretly on whether it should be a national policy to use these means. Would we vote for it?

Presumably parents whose children were not doing well in school would vote yes. Social agencies, in their official capacities at least, would see an opportunity for the abolition of all social evils that result from ignorance. Politicians with an itch for controlling the electorate might vote yes, if they could control the input. Exasperated teachers—especially around three in the afternoon—would be sorely tempted to vote for it.

I dare say all of us might want to vote for it, provided it were restricted to didactics, to learning painlessly particular necessary facts, rules, and skills. Who, for example, would object to learning spelling by ingesting a pill or arithmetical computation by electrical stimulation of the brain or the facts of history and geography by minor surgery? Who would object to having his parents select a set of genes for him that would enable him to learn these things at a single exposure?

Our reservations would emerge when it came to using drugs, neurosurgery, or the manipulation of the genetic pool in heuristics and philetics—the processes that shape the forms of the mind and of feeling. Here the crucial matter is not achievement of the right thought or feeling but the process of becoming aware of what is right. This, in turn, necessitates the possibility of error, of alternatives conjured up by imagination. In short, it necessitates freedom and indeterminacy. But this is precisely what the perfect control of all types of learning might so easily choke off.

Without being unduly Freudian about it, one might say that consciously we are for efficiency, and efficiency in learning and teaching would be greatly enhanced if we could control these processes as well as we control some of our physiological processes. But when we are confronted with images of societies that presumably carry out the potentialities of social control by intelligence—for example, B. F. Skinner's *Walden II* and *Beyond Freedom and Dignity*—we shrink from them. Perhaps subconsciously we don't want to unravel the mystery of learning too far, and maybe that is why we have not done so.

CONCLUSION

I must apologize to the reader for the unspectacular future herein predicted for education, but this comes from the notions set forth in the early paragraphs of this chapter. Among them was the notion that education may not develop isomorphically with the developments in what W. F. Ogburn called the "material culture." Thus education may confront complexity with greater efforts at simplicity; it may confront the increased threat of robotism with imaginative ploys for freedom; people may rediscover a moral and esthetic sensitivity that the developments of the technological society should, in principle, preclude.

To borrow a concept from physiology, human experience also tends toward a stable state, toward homeostasis, but the stable state is what has always been called human nature or the human essence. That essence has as its most unique power the imagination by which we can disengage ourselves from actuality and create the whole realm of possibility. Science and technology, which are themselves energized by the imagination, hastily disown this parent in favor of the other one, reason. But the human adventure continues to be instigated, organized, and renewed by imagination, and so long as this is true, the education of human beings will be by, for, and by means of the fruits of that imagination—the cultural heritage husbanded, nurtured, and transmitted by the school.

NOTES

1. In the words of a noted futurist, predicting the future is a construction, although perhaps I would not want to claim as he does that "the intellectual construction of a likely future is a *work of art, in the full sense of the term* . . ." Bertrand de Jouvenel, *The Art of Conjecture*, trans. Nikita Lary (New York: Basic Books, 1967), p. 17.

2. D. H. Meadows et al., *The Limits to Growth*, a report for the Club of Rome's Project on the Predicament of Mankind (New York: Potomac Associates-Universe Books, 1972).

3. Philip H. Abelson, "Limits to Growth," *Science*, vol. 175, 17 March 1972, p. 1197. Copyright 1972 by the American Association for the Advancement of Science.

4. *Ibid.*

5. Glenn T. Seaborg, "For a U.S. Energy Agency," *Science,* vol. 176, 16 June 1972, p. 1189. Copyright 1972 by the American Association for the Advancement of Science.

6. For example, Ivar Berg, *Education and Jobs: The Great Training Robbery* (New York: Praeger, 1970).

7. Sterling Livingston, "The Myth of the Well-Educated Manager," *Harvard Business Review,* January–February, 1971.

8. The main arguments for de-schooling, especially for the poor of undeveloped countries, can be found in Illich's *Celebration of Awareness—A Call for Institution Revolution* (New York: Doubleday Anchor Books, 1971).

9. Thus it is reported that in Budapest the labor unions foster a number of symphonic, choral, and dance groups, and that in this country the AFL-CIO has established professional offices in New York, Buffalo, Louisville, and Minneapolis to encourage esthetic relationships between their members and community resources. Max Kaplan, "Work, Leisure, and Aesthetic Education," *Journal of Aesthetic Education,* January 1970, p. 48.

10. The role of the imagination and the arts in enlightened cherishing is discussed in some detail in my *Enlightened Cherishing: An Essay on Aesthetic Education,* Kappa Delta Pi Lecture (Urbana: University of Illinois Press, 1972).

11. Lewis Mumford, *Technics and Civilization* (New York: Harcourt Brace Jovanovich, 1934).

12. Horatio Greenough, *Form and Function,* reprint (Berkeley: University of California Press, 1957).

13. For the role of art and artists and esthetic education in the future, see the special issue of *The Journal of Aesthetic Education,* January, 1970.

14. One might argue that in meritocratic, technologically mature society, the difference between the masses and classes would give way to a single ladder of achievement—a continuum. I have so argued in *The Real World of the Public Schools* (New York: Harcourt Brace Jovanovich, 1972), but this continuum may describe the economic vocational aspect of the culture better than it does the quality of individual life.

Jack R.
Frymier

Jack R. Frymier

*Dr. Frymier is chairman of the
division of curriculum and
foundations in the College of
Education at Ohio State
University and is co-director of
the Center for the Study of
Motivation and Human Abilities
there. Author of a number of
books in education, including*
Curriculum Improvement for
Better Schools, *he has also been
active in professional
organizations, especially the
Association for Supervision and
Curriculum Development and the
Alliance of Associations for the
Advancement of Education,
serving as president of each of
these. He also edits* Theory Into
Practice *and* The Educational
Forum.

a curriculum manifesto

INTRODUCTION

It is fashionable today for speakers to talk about change and for writers to write about change. Alvin Toffler's exciting book, *Future Shock*, begins this way:

In the three short decades between now and the twenty-first century, millions of ordinary, psychologically normal people will face an abrupt collision with the future. Citizens of the world's richest and most technologically advanced nations, many of them will find it increasingly painful to keep up with the incessant demand for change that characterizes our time. For them, the future will have arrived too soon.[1]

Change has been a part of man's life since the beginning of time. Today the pace of change is accelerating phenomenally. We understand Norman Cousins when he maintains "that 1940 was more than a hundred years ago."[2] Being in Washington today, San Francisco tomorrow, and Columbus the next day is more typical than unusual. Communication, transportation, social relations, conceptualization—these are the areas of fantastic change.

It has been suggested that man now has developed, to the theoretical level, the capacity to transmit people by means of electronic impulse. And before this century is out, the odds are very great that we will have developed the hardware to communicate objects by electronic means. Imagine the changes that will come about when man can transmit objects through space at the speed of light. Think of the changes that will have to occur when people are able to send themselves from here to there electronically. Perhaps we will eventually be able to enter a booth, dial a set of numbers, and—zip—we will leave that spot and find ourselves in another booth thousands of miles away in less than a second. Sound fantastic? Of course! The idea of sending men to the moon at speeds of thousands of miles an hour sounded fantastic at the time of the Civil War. But the Civil War and man on the moon are both history now. Both have been accomplished and are part of our past.

Speculation that man can devise a means of sending himself at the speed of light along the waves of light is not idle. And what will the world be like when such technology has been made operational? What will the world be like when transportation and communication are the very same thing? What will happen to our cities? What will become of the automobile industry and the aircraft industry and our highway system? What kinds of social problems and educational problems and employment problems will we face?

Questions such as these are almost unthinkable. Most of us can hardly comprehend the idea that transportation may become synonlymous with communication. Sorting out the implications of such a proposition is even more difficult. And yet we must. The people who will have to live in that kind of world and cope with those kinds of problems are in our schools right now or will be in our schools during our teaching years. The obligation to help them equip themselves for that world is ours. We may not live to see transportation become synonymous with communication, but we know it is likely to happen. When it does, will our responsibilities to the young have been fulfilled? Will we have provided them with opportunities and experiences for developing attitudes and skills and understanding which will serve them well? That is our charge, our professional responsibility. What can we do?

We are halfway between the end of World War II and the year 2000. We live and work in one of the most technologically advanced and urbanized societies in the world. The American culture is changing, as Toffler maintains, at an unbelievable pace and in unpredictable ways.

Some persons argue that all of the changes add up to fewer freedoms for individuals and more institutional and governmental control. Freedom inheres in opportunities individuals have to exercise personal choice, to make decisions. Those forces and factors which limit choice move us away from freedom toward authoritarian or external control. Those forces and factors which expand the opportunity of individuals to exercise personal choice and which make more alternatives available move us in the direction of freedom, toward democratic or internal self-control. My understanding of the American scene during the final third of the twentieth century suggests that Americans have expanded and extended both the range and depth of personal choice for all individuals to an unprecedented degree. But the expansion of human freedom has created a paradox that few of us have been prepared to face: qualitatively more and qualitatively worse problems than almost anyone had thought would ever occur. How did this happen?

Expanding and extending freedom has meant that more people have more opportunities to exercise more personal choices in more areas of human endeavor than ever before. Choices, however, always create consequences. Decisions by one person, for example, almost always affect other people. That is the reality of human affairs. And more opportunities for more individuals to make more personal choices have resulted in more bad decisions as well as more good decisions. Further, many decisions were bad because people have been hurt or killed, and property and human relationships have been defaced or destroyed.

Choices and decisions require information, and information is readily available as a commodity today. We can obtain more facts, more knowledge, more concepts, more information of every kind now than ever before. Access to information is part of the choice-making process today. But as the amount and availability of accurate information have increased, so too have the amount and availability of inaccurate information and of information-distorting phenomena such as whiskey, heroin, and LSD.

In America at the present time, we have more personal freedoms but also more social problems than ever before. Overwhelmed with information but prodded and pulled in a million directions, we grope our way toward the twenty-first century doing some things right and some things wrong. Furthermore, we are seldom clear about which is right and which is wrong, because standards and values and even factual knowledge seem to change all the time.

Two courses of action, at least, have been set forth from which we might choose. The first possibility goes something like this: "If people do not know how to use their freedoms wisely and well, then take the freedoms away." That notion has been advocated by many people in various ways. Such proposals are often expressed in statements such as these:

> *If those long-haired kids don't know how to dress right and act decent, then kick them out of school.*
>
> *If those stupid people on welfare can't hold a job, then let them starve.*
>
> *If those left-wing liberals or radical blacks don't like it here, why don't they go to Russia or Africa and let us be?*
>
> *America—love it or leave it (as if "love it" meant agree with, approve of, and conform to whatever most people or particular people feel and say).*

Given the proliferation of facts and places and things from which to choose, some people argue that anyone who cannot or will not make decisions which conform to their own values ought to be restrained. Dissidents ought to have their freedoms curtailed. They should be restricted, cut off from subsequent choices, and denied.

An alternative to this way of thinking goes like this: "If people do not know how to use their freedoms wisely and well, then we must help them to learn, to understand, to develop intellectually and emotionally, to grow. We must help them learn to make rational decisions that will serve them and their fellow man in creative, loving, humane ways.

The learning route, of course, means more education, better teaching, and an upgrading of curricula and schooling in every conceivable way. Such a way of thinking is expressed in propositions such as these:

> *If hard drugs are a problem among young people, then we ought to have a drug education program in the schools.*
>
> *If pregnancy and venereal disease among teenagers is increasing, then perhaps we need more sex education in the curriculum.*
>
> *If high school graduates cannot get and hold a job, maybe we should build more vocational schools.*
>
> *If more and more students think the Russian economic system is better than ours, then we probably need to develop new curriculum materials in the area of economic education.*

Schools have often been asked to deal with social problems that cannot be solved by education alone. Juvenile delinquency, drug addiction and distribution, poverty, and segregation, for example, are all affected by education to some degree. But none of those problem areas can ever be solved completely or even primarily by educational means, unless that term is defined very broadly to include therapeutic rehabilitation, penal system reform, and the enlightenment of senators, representatives, presidents, governors, sheriffs, judges, city council members, and the like. Granting these difficulties and limitations, education is still a very different and more positive approach to dealing with the problem of poor decisions and irrational choice-making than the curtailment of choice. Further, helping people learn to make intelligent, compassionate decisions is clearly a goal that schools can and are expected to pursue. Curriculum is a means to that human end. Improving curriculum, dramatically and demonstrably, is a responsibility which teachers and administrators must assume. And we have to do it better in the future than we have ever been able to do it up to now.

We must try to be perfect. We know that we cannot be, of course, but we have to try. Such idealism, of course, makes for problems and potentialities. The problems arise because we are never satisfied—we fall short of our goals and strive and strive again. Even though we may be moving in a positive direction consistently, we criticize both our leaders and ourselves for not moving far enough, fast enough, or often enough. Idealism is an absolutely marvelous disease.

But there are reality factors with which we have to deal, too. Gravity cannot be ignored if one wants to fly a plane, for example. Ingenuity, hard work, understanding, and careful planning make it possible to overcome the force of gravity and in fact to fly—but the reality factor cannot be ignored.

The trick to making a difference and being effective, if there is a trick, is to merge the reality factors with the idealistic conceptions so that ideals are reality based and reality is rooted directly in the core of idealism. Such a proposition is simple to state but difficult to achieve. For example, the Golden Gate Bridge is an architectural wonder and breathtaking to look at, but it is rooted in engineering principles and mathematical formulas which are consistent with reality factors as well as with aesthetic considerations. Semmelweis' search for the cause of death from childbirth fever or the safe return of the Apollo 13 crew from their ill-fated voyage are other examples of the fusion of idealism and reality. Our history, as a people and as a profession, has been a continuous and relentless search for goals and means which embody the essence of idealism and practical forms.

During recent years all of our social institutions have come under vigorous attack. Schools are not alone as the objects of fault-finding today. Churches, government, industry, the professions, and even philanthropies have been severely criticized. However, it is important to note that public institutions have been criticized primarily for the *means* they have employed, while private institutions have come under attack for the *goals* they have pursued. Schools, courts, legislatures, hospitals, and prisons, for example, have been roundly condemned because their techniques, procedures, and methods have been inadequate or ineffective or worse. Private institutions, such as corporations, churches, even law firms, have been viciously criticized for their objectives and goals.

For example, not many people doubt that the United States needs some kind of military force, given the state of affairs in the world today. There are some who question the wisdom of any army or navy or air force, but most Americans accept the general goals which the military seek to achieve. It is the means the armed forces employ which arouse public indignation. Is bombing necessary? Is defoliation imperative? Is continued underground testing of nuclear weapons essential? Do we need a large standing army in Western Europe today?

The same kinds of questions have been raised about education and schools. Few people doubt that education is important and that we need schools. Few people question the goal of doing whatever we can to help children learn. What people are concerned about is how we are going about the job. People are disturbed about the methods and the curricula—the means—that we have chosen to utilize.

It is within this framework and from this perspective that we must try to respond. Furthermore, we need to conceptualize our undertakings in such a way that we are deliberate and farsighted and active, rather than irrational and myopic and reactive, in anything we choose to do. Our fiber and our mettle are being tested. The time has come for us to pour everything we know and everything we can do into a new and creative effort to completely transform the curricula in our schools.

My purpose here is to issue a call for curriculum development and curriculum change. The developments and changes which I sketch in outline form are basically different in conception and implementation from those we have experienced in recent years. If we can find new and more powerful ways to do better what everybody agrees we ought to do—help children learn—then we can make a significant contribution to our students, to our profession, and to ourselves.

We need all of the intelligence, conviction, creativity, and motivation that we can muster. The task is difficult beyond belief, and tinkering will not suffice. We have piddled around with curriculum development for far too long. We have spent millions and millions of dollars on curriculum efforts that are going straight down the drain. Some residue will typically remain, of course, and we can always hope that what has been created and pressed on schools is not worse than what was there before. We are a rich nation. We can afford the cost. And as Edison said, "There are a lot of things we know now that will not work."

Our problem, our task, our challenge must be to learn what we can from the curriculum ventures of recent years, and to go beyond, far beyond, to a new and different conceptualization of what curriculum might become. To say it another way—our activities and our goals were far too modest in the years gone by. We need to find different conceptual handles with which to generate curriculum. We need new assumptions, new language, new metaphors to think about the curriculum realities and the curriculum ideals that are involved. We need new propositions, new analyses, and new insights into whatever it is that we refer to when we use the word *curriculum.*

I will not be able to provide many of those new things that I think we so sorely need. I intend to do the very best I can, but what I really hope is that our profession, as an intelligent, hard-working group, can find ways to work together to break out of our old ways of thinking and feeling and acting about curriculum so that we can generate some completely new theoretical possibilities and practical realities.

This paper outlines three things: where we are now; where I think we ought to go; and how I think we ought to try to get there. I am going to share with you some of my assessments about curriculum as it exists today, and something about my hopes of what it might become. In this sense, the paper outlines my perceptions and my dreams. It is not complete. There are a thousand other topics that might have been included, and at least a hundred other possible paths that we might pursue. Even so, the paper represents a call to action, a plea to focus hard on curriculum development in new and different ways in the days and months and years ahead.

MAN SHAPES AND IS SHAPED BY HIS ENVIRONMENT [3]

Let me begin by outlining a concept of environment which I think has relevance for curriculum workers today. Human behavior is a function of the interaction of the individual with his environment. The individual has both a time span and a life space, and he lives and functions in an environmental setting. Man is a part of the universe, yet apart from the universe, too. As part of the natural phenomena of the universe, man interacts with his environment and is profoundly affected by both the nature and the quality of those interactions. He looks at the stars and writes sonnets and songs. He pollutes rivers and air and gets ill and complains. By deliberate and unconscious endeavor, he creates and recreates environmental artifacts which, in turn, affect the way he thinks and acts and feels. Probably no other organism exercises as much control over those aspects of the universe with which it interacts as does man. The result is that man shapes and is shaped by his environment day after day.

The story of Winston Churchill's ideas about reconstructing the House of Commons during the height of World War II has been described by Max Ways as follows:

The old House had been blasted by a German bomb, and the question was how it should be reconstructed. A more spacious chamber, perhaps? One with a semicircular arrangement of comfortable chairs and useful desks, such as many of the world's parliaments enjoyed? Churchill thought not. What he wanted, essentially, was a replica of the old House with its rows of facing benches that symbolically expressed the party structure, emphasizing the contrasting roles of the Government and the Opposition. The new House, like the old, should have far fewer seats than there were members, so that in an ordinary ill-attended session speakers would not be discouraged by addressing empty benches. On great occasions, members flocking in would be crowded standing in the aisles, thus encasing debate and decision with visible signs of gravity and urgency.[4]

Churchill's summary argument was: "We shape our buildings, and afterwards our buildings shape us." Man shapes his own environment, then is shaped by it in turn.

Man affects what is around him, then is affected in return. That point is simple and yet profound. It is so obvious that it hardly seems worth mentioning, but it is so important that those of us who are environmental builders—curriculum construction is the term we usually employ—must grasp its significance or we lose our sense of perspective and our sense of influence and control.

Beliefs and assumptions are part of our environment, too. We are imprisoned by the assumptions which we hold. Willis Harman[5] argues that within the framework of prevailing values and basic cultural assumptions, the major problems of the world are essentially unsolvable. As long as we hold to what he calls "pathogenic premises"—the reductionist view of man, the separateness of men, the separateness of man from nature, the economic image of man, the belief that the future of the planet ought to be left to autonomous nation–states—we immobilize ourselves. Everything can be explained away as a function of the fact that everything lies outside of our sphere of control. It is a fatalistic, pessimistic set of notions, hardly worthy of creatures who claim to have been created in God's image.

It shows up in many ways. For example, in the area of curriculum innovation, for years we have said: "If you will give us more money, we will innovate." Implicit in that proposition is the notion that "if you do not give us extra funds, we will stay the same." That argument is both irrational and irresponsible. It absolves us of the responsibility for improving what we are doing, and simultaneously places us in a dependent rather than an independent role. All over America there are school people who say, in effect: "Tell me what the guidelines are and I will put together a proposal on any topic right away." Such a willingness to do almost anything for extra money has allowed us, over the years, to slip until we are following other people's leads rather than setting our own courses of action.

For example, how many times have you heard somebody say: "We would offer more vocational programs (or special classes for retarded children) if the state would give us extra units under the minimum foundations program. We would really like to do it, but the state won't give us the extra funds." Or: "We would like to buy special curriculum materials for use with youngsters who come from economically disadvantaged backgrounds, but our special project was not approved."

These are examples from within our experience of pathogenic premises at work. The beliefs and assumptions we hold about people and institutions and things shape and frame our lives in inexorable ways. If we believe that we can act, if we assume that we have latitude and flexibility, if we are convinced that we have considerable control over who we are and what we do, then we can shape our environment in such a way that it shapes us as we want it to. We can build into our environment those ideas and those people who will enable us to become what we hope to become. But only if we believe that this is possible can it become so.

We are prisoners of our beliefs. But beliefs are learned—at home, at work, at play. Experience resides within us as achievement: a residue that we call memory, or what we have learned. Our knowledge about the process of perception makes it obvious that past experience exerts a pervasive effect on present experiencing. As Earl Kelly taught us so dramatically,[6] our previous experiences with rectangles and right angles "will not go away" when we look at the rotating trapezoidal window, so we see it go back and forth instead of going all the way around. We are prisoners, so to speak, of what we have done and where we have been and what we have seen and heard. The basic purpose of education is to help us learn to use past experience as a basis for acquiring new meanings that will free us from what restricts and enslaves. In this sense, we are like prisoners who use their imprisoning experience as a basis for developing new understandings (conceptual tools) and skills (physical tools). As we add meaning to incoming stimuli, we broaden our experiential base. As we reinterpret and relate and create new meanings and new significances, we grow. And growth is the driving force which frees us from the limitations of our pasts.

WHERE ARE WE NOW?

Some persons maintain that curriculum has been a changing field in recent years. That is probably correct. In a "back and forth" sense, anyway, curriculum has seemed to be different at various points in time. It is very difficult, however, to not believe that we are in a rut. We shift back and forth between what I have referred to in another place[7] as Assumption Number One and Assumption Number Two—subject matter-oriented or society-oriented programs, both of which are essentially curricula for the purpose of vocational or social control.

Herrick talks about these two approaches this way:

A preoccupation with subject fields leads directly to the problems of generalizing, the cognitive processes, the logical structures of subject matter, transfer of training, mental discipline, readiness, repetition, reinforcement, retention, and the ability of this individual to learn. A preoccupation with a socially centered curriculum leads to an examination of the nature of persistent and recurring social and democratic processes, group dynamics, valuing and normative behavior, organismic and topological concepts of learning, and status- and role-determining processes.[8]

As I understand these two assumptions in action, both reflect a pervasive and persistent concern for control.

In Assumption Number One, the disciplines are used to discipline the learner, to channel and focus his behavior in what are essentially vocational ways. That is, if a person wants to be a mathematician, then he has to study mathematics. If he wants to be a farmer, then he needs to study farming. If he wants to be a poet or a plumber or a pilot or a physicist, then obviously it is both appropriate and necessary to study those particular areas of academic inquiry. Once a student has made a vocational choice, once a student is sure that he intends to be a pharmacist or an engineer, a short order cook or a newspaper writer or a styler of hair, then those who have responsibility for helping that student learn can mold and shape and direct his behavior in precisely predetermined ways. Complete control of what the learner does is the instructor's goal.

In Assumption Number Two, social considerations and social needs give form and substance to programs so that social purposes are achieved. The prevalent language is learned. The customs, traditions, sentiments, and norms of the immediate group are instilled in the learner in ways that make people become as alike as peas in a pod in an anthropological sense.[9] The basic tendency of every society is to induce conformity among its members. When the school functions on the basis of Assumption Number Two, then the curriculum becomes a program for social purposes and the school becomes an instrument of social control.

For centuries, schools have served these two primary purposes—vocational training and socialization of the child—with first one purpose and then the other being emphasized at different points in time. Any careful study of educational practice will reflect that point. Less obvious but equally important is that both approaches are essentially programs for restricting and controlling what the learners do. The control is always "for the students' welfare," of course, but even so, it is control.

Sometimes those who advocate inquiry training or learning by discovery imply that such techniques are less concerned with control than other approaches might be. Not so. One of the observers at a national conference on learning by discovery makes the point this way: "Students can be encouraged, prodded, and shaped to discover. In short, learning by discovery implies controlling the behavior just as does the old-fashioned drill method. The only difference is the pattern of control."[10]

In practice, the emphasis on behavioral objectives, career education and vocational training—learning mathematics as a mathematician learns it, or exploring economics the way an economist would—are all illustrations of the control-oriented aspects of curriculum today. I do not make that point to suggest that control is wrong. Sometimes teaching that is designed to control the behavior of the learner is most appropriate, and, in fact, exactly what the learner himself desires. Sometimes it is necessary. The question is: Are control assumptions the ones that ought to characterize most of the curriculum considerations from kindergarten to grade twelve? I do not think so.

Look at other so-called innovations that exist in curriculum now. Although they are not particularly widespread, consider the assumptions and operations in evidence behind the performance contracting efforts and the accountability talk today. The talk that men employ affects their conduct.

Benjamin[11] Whorf argues, in linguistic theory, that language shapes behavior. The words men use to describe reality to themselves dictates what they do or do not do. Men will smoke around gasoline drums marked empty, for example, more readily than around drums labeled full, even though the gasoline vapors in and near the empty tank make that vicinity more dangerous. It is the word, not the reality of the situation, that prompts the response.

In our society and in our schools, the language of relationships might be dichotomized this way: conditional relationships, and relationships without conditions. The first is a language of control. The second is a language of love and growth.

The language of conditional relationships sounds something like this:

I will love you if you will do what I say.

I will give you a dollar if you get an A in school.

If you will read this book, then I will let you play.

If you keep your room neat and tidy and don't tell any lies, then Santa Claus will bring you a present on Christmas Day.

The language of conditional relationships is an if-then language—"*if* you do this, *then* I will do that." It assumes the logic of cause and effect. In actual practice it fosters dependent-prone behavior because it invites manipulation of other persons, deception, and control. Such relationships are basically utilitarian—each person attempts to use another to achieve his own purposes or goals—and ethical values are reduced to practical considerations.

Will it work?

Does it get results?

How much does it cost?

Will it take too much time?

Consider the language of the Texarkana performance contract:

The stimulus for the refinement of contingency management was, quite basically, the difficulty of motivating students to complete PI (programmed instruction) sequences. . . . To considerably oversimplify, it was found that a great many activities could be identified which the student would prefer to engage in (rather) than going through a PI sequence. These activities, called high-probability behaviors, can be specified by observing students, asking them, or sometimes prompting them through the use of a "reinforcement memo." Once an appropriate high-probability behavior is identified, it can be used to reinforce the lower probability behavior of attending to an instructional unit.

This system sounds deceptively simple. Many will say that this is how they've always managed behavior. But the key is to let the student himself identify the desired high-probability behavior, and then to make a "performance contract," either written or verbalized, in which the student agrees to perform a certain amount of low-probability behavior in return for the consideration of being permitted to engage in a higher-probability behavior for a specified period of time.[12]

What does that language say to you? It says to me that those who use such relationships to help young people learn are treating people as things—as objects to be used.

I know that such concepts and techniques will work to help a six-year-old who cannot control his bowel movements learn not to soil his britches, but is that any reason to urge that they be adopted in more normal circumstances? I think not.

A friend of mine tells the following story about conditional relationships and learning. This friend had been interested for years in language and vocabulary development among the young. One day he was visiting a neighbor, and as he talked with his neighbor's child the little girl told him about a game her parents played to help her learn new words. For every new word for which the child would learn the spelling and the meaning, her parents would give her a quarter. My friend is interested in children learning new words, of course, and he wanted to go along with things, so he spelled out a big word for the youngster and said: "If you will learn how to spell that word and what it means, I'll give you a quarter." The little girl studied the word and thought for a moment, and then she replied: "I think that word is worth fifty cents."

That is what happens when we use conditional relationships to facilitate learning. Students sense that they are objects rather than beings. What they do becomes more important than what they are. The logic encourages them to respond in kind. When we attempt to manipulate other people and control their behavior, they attempt to manipulate us and control what we do.

The logic of unconditional relationships, on the other hand, is the logic of growth rather than the logic of denial or control. Jesus said: "Love thy neighbor." He did not say, "If your neighbor loves you, then love him in return." He did not say, "Do good unto others if they do good to you." Jesus urged men to "do unto others as you would have them do unto you."

The language of relationships without conditions might look something like this:

> *I will love you whether you do what I say or not.*
>
> *I will honor and value you as a person of dignity and worth, whatever you do.*
>
> *If you kill other people, I will attempt to restrain you, but I will not take your life.*
>
> *You are important because you are you.*

The relationship without conditions is a voluntary relationship. Only when people are free to separate is there meaning in being together. Compulsory relationships rob both parties of their integrity. Both the captor and the slave are prisoners of the compulsory system. The power of a voluntary relationship, on the other hand, is absolutely fantastic. Physician and patient, man and wife, friend and friend. The freedom to go apart—to separate and leave—gives significance and strength to the relationships that generate and are maintained. People who come together and stay together, without conditions and without bonds, are able to help one another develop and grow in ways no conditional relationship can ever assure.

There are many occasions, of course, in which people deliberately place themselves in a learning situation where they are extremely dependent upon the teacher. This sense of dependence may be a function of the fact that decisions and actions of great impact are involved. It may arise because of complete novelty or lack of experience in the situation, or because of the detail and complexity of information being utilized. Any combination of these factors heightens the sense of dependence of student on teacher in the teaching-learning situation.

A medical student, for example, or a student pilot, will find that almost any learning situation is potent with possibilities which could affect or curtail human life, sometimes his own. The student pilot, for example, is dependent upon his instructor for information and assistance, because anything the student does affects life and limb. The same would be true if a person were learning to fire a 4.2-inch mortar, take LSD, drive an automobile, scuba dive, or jump from an airplane with a parachute. The sense of danger makes a learner feel dependent on the teacher.

Likewise, if a person wants to learn to play the trumpet, build an electronic organ, write a novel, or program a computer, lack of experience in any of these endeavors may make him feel completely dependent on his teacher. Even if he has had some experience and no actual danger to persons is involved, if the goal to be achieved requires intricate patterns of information, awareness of nuances and subtleties which are not easily observable, or vast sums of factual knowledge which he does not possess, he would be forced to be dependent on his teacher. If a student wants to test a biological theory, analyze the content of a chemical solution, read a foreign newspaper, repair an airplane engine, or navigate the open ocean in a sailboat, he needs precise technical data and particular problem solving skills. Lacking these, he has a sense of inadequacy; he is dependent on those who are helping him learn to do those things.

If a learner feels dependent in a teaching-learning situation, and if he hopes to master factual knowledge or concepts or skills, then over a period of time (the learning period) he must move from a state of dependence to a state of independence. If he does not, his teacher will have failed.

In other words, mastering the intricacies of flying an airplane, for example, is not enough. If after completion of that learning the student pilot is still afraid to fly unless his teacher is there to "bail him out," then the student is incompetent or a failure. And such labels are appropriate despite the fact that "he knows" most if not all that he is "supposed to know."

What I am arguing for is a direction, an inclination, a tendency. It is extremely difficult, in our condition-laden culture, to place oneself and function in a completely nonconditional role. Even so, I am urging a deliberate shift, from conditional relationships between teacher and child and between supervisor and teacher toward relationships without conditions, relationships in which honest interaction and noncoercive efforts would always prevail.

To make that shift, we must change our attitudes. We do not need any special understandings or particular facts or unusual skills. All we need is a set of assumptions which characterize those with whom we work as persons of integrity and worth. If we believe that they want to learn, they will. If we believe that they want to work, they will. A child on drugs or a youngster conditioned for years by evasive or deceptive treatment will have a resistance to change which must be overcome. But that can be done. Most people are not in one of those extreme categories. Most people are honest and open. They look forward to new experiences, and they want a chance to learn. Most

people are intrigued if another person relates to them in a nonconditional way.

Now consider these ideas in relation to some of the propositions
which are inherent in the concepts of accountability as those are being
propounded today. Accountability is an important idea. It must be
explored and debated in every way. We learned from the Nuremburg
war trials that men must be held accountable for what they do. The
Mai Lai incident carved that concept deeply in our conscience again.
As a people, our history is an oft told story of responsibility and freedom. Holding people responsible for their actions is a notion almost
as old as time.

But holding one man responsible for what he does is not the
same as holding one man responsible for the deeds of another. No
man should be held responsible for what another person does or does
not do. Even parents cannot be held responsible for the deeds or mis-
deeds of their children. Recently ordinances were passed in Michigan
holding parents responsible for what their children do. A story[13] about
those ordinances attests to the fact that the concept of assigned responsibility is not a part of our heritage. One of the commissioners who
passed the ordinance even feels that it is unconstitutional, but he
wonders aloud: "If parents aren't responsible for their children, who
the hell is?" The answer, at least in some people's minds, is the school.

The schools and school people are thought by many to be
responsible for what children do. Learning has always been defined
in terms of behavioral change. The father who complains to the teacher,
"Our boy is in the third grade now, and he still sasses his mother,"
is suggesting that the school is to blame. How arrogant and impudent
can people be?

Obviously school people are responsible for what they do, for
how they teach and administer and supervise in schools. Obviously
school people must give an accounting for their behaviors, for their
personal and professional conduct, for what they do or do not do.
It is completely inappropriate, however, to argue that one man ought
to be held accountable for the thoughts and deeds of another person.
That is guilt by association under a new and fancy name.

For example, hold my feet to the fire for what I write in this
chapter. Insist that my statements and my logic in this chapter are
soundly reasoned and validly based. Be adamant if I do not present
my propositions with strength of conviction and clarity of prose. But
do not hold me responsible for what you do with these ideas after
you have finished reading what I have written. Do not insist that it
is my fault if you do not do my bidding. Do not argue that I am
responsible if you fail to heed my suggestions.

This is a curriculum manifesto—a call to action. And I sincerely hope that, when you have finished reading this paper, you will weave some of what I say into your professional efforts and your understanding about what education is and what it could be. But if someone tries to hold me responsible for what you do, then I may be forced to go beyond the reasonable limits of persuasion and communication. I may have to manipulate not only the environment but also you. If I were responsible for what you do, then I would work in every way that I know to control your behavior, to limit your choice, to channel your thoughts and feelings and actions along lines that I approve. Without those limitations, you might do what you want to do. And if I have to be responsible for your behavior and being, that cannot be condoned; not even allowed.

Our laws and our customs, our beliefs and our heritage all argue convincingly that each man can be held accountable for his own behavior, but not for the actions or inactions of others. In his famous Cooper Institute address, Lincoln dealt with the concept of individual responsibility. His arguments were aimed at the Southerners of that time, but his logic holds for all Americans today. He said:

You charge that we stir up insurrections among your slaves. We deny it; and what is your proof? Harper's Ferry! John Brown! John Brown was no Republican; and you have failed to implicate a single Republican in his Harper's Ferry enterprise. If any member of our party is guilty in that matter, you know it or you do not know it. If you do know it you are inexcusable for not designating the man and proving the fact. If you do not know it, you are inexcusable for asserting it, and especially for persisting in the assertion after you have tried and failed to make the proof. You do not have to be told that persisting in a charge which one does not know to be true, is simply malicious slander.[14]

The most violent rending in our nation's history was a wild and mauling war fought to grant personal freedom to hundreds of thousands of men and women. It is not to our credit today that Lincoln preserved the union and freed the slaves. It is not to our credit that Nixon bridged the gap in time and space between America and China. Nixon took that step, not us. He led the way. Whatever credit or blame is involved rests on his shoulders. We can be neither proud of nor blamed for what other men have done. And that is precisely how it ought to be. The president of the United States is accountable to the people of the United States for what *he* does. If we approve of political figures' efforts and think well of their actions, we will vote them into office again. If we disapprove of their efforts and disagree with their actions, we will not vote them into office again.

I am not responsible for what my forefathers did to Blacks or women or Jews. I am directly responsible for what I do. I am not accountable for what my grandfather or my wife or my administrative superiors or my colleagues do. I am responsible for my teaching, my arguments, my interpretations, my learning. But not for yours.

Nor do I want to be. You have your life to live, your commitments to cherish, your proposals to make, your own ways to behave. We need persuasion, not coercion; discussion, not demands. Accountability is an important and powerful concept, but we must not misuse it.

WHERE SHOULD WE BE GOING?

Herbert Kliebard[15] maintains that the new epoch of curriculum inquiry is long overdue. I wholeheartedly agree. But finding fault with the old rationale is not enough. Kliebard's dissection of the conventional theory is so precise and so effective, no further attention will be devoted to it here. Let me shift, instead, to a series of propositions that have been developing in my own mind over the past several years. As I have interacted with my colleagues and students at Ohio State,[16] and as I have met with many educational groups around the country, my understanding of curriculum has broadened tremendously. What follows is a broad-brush portrayal of some of the central concepts and considerations which may be important as we struggle to reconceive that with which we work each day.

Curriculum is like a soap bubble.[17] It is a bounded entity—it includes some things and excludes others—and it has properties, forces, and ingredients which we can attempt to identify. But when we try to study a soap bubble, it invariably bursts and disappears. Something similar occurs when we try to study curriculum. With analysis, some of the essence of the reality slips away. Just as a description of a soap bubble in mathematical or physical terms may miss the point, our observations of curriculum miss the point sometimes too. Nevertheless, we need to know what curriculum is.

Aside from the Tyler rationale,[18] the two most frequently employed definitions of curriculum are probably *the courses taught* and *everything which happens to the child under the aegis of the school.* The first is obviously too narrow, but the second is obviously too broad. No one really doubts the fact that the experiences a youngster has on the playground during recess, in the lunchroom, or while working on a school dramatic production, for example, are terribly important and need to be brought under the rubric of curriculum. However, no one really believes that curriculum is involved if a child rides home on a school bus, gets off, walks in front of the bus and drops his books, stoops down and is run over by the bus and killed. Even though being killed is, without question, the most significant experience that child ever had, and even though the experience took place under the aegis of the school, it is stretching the point to describe that tragic event as curriculum. Such a definition simply will not do.

The Tyler rationale[19] posits the ideas of purposes, content, experiences, organization, methods, and evaluation as the fundamental components of curriculum, and those ideas are familiar to us all. I would like to suggest as an alternative to the Tyler rationale that the fundamental elements in curriculum are *actors, artifacts,* and *operations.* The choice of terms here is intentional. Actors are people, but more is implied by actors than by people. Artifacts are things, but more is implied by artifacts than by things. Similarly, operations implies more than processes, although processes are obviously involved. These implications can be summed up under the ideas of intent, purpose, and ends—qualities assumed to be inherent in the elements of curriculum.

I am proposing that actors, artifacts, and operations be considered the basic ingredients of curriculum. Examination of these concepts may help clarify their nature and justify this position. Actors refers to those people directly involved in curriculum—students, teachers, materials producers, supervisors, and administrators. (Many others are not directly involved but affect curriculum indirectly, and often profoundly—for example, school board members, publishers, parents, or legislators.) One purpose of the term actors is to define some people as inside curriculum and others as outside, thus helping to establish a bounded concept. Actors, then, denotes an element of curriculum. As such, it implies intent or purpose and direct involvement.

Artifact refers to a "product of human workmanship." I use this term to refer to what we normally think of as subject matter or content. Implicit is the notion that ideas are products of human workmanship. These ideas, however, are also typically represented by a thing, such as a textbook or film. Thus, any kind of symbolic representation of ideational phenomena can be considered as an artifact. Artifact, like actor, implies purpose or intent—made for a reason. Artifacts are bounded with respect to curriculum by the relationship they have to actors. In other words, an artifact becomes a curriculum artifact because of its relationship to a person directly involved in curriculum.

An operation is a process involving modifications over time in the relationships between elements, actors, and artifacts, or some modification of an element itself. That Johnny knows "7 × 6 = 42," when at some prior time he did not, is after-the-fact evidence of the existence of an operation. The teacher's act of teaching Johnny "7 × 6 = 42" is also evidence of an operation. An infinite variety of groupings of actors and artifacts may occur.

If it is assumed that a curriculum event includes actors, artifacts, and operations, then it is important to conceptualize a way of observing curriculum which will illustrate the reality in action. Perhaps it would be useful to think of curriculum in terms of systems theory. Systems theory suggests that something is planned, something occurs, and something is evaluated.[20] In terms of curriculum, this means that curriculum is planned, curriculum occurs, and curriculum is evaluated. That which is planned is deliberate, rational, and premeditated. That which occurs may be planned or accidental, relevant or irrelevant, deliberate or incidental. That which is evaluated must include both what is planned and what actually occurs. Assessing curriculum in terms of intentions alone is naive and futile. What is intended and what takes place must both be comprehended and thoughtfully judged.

These propositions have been developed more elaborately in other places,[21] and I will not review them here. For the purposes of this paper, curriculum means spatial realities in process over time: actors, artifacts, and operations in terms of that which is planned, that which occurs, and that which is evaluated.

Given such a definition of curriculum, what should the process of curriculum development be like? Analogies are dangerous, but they are useful, too. Suppose we think about curriculum development as a construction problem; *curriculum construction* is a term that we often employ.

Construction means building. If we think about curriculum development as analogous to constructing a temple, there seem to be at least four fundamental functions or processes involved:

1. envisioning the temple   (architect's job)
2. constructing the temple   (contractor's job)
3. producing materials   (manufacturer's job)
4. Extracting materials   (miners' and other jobs)

The architect has a dream. He has to envision a totality, and he must articulate that totality into particulars (blueprints, specifications, and so on). The contractor and his workers create the totality. They take the bricks and mortar, the glass and wire, and put it all together in precisely related ways. The manufacturers make the materials that are employed in the construction. They produce the bricks; they make the glass and fixtures and pipe. The extractors collect the raw materials from the earth itself. They mine the copper, scoop up the silicone, cut down the trees, and the like.

The model holds if we look at other construction fields. Consider automobile development or airplane development. In those endeavors somebody has to be the master dreamer, the coordinator of conceptualizing efforts. Many persons participate in the dreaming stage, many in the extraction stage. If the communication patterns within and between the stages are effective, the ultimate result should be a more effective or a higher quality product, but better communication is not a sufficient condition. There must also be evaluation and modification of plans of construction and other phases for the resultant product to be consistently improved. And if we can understand the motivation dynamics inherent in good systems as opposed to poor ones,[22] we may be in a still better position to know how to build curriculum more effectively, too.

The aircraft designer (architect), for example, is supported by a very large staff of highly competent engineers, many of whom function in different ways. Some engineers have to determine information about landing gear only. What will normal stress be on the landing gear when 50,000 pounds hit the runway at an angle of 19 degrees and at a speed of 136 miles per hour? What if the speed is 175 miles per hour and the angle of touchdown 24 degrees? How much safety factor must be built in to make the plane reasonably safe, and what is "reasonable"? Others engineer the communication systems for the plane. How many radios, what kinds of transmitters and receivers, how many backup systems should be placed in what kinds of locations, and so on?

Many different people with different talents and skills help conceptualize and design the plane. They are architects, if you please. They work closely with construction personnel and the manufacturers to determine materials strength, durability, effects of corrosion, or fatigue or wear, but their basic responsibility is conceptualization and design. Such an operation requires superb lateral and vertical communication, good feelings and relationships among the participants, quality data and timely decisions so that the right decision will always occur. The right decision will ensure safety and economy, as well as long life and effective functioning.

When we educators build program (that is, construct curriculum), sometimes we operate as if each of us has to engage in all of these functions. We try to envision the temple and specify the particulars, select the materials and relate them in a particular way, and sometimes we even "create the knowledge" that we intend to use. Is it reasonable to suppose that each curriculum worker can do all things equally well? Can we borrow from other construction fields and recognize the power in developing specialties according to function rather than specialties according to subject matter or grade level? Can we capitalize on the advantages of specialization without submitting to the obvious difficulties that accompany it? The generalist's role in curriculum development is an important one, comparable to the role of the architect in this analogy. But competence as a generalist requires many specialized abilities in many roles and fields. Superficial awareness of or knowledge about the various areas is not enough.

What I am suggesting is that we try to learn from other fields. Some people will argue that we should not try to learn from fields that are concerned with things rather than people. I disagree. People who build automobiles and airplanes, for example, are building machines that will help people, and they themselves are people, too. Further, a textbook or film is not a person, it is a thing. School people deal with things, too. We can learn from many different situations, and we must.

What has been talked about here as curriculum development and what was examined at some length earlier as relationships without conditions fit under the concept of operations as it has been defined in this paper. The artifacts are also a major component of curriculum. As schools exist today, the most common artifacts are such things as textbooks, workbooks, films, recordings, and diagrams on the blackboard.

In my judgment, the curriculum of the schools of the future ought to be quite different from the curriculum of the schools today. Rather than focusing on curriculum for control, curriculum in the years ahead should be growth-oriented. Curricular conceptualizations ought to be rooted in primary attention to the learner as the major source of information in curriculum development. Herrick states it this way:

A preoccupation with the learner as the initial consideration in curriculum building leads to examination of the self-perceptive process, the mechanisms for the identification of persistent and recurring concerns of the individual, questions of creativity, phenomenological fields, biological growth processes, and what constitutes maturity and development in the human organism.[23]

Artifacts imply intentions. Curriculum in the years ahead must be growth-oriented rather than control-oriented, rooted in the nature of human tissue and human need rather than in subject matter concerns or social concerns. And so curriculum artifacts of the future should differ considerably from the artifacts that are present in schools today. Figure 1 outlines some of the crucial differentiating characteristics which ought to be apparent, as well as some of the theoretical dimensions that are involved.

Some curriculum development efforts in recent years reflect some of these characteristics in programs and materials now. By studiously examining new and existing materials, it should be possible to infer other useful dimensions, and it may be possible over time to invent a completely new way of thinking about and looking at curriculum artifacts. The dimensions listed below, therefore, are suggestive and not definitive—they are illustrations, not finalities.

FIGURE 1. CHARACTERISTICS OF CURRICULUM ARTIFACTS IN SCHOOLS OF TODAY AND HOW THEY MIGHT BE IN SCHOOLS IN THE FUTURE*

CURRICULUM ARTIFACTS IN SCHOOLS TODAY	THEORETICAL DIMENSIONS	CURRICULUM ARTIFACTS IN SCHOOLS OF THE FUTURE
large, few	size of artifact	small, many
fixed	nature of sequencing	variable
few	combinations possible	many
boring	consequence for teacher	exciting
for scholar	purpose of organization	for teacher
storage	nature of organization	for retrieval
reliable, acceptable	quality of artifact	valid
irrelevant, delayed	significance of artifact	relevant, immediate
few	number of options possible	many
recognition, recall	purpose of artifact	understanding
teacher controlled	pacing of use	student controlled
certain	predictability	uncertain
tidy	physical appearance	messy
changing	focus	continuing
abstract	concreteness	concrete
disparate	relatedness	integrated
limited	availability	readily
most or all	extent to which used	some
maximal	degree of requirement	minimal
uniform	form of artifacts	varied

*The concepts outlined in Figure 1 must be seen as a beginning effort to characterize curriculum artifacts in ways that are different from the conceptualizations which are traditionally employed. For example, concerns for "scope and sequence" are concerns of the school as it generally exists today. Breadth of topic and nature of sequencing will be so different in a school for tomorrow that such conventional terminology is not even appropriate. This listing simply describes a way of thinking. Further thought along this line would undoubtedly result in additional illustrations. Or, these ideas might cluster themselves into factors or more general categories. The point is, there are different ways of thinking about curriculum than those that we have used before. We need to keep generating new possibilities for seeing curriculum in different and perhaps better ways.

Curriculum artifacts today come in large pieces, whereas artifacts in schools of the future will be much smaller in size. The most obvious illustration of a large chunk of curriculum today is the textbook, or even larger, a series of textbooks for several grade levels. Schools in the future will have curriculum artifacts which will be much more limited in size: one page, a single picture, a three-page graph, a single concept film loop, fifteen-minute cassette recordings, and the like.

Artifacts in today's schools are typically sequenced in precise, predetermined, or even rigid ways. Sequencing of curriculum artifacts in schools of the future will be variable and not predetermined. Again, the textbook illustrates the fixed nature of sequence of artifacts in the schools of today. The edges are glued, and the sequence is firmly fixed. Theoretically, of course, a teacher is free to start on page 243, then move to page 76, and after that to proceed to pages 118 and 4 and 195 in that order. Actually, however, that seldom occurs. Sequencing of artifacts in the schools of the future will be quite different indeed. Because the pieces will be small, it will be possible to combine them in many different patterns and unique sequences, to match the logic of a growing youngster's mind. Variability of sequence will be the rule rather than the exception.

A third theoretical dimension that will differentiate the curriculum of schools in the future from the curriculum in schools of today relates to the number of combinations of artifacts that teacher and student will be able to make. Because curriculum artifacts today tend to come in large pieces and fixed sequences, the opportunities for teachers and students to arrange these in varying patterns and different forms are severely limited. In the schools of the future, small pieces and variable sequences will mean that teachers and students will have an almost infinite number of ways of bringing the artifacts together temporally and spatially to facilitate each youngster's unique learning needs.

As a direct consequence of these theoretical differences, teachers in schools of today tend to become bored with curriculum, whereas teachers in the schools of the future will be able to maintain a high level of personal and professional interest in the curriculum at hand. That is, given the nature of large chunks of materials arranged in fairly rigid sequential patterns with little flexibility possible, teachers in today's schools tend to experience the same curriculum year after year. Variety may be introduced by adopting a new textbook or deliberately deviating from the predetermined plan, but a very real (even though seldom talked about) problem for teachers in the schools of today is that they themselves become uninterested in the ideas with which they are working. Because the opportunity to continuously create new and different arrangements of artifacts for each child will characterize the curriculum of the schools of tomorrow, the professional's interest in curriculum materials will stay at a reasonably high level. Even learning by discovery gets to be old hat for a teacher after four or five times through the precisely arranged sequences. In the schools of the future, there could be much more opportunity for ingenuity and creativity on the part of teachers. This will foster and maintain high interest levels.

Another aspect of curriculum relates to its storage and retrieval characteristics. In the conventional curriculum today, the emphasis is on storage. In the schools of the future, the emphasis will be on retrieval. Now, for example, curriculum artifacts reflect an organizing construct which suggests that the component parts were stored (that is, put into the curriculum system) according to the author's interests or the curriculum worker's inclination. Sometimes it is argued that the topical approach, or the thematic considerations, are really related to children's interests or some such thing. Because children differ so greatly in every conceivable way, it is hard to imagine one way of organizing content so that it would be most useful for all children. In the schools of the future, the emphasis will be on random storage and random access. Artifacts will be stored in such a way that they will be convenient for the teachers' use. Availability will be a crucial criterion. With many more artifacts in smaller pieces, and with capability for combining these pieces in many different ways, the important considerations will be for access and retrievability of particular artifacts in very short periods of time.

This discussion has suggested how these theoretical dimensions might be conceptualized and operationalized in curriculum in the years ahead. Let us turn our attention now to what curriculum workers might do.

WHAT CAN CURRICULUM WORKERS DO?

Implicit in these pages are many possibilities. I would like to spell out two ideas that may have merit, then illustrate each of those ideas in one or more ways. I would suggest that: (1) we need to study developmental efforts outside of education, and (2) we need to invest in ourselves for growth. Each of these ideas is explored on the following pages.

Study Developmental Efforts

The American social, industrial, and governmental scene is characterized by many kinds of major developmental efforts. The Apollo project, for example, has probably been the biggest single developmental effort undertaken by men anywhere at anytime. Furthermore, the project was conceptualized and accomplished within 10 percent of the projected budget and in less than the projected time. Considering the fantastic complexities and difficulties involved in this project to do what had never been done before—put men on the moon and bring them home safely again—and considering the factors of long-range projections, monetary inflation, and the need for development of literally hundreds of new concepts and devices (heat shields, lunar lift-off machines, reentry procedures, insertion in orbit, weightlessness, and the like), the accomplishments of the project seem little short of unbelievable. But they did occur. When we compare that to the fact that construction of the Sam Rayburn Memorial Office Building, for example, exceeded projected time limits and estimated costs far in excess of those of Project Apollo, the Apollo effort is dramatized still more. We should have known how to build an office building and to do it within our planned budget and schedules. The point is simple: the men who conceived and operationalized Project Apollo must have done something right. If we could study their developmental efforts carefully, perhaps we could learn something which would enable us to make breakthroughs in curriculum development.

I pointed out earlier that some persons will probably object to looking carefully at developers who work in nonpeople ventures. I think we ought to try to hold those reservations in abeyance, if we can, and learn whatever can be learned from every possible source. For example, Tom Alexander[24] reports that the real payoffs from Project Apollo may be in the realm of management theory, an area of direct concern to people in curriculum work and supervision today. He describes in detail some of the structural relationships and communication patterns which developed as the project evolved. He points to rigid delineations in hierarchical terms at any given point in time, but also to flexibility which allowed for—even fostered—changes in the hierarchical arrangements very quickly, even several times a day. Elaborate and permanent communication procedures existed, but almost every decision—thousands every day—was talked through informally and personally by the people involved. There was superb lateral communication among persons who were hierarchically related, and detailed recording admidst constant recording of people and events and things. Furthermore, the allegiances which thousands of professionals and other workers came to feel, and the motivations they brought to the project each day, helped carry the project forward in a very human, idealistic way. Obviously these persons were caught up in an exciting, bold, new venture. But there are exciting, bold, new ventures in curriculum development, too. Anyone who has worked closely with some of the major curriculum development projects senses that spirit, but certainly not all curriculum development efforts can be so described.

And the problem is more basic than money. In fact, money is probably not the crucial factor at all. The assumptions that the developers hold about the nature of man, their attitudes toward themselves and others, and their beliefs about the power of information and good data are more basic than financial support. The military, for instance, got vast sums of money for special projects, but their developmental efforts were feeble compared to those which the Apollo team was able to bring to life. The work of Rensis Likert,[25] Douglas McGregor,[26] and Peter Drucker,[27] and even the work of Robert Ardrey[28] are all pertinent. The new thrusts in management theory are not contingency based, despite what many say. The most effective approaches start from the premise that people are important, they like to work, they can be depended on, and they are able to develop and learn and grow.

Other developmental efforts should be studied, too. Arthur Hailey's novel *Wheels*[29] portrays the development of a new automobile project. Case studies like Hailey's might contribute to our understanding of idea generation, planning prototypes, testing, refinements, and other phenomena. More limited developmental projects might be studied, too. The story about the development of the Link Trainer,[30] for example, tells something of the frustrations and successes of one man as he worked to get a novel idea off the ground and into practical use. And anyone who has spent time at the factory where simulators and trainers are built for the men who fly the Boeing 747 or the other planes realizes some of the factors with which those developers work. They go from theory to practice and back to theory and back to practice a thousand times each day.

Another kind of developmental project that we could study carefully would be some of the medical breakthroughs which are being attempted in research and development centers around the country. The report of a project being conducted by the National Institutes of Health[31] in the area of heart disease, for example, sounds promising as a developmental project in a very different, people-centered field. The researchers in that particular project "know," for instance, with the assurance that every developmental researcher "knows" that their proposed therapies are more likely to save prospective cardiac cases' lives than are the conventional therapies, even preventive ones, in use today. Even so, the researchers are committed to submitting their knowledge to empirical test. They know full well that in doing so they are probably creating situations in which people randomly assigned to control groups are more likely to die. In fact, only if more members of the control group die will the experimental hypothesis be verified. But medical practitioneers will not buy a pig in a poke; they will not adopt any proposed new therapeutic procedure unless it has been experimentally confirmed. Such commitment to scientific inquiry, such developmental schemes, could very well be pregnant with hypotheses about how we might step outside of our own field and learn from others as they engage in developmental chores. Studying the developmental process in developing countries would be still another very promising approach.

We should try to learn from others who spend their lives in developmental roles. We are imprisoned by our own experiences; we have to struggle against the narrow confines of the lives we have led and the places we have been and the people we have known. Most of the important developmental projects that have taken place since the beginning of time have taken place outside of the limits of the school. I am arguing for systematic study of some of those projects, with a view toward generalizing what development means in educational terms.

Investing in Ourselves for Growth

The greatest resource we have in education is ourselves. The greatest resource any professional group has are the talents and creative energies and motivations of its members. We tend too often to think of resources as time and money. Those are important, it is true, but it is also true that what counts in any operation are the people who are involved. Our problems and our possibilities inhere in our efforts to find ways to tap those talents and unleash those motivations which lie idle or are only partially functioning. Fred Wilhelms[32] has reminded us again and again of the enormous potential that resides within us all, begging for further development and almost unlimited growth. Can we find a way to cultivate our own capacities? I think we can.

Let me suggest one proposition which is along the directions I have been outlining here. It is simplistic, involving organizational schemes, and I do not personally have much confidence in organizational arrangements as effective ways to make a difference in things. But sometimes restructuring the temporal and spatial components of an enterprise makes it possible to bring both focus and power to what men do. For example, accommodation in the lens of the eye means that—regardless of the distance of the object from the retina—a clear, sharp image can be perceived. To see objects at different distances, the eye *reorganizes* itself to be more effective. In a somewhat different vein, regular savings add up, as anyone who has thought about teacher retirement programs knows, and insurance, as an idea, is nothing more than the principle of sharing the risk. Those are all organizational propositions. I am not enthusiastic about organizational changes, but if they can help us do better what we are trying to do, then we ought to consider the possibilities.

I want to talk about in-service education and staff development. The problem, as I see it, is to find a way to guarantee that the people in education have opportunities for self-renewal and continuous growth. In most school situations today, every teacher is expected to work with children almost every hour of every working day. Teaching is a relentless activity, as it typically occurs, with little letup, with only snatches of time here and there to get on top of things. There is seldom opportunity to renew oneself with the current literature and new development in one's own field. Perhaps we could think about building up or actually creating a group of professionals in reserve.

We need a concept of staff development in which a portion of the professional staff (perhaps 10 percent) is scheduled for a specified period of time (perhaps 10 percent) for professional growth and development. We are not going to get extra funds for such a purpose, so we must do it with the resources we presently have. A policy to schedule professionals' time to learn would mean, therefore, a slight increase in class size. However, if ten teachers in a one-hundred-teacher school had eighteen full days of in-service time to work together and plan and grow, who knows what powerful personalities and excited teachers might be interacting with youngsters day by day? The sabbatical idea is sound, but you cannot wait for seven years to pass before you renew your understandings. We have to schedule time and stimulation and support for professional growth on a regular basis.

The logistics of such an arrangement might vary greatly—five teachers might work together on nine occasions during the year for two days at a time, or any other combination that seemed to make sense could be used. But the basic principle of scheduling regular opportunities for staff development is imperative. Now many systems schedule the entire school district or one building faculty for one day before school in the fall and another at midyear. By using the concept of professionals in reserve, it should be possible to arrange schedules so that hard-working teachers could escape from the demands of six hours of contact with classroom groups, five days a week. Small groups of staff, working as a team over extended periods of time as part of a staff development plan, could undoubtedly cope with some of the very difficult problems of personal growth, materials collection and development, and meaningful visits to other institutions or experts for consultation and advice. Such a procedure would not cost a district any more money than it presently spends, but it would provide a deliberate scheduling of time for small groups of staff to learn and grow in their own varied professional ways.

A CALL TO ACTION

Curriculum workers of the world—unite! Pool your talents! Share your dreams! Create the ways and map the routes we need to follow. We are fast moving toward the year 2000 and then beyond. The children we teach today will be living then. The teachers with whom we work will be teaching then. The schools we are building now will be utilized then. We have to change. We need to learn. We must work in different, more effective ways.

The time to start these things is now. The place to start is with ourselves. The ones to make it go are you and me. We count! We can do it! If we don't do it, it won't get done.

The challenge and the opportunities are real. We must be architects and we must dream. We must invent ways to invest ourselves and our energies in project efforts that will make a difference. The future for curriculum workers rests squarely on the decisions and directions we set today. We must turn our attention to curriculum concerns. We must use ourselves, powerfully and creatively, to shape our own environment in ways that will enable us to become what we hope to be—compassionate, creative curriculum workers.

Human freedom is expanding. Education and schooling must be expanded and developed, too. Building learning environments, devising curriculum artifacts, and generating techniques for helping children learn and grow will guarantee all men the fruits of freedom and the advantages of access and the opulence of opportunity. Curriculum development can be the anthem of a better world. All that it takes is all that we are, plus all that we might ever be.

NOTES

1. Alvin Toffler, *Future Shock* (New York: Random House, 1970), p. 11. Copyright 1970 Alvin Toffler.

2. Norman Cousins, "The Age of Acceleration," in *Issues 1968*, ed. William M. Boyer (Lawrence: The University Press of Kansas, 1968), p. 3.

3. Portions of this section are drawn directly from Jack R. Frymier, et al., *A School for Tomorrow* (Berkeley: McCutchan, 1973), chap. 3.

4. Max Ways, "How to Think about the Environment," *Fortune* (February 1970), pp. 99–100.

5. Willis W. Harman, "Context for Education in the Seventies," paper prepared for the U.S. House of Representatives General Subcommittee on Education, mimeographed (Palo Alto: Stanford Research Institute, 1969), 14 pp.

6. Earl Kelly, *Education for What is Real* (New York: Harper, 1947).

7. Jack R. Frymier and H. C. Hawn, *Curriculum Improvement for Better Schools* (Worthington, Ohio: Charles A. Jones, 1971), chap. 10.

8. Virgil Herrick. *Strategies of Curriculum Development* (Columbus: Charles E. Merrill, 1965), p. 6.

9. For example, in Ruth Benedict, *Patterns of Culture* (New York: Houghton Mifflin, 1934), p. 2, the author makes the point this way: "The life history of the individual is first and foremost an accommodation to the patterns and standards traditionally handed down in his community. . . . By the time he can talk, he is the little creature of his culture, and by the time he is grown and able to take part in its activities, its habits are his habits, its beliefs his beliefs, and its impossibilities his impossibilities."

10. Howard H. Kendler in *Learning by Discovery*, eds. Lee S. Shulman and Evan R. Kelsiar (Chicago: Rand McNally, 1966), p. 172.

11. Benjamin L. Whorf, *Language, Thought, and Reality* (Boston: The Technology Press, and New York: John Wiley, 1956).

12. Leon M. Lessinger, *Every Kid a Winner: Accountability in Education* (Palo Alto: Dorsett Educational Systems, Inc., 1970), p. 203. Reprinted by permission of Loyd G. Dorsett.

13. "A Father Is Tried for What His Son Did," *Life* (February 18, 1972), pp. 61–64.

14. Reprinted by permission of World Publishing Company from *Abraham Lincoln: His Speeches and Writings* by Roy P. Basler. Copyright 1946 by The World Publishing Company.

15. Herbert M. Kliebard, "Reappraisal: The Tyler Rationale," *School Review* 78 (February 1970), pp. 259–272.

16. Donald Anderson, Kelly Duncan, Jack Hough, Gerald Reagan, and Charles Galloway have been particularly inspirational and helpful.

17. Much of this section is drawn directly from James K. Duncan and Jack R. Frymier, "Explorations in the Systematic Study of Curriculum," *Theory into Practice* 6 (October 1967), pp. 180–199.

18. Ralph W. Tyler, *Basic Principles of Curriculum and Instruction* (Chicago: University of Chicago Press, 1950).

19. *Ibid.*

20. Jack R. Frymier, *Fostering Education Change* (Columbus: Charles E. Merrill, 1969).

21. Duncan and Frymier, *op cit.* (no. 17, above).

22. Douglas McGregor, *The Human Side of Enterprise* (New York: McGraw-Hill, 1960).

23. Herrick, *op. cit.* (no. 8, above).

24. Tom Alexander, "The Unexpected Payoff of Project Apollo," *Fortune* (July 1969), pp. 114–155.

25. Rensis Likert, *New Patterns of Management* (New York: McGraw-Hill, 1961).

26. McGregor, *op. cit.* (no. 22, above).

27. Peter Drucker, *The Age of Discontinuity* (New York: Harper and Row, 1969); and Drucker, *Managing for Results* (New York: Harper and Row, 1964).

28. Robert Ardrey, *The Social Contract* (New York: Atheneum, 1970).

29. Arthur Hailey, *Wheels* (New York: Doubleday, 1971).

30. Lloyd L. Kelly, *The Pilot Maker* (New York: Grosset and Dunlap, 1970).

31. "Five New Diets to Save Your Heart," *Look* (February 9, 1971), pp. 53–54.

32. Fred T. Wilhelms, "The Influence of Environment and Education," *The Bulletin of the National Association of Secondary School Principals* 53 (April 1969), pp. 1–37.

Robert J. Havighurst

Robert J. Havighurst

Author and co-author of over a dozen books in the field of education, including several that deal with the schooling of members of ethnic minorities, Dr. Havighurst is professor of education and human development at the University of Chicago, a position he has held since 1941. His research in the area of human development has contributed importantly to teachers in their efforts to understand the children whom they teach.

the future
of education:
image
and reality

In speculating about the course of education during the
period from 1975 to 2000, I will use a combination of
images and extrapolations. The images are more or less
disciplined speculations or expectations that express my
hopes and fears about the future. The extrapolations
are extensions of well-established trends and will not be
pushed very far—possibly not beyond 1990. I remember
what happened to predictions, made during the 1930s
and based on extrapolations of the trends of that day,
of the future size of the American population. Some
sociologists confidently proclaimed that the population
of the United States would reach a stable maximum of
about 165 million by the year 2000. Extrapolation of
population figures for 1970 to the year 2000 appears to
be reasonably safe and predicts a population of 288
million at the end of this century. I will take 1985 as a
fulcrum for my guess about the remainder of the
century. That is, I will try to describe the 1985 situation
in education with a fair degree of assurance, and then
I will speculate about the fifteen years that will follow.

     Images of the future determine present actions,
but they do not determine future reality. Thus, we act
on our notions of what is likely to happen, and what
we want to happen, and our actions have some weight,
but they are not sufficient to guarantee the shape of

future reality. Events which we do not expect and cannot control have a major bearing on the future reality. Furthermore, we know too much to be confident about our predictions. Our view of the future is clouded by our knowledge, not by our ignorance. We have learned so much about social change—its complexity and the many interrelated forces— that we cannot say with any assurance what shape the future will take. Also, we have enough power to alter the man-made forces that partially control the future. But "we" are a diverse group of people, with diverse values and attitudes.

FIVE POLITICAL IMAGES OF THE FUTURE

The shape of education depends on the sociopolitical situation—we cannot usefully think about the future of education unless we make some assumptions about the sociopolitical future. Willis W. Harman(5) has sketched out five alternative responses of the society to the counterculture and the social unrest of the 1960s:

1. *Anarchy*—a breakdown of the social and political machinery of the society. Extremely unlikely.

2. *Massive repression of militant unrest—garrison state.* Also extremely unlikely, since the anarchistic forces are not powerful enough to provoke this kind of repression in a democratic society.

3. *Some disruption, followed by social restriction.* A period of unrest with some violence during the 1970s, followed by legislation and institutional changes which give more power to previously disadvantaged groups. This produces a stable situation.

4. *Gradual, peaceful evolution toward a new social structure and values system.* This differs from no.3 in being more gradual, with less overt conflict.

5. *Maintenance of the present power structure through dissident groups gaining "rewards" or concessions to make them content with the present basic economic and political structure.*

We can dismiss the first two alternatives and can expect some variation of the last three, which shade into each other. They all anticipate a resolution of the conflicts of the 1960s during the 1970s, with the appearance of a greater degree of stability in the 1980s.

THE DEMOGRAPHIC SETTING

The decade of the 1960s has made us keenly aware of the diversity of problems when a heterogeneous population seeks a modern education. With universal schooling to age sixteen and quasi-universal school attendance to age eighteen, the educational system must be adapted to the needs and desires of all social classes and all ethnic groups. It is no longer possible to assume that as many as 30 percent of the young people over the age of fifteen will find their way to adult-hood outside of the educational system, through employment or marriage.

And it is not possible to ignore the cultural pluralism represented by Blacks, Puerto Ricans, Chicanos, Cuban-Americans, American Indians, Appalachian Whites, Chinese-Americans, Japanese-Americans, Filipino-Americans, and also by European ethnic groups—Poles, Yugoslavs, Lithuanians, Italians, Greeks, and Czechs. Some members of these groups are acutely conscious of their subcultures, and they want to preserve their ethnic identity while participating in and "making good" in the American economic system. Ethnic and socioeconomic diversity must be recognized and dealt with in the educational system with a creative and dynamic combination of pluralism and integration.

The demographic composition of the society, as of about 1985, is portrayed in Tables 1, 2, and 3. The important differences between 1970 and 1985 are:

1. Substantially more Black and Spanish surname people are in the middle socioeconomic classes. As these groups move into the middle classes from the working classes, they will become less separatist and more integrated into the mainstream of society.

2. Fewer people will be living in conditions of economic poverty, as defined by the official income data of the Department of Health, Education, and Welfare. A basic annual income plan will have been adopted by the federal government during the 1970s.

DEMOGRAPHIC TRENDS AND EDUCATION: 1970–1985

The population will increase 25 percent between 1970 and 1985, and most of this increase will take place in the suburbs of the larger

TABLE 1. SOCIOECONOMIC AND ETHNIC STRUCTURE OF THE POPULATION

Socioeconomic group	White[a]		Black		Spanish surname[a]		Oriental		TOTAL	
	1970	1985	1970	1985	1970	1985	1970	1985	1970	1985
(High) I	13%	15%	0.6%	1.0%	0.3%	0.5%	0.1%	0.2%	14%	17%
II	24%	25%	2.0%	2.5%	0.7%	1.0%	0.2%	0.3%	27%	29%
III	34%	32%	4.0%	4.5%	2.0%	2.5%	0.3%	0.4%	40%	39%
(Low) IV	13%	10%	4.5%	4.0%	1.5%	1.0%	0.1%	0.1%	19%	15%
Total	84%	82%	11.1%	12%	4.5%	5.0%	0.7%	1.0%	100%	100%
Total number (millions)	179	207	22.7	30.2	9.2	12.6	1.4	2.5	205	252

[a] The White category omits those with Spanish surnames, most of whom are White.

SOURCE: 1970 census, and estimates by the author for 1985.

TABLE 2. DEMOGRAPHIC STRUCTURE OF AN AVERAGE LARGE METROPOLITAN AREA: 1970 AND 1985

CENTRAL CITY

Socioeconomic group	White and Oriental[a]		Black		Spanish surname		TOTAL	
	1970	1985	1970	1985	1970	1985	1970	1985
(High) I	9	10	1.5	3.0	0.8	1.8	11	15
II	21	19	2.5	5.0	1.8	3.2	25	27
III	28	27	10.0	10.0	5.5	5.0	44	42
(Low) IV	12	9	6.0	5.0	2.0	2.0	20	16
Percent of population	70	65	20	23	10	12	100	100

SUBURBS

	White and Oriental		Black		Spanish surname		TOTAL	
	1970	1985	1970	1985	1970	1985	1970	1985
(High) I	20	18	0.5	1.7	0.1	0.3	21	20
II	29	26	0.9	3.5	0.2	0.5	30	30
III	36	35	2.6	2.5	0.5	0.8	39	38
(Low) IV	9	9	1.0	2.5	0.2	0.5	10	12
Percent of population	94	88	5	10	1	2	100	100

[a] The category "White and Oriental" omits the Spanish surname group, most of whom are White.

SOURCE: Census data for large metropolitan areas, 1970, and estimates by the writer for 1985. This is a "mythical" metropolitan area.

TABLE 3. EDUCATIONAL STATUS OF THE COHORT BORN IN 1960, AS OF 1990 (PERCENT STOPPING AT A GIVEN LEVEL)

SE GROUP

Highest educational level	Total	I (Hi)	IV (Lo)	White and Oriental[a]	Black	Spanish surname
Dropped out before completing high school	15	2	65	11	32	32
High school graduate only	33	8	20	34	30	30
Some college only	27	40	12	28	20	20
College graduate only	15	30	4	16	11	11
Some professional or graduate work	10	20	2	11	7	7
Percent of total cohort	100	18	13	81	13	6

[a] The White category omits those with Spanish surnames, most of whom are White. Orientals include Japanese, Chinese, and Filipinos.

SOURCE: Estimates by the writer, based on census data and educational statistics.

cities. At the same time, the proportion of white-collar jobs will increase, and the proportion of jobs that use unskilled labor will decrease. During this same period, young adults from the Black and Spanish surname groups will be getting better jobs, because discrimination against them will decrease and because they will achieve increasing levels of education. These three changes will cause changes of two general types in the educational system.

Upgrading of the social status of the population will increase the rates of high school graduation and college attendance. Table 1 shows how the socioeconomic structure of the population may be expected to change during this fifteen-year period. Group I, consisting of professional and managerial workers (upper and upper middle class) will grow both in proportion to the population and in absolute numbers. Group II (lower middle class) will also increase. Group III (the upper working class) will maintain its proportion of the population and Group IV (the lower working class) will decrease substantially.

The chief carriers of this broad rise in socioeconomic status will be the Black and Spanish surname groups, which will increase their shares of middle class positions more than the Whites will. Concomitant with this upward social mobility of Blacks and Spanish surname youth will be an increase in the number of high school graduates and college entrants, as shown in Table 3. Almost 40 percent of Black and Spanish surname youth will be entering college by 1980, compared with 20 percent in 1970.

Big cities and their suburbs will become more nearly like each other in socioeconomic composition and in educational programs. Table 2 compares the socioeconomic and ethnic composition of a typical large city in 1970 with its probable composition in 1985, and does the same thing for the suburban area surrounding this large central city. Suburban population will exceed central city population. Suburbs will attract more working class and ethnic minorities. Central cities will raise their average socioeconomic level, due both to successful efforts at urban renewal—which make the cities more attractive to middle-income people—and to the success of the society in reducing the proportion of people who live in poverty. This table predicts that the proportions of Blacks and Spanish surname people in the suburbs will double during this fifteen-year period, and that these groups will improve their socioeconomic status.

These demographic predictions are based on clearly discernible trends of the 1960s, but they also depend very much on the sociopolitical decisions that are made during the 1970s concerning urban renewal, racial segregation in housing, and financial assistance to students from low-income families for college attendance.

THE VALUE STRUCTURE OF THE POPULATION

To write of values in relation to the future of education, it is necessary to point out the major social and personal values which have the most implications for education. It is also necessary to point out the values that are changing and thus creating educational changes. Emerging values and receding values which have the most educational significance seem to be related to the fact that the American society has moved, within a few decades, from an economy of scarcity to an economy of abundance.

The productivity of the American economy is so high that it is now controlled and held down to avoid overproduction. This has meant that there is less work to be done, and has created a relatively high level of unemployment for people under twenty-one and for the lower working class. In this situation, the value placed on work is bound to change. If work is seen primarily as a means to the production of goods and services, and if plenty of goods and services are produced by less and less work, people will value work less in their lives. On the other hand, if work is valuable *in itself*—if people enjoy working—then they will value work more highly when there is a scarcity of work.

Both things are now happening. Probably the majority of people value work less than the majority did a few decades ago, because they can get the goods and services they want with less work. They can take longer vacations. They can take longer weekends. They can retire earlier. And the majority of Americans seem to be doing these things. On the other hand, a minority of people have what is called the *attitude of the artist*. They enjoy their work; they want to do it as well as possible, and they want to keep on working as long as they are physically able to and under conditions that provide reasonable rest, relaxation, and payment.

This distinction between two valuations of work illustrates the basic distinction between *instrumental* and *expressive* activity which underlies the contemporary change in the value structure of American society. An instrumental act is one that aims to make an improvement in the present situation, or to create a new situation that is better than the present one. It is a means to an end which is beyond and outside of the act itself. Thus, the American pioneers broke the sod of the Great Plains and planted wheat and corn to produce materials they could sell at a profit to achieve a better standard of living. The American society of the nineteenth and early twentieth centuries has been known as the society which grew wealthy by means of instrumental action.

Education has been seen as an instrumental activity and valued accordingly. A boy or girl studied in order to progress up the ladder of school and into a good job. A high school student who studied algebra and trigonometry and got good marks might be asked, "Why do you work so hard on mathematics?" He would reply, "Because I need these subjects to get into an engineering school, and I wish to become an engineer because that is a job that pays well." Thus, he valued mathematics as an instrumental activity.

An expressive activity is one that carries its own reward. It is done for its own sake, not as a means to an end beyond the activity. An expressive activity is fun, rather than work. A high school student may study mathematics and get good marks as an expressive rather than an instrumental activity. In this case, he answers the question, "Why do you work so hard on mathematics?" by saying, "I *like* mathematics. It is fun to play with numbers. I don't know whether I will make use of mathematics for my future occupation. I don't really care very much about my future work. I just like mathematics and other studies, and so I choose them."

American society seems to be moving toward a value system which places *expressive* activities higher than *instrumental* activities. This is due mainly to the very efficient technology and the high productivity that give us the goods and services we want at a cost of much less work or instrumental activity than was required in the past and therefore leave more time and energy for other things.

Other value changes arise from the social and economic and intellectual changes of the current century. We are placing more value on international cooperation, as opposed to nationalistic political and economic action. We are placing more value on ecumenical cooperation in religion, as opposed to separate and competing religious denominations.

A list of emerging values stands in sharp contrast to a list of receding values, as can be seen in the following tabulation:

Emerging Values

Experience for the sake of experience
"Doing your thing"
Esthetic activity
Tolerance of complexity and ambiguity
International cooperation among
   religious groups
Domestic justice and opportunity for
   the disadvantaged
Service to the society

Receding Values

Individual saving and thrift
Work as a major source of self-respect
Nationalistic attitudes and policies of
   national military power
Religious separatism and sectarian
   loyalty

THE EDUCATIONAL SYSTEM OF 1985-1990—HOW IT RELATES TO VARIOUS AGE LEVELS

With this perspective on trends in American society which bear on education, I now turn to some specific predictions about the future. Before doing that, though, let me ask two bothersome questions: Will there be any school system in 1985-1990? And if there is, will it make any difference to the students? After all, many copies of *Deschooling America* by Ivan Illich[7] have been sold; and Christopher Jencks, in his book entitled *Inequality: A Reassessment of Family and Schooling in America* (1972) has proclaimed:

The character of a school's output depends largely on a single input, namely the characteristics of the entering children. Everything else—the school budget, its policies, the characteristics of the teachers—is either secondary or completely irrelevant, at least as long as the range of variation among schools is as narrow as it seems to be in America.[8]

On the first part of the question—will there be a school system that is recognizable?—we need hardly dwell. Illich's proposal of four educational networks to take the place of schools is so obviously unworkable for poor and uneducated parents that a society which makes any claim to equalizing opportunity through education will ignore it. Michael Rossman in his new book, *On Learning and Social Change*[10] describes an "alternative system" of higher education which has something in common with Illich's proposal. But *Saturday Review of Education* (August 19, 1972)—which apparently approves enough to publish an article by Rossman that previews the book—perhaps unconsciously calls him, in reference to the counterculture, "one of its leading visionaries." There must be some place in a discussion of the future of education for attention to the visionaries, but not in this particular essay. Americans have a penchant for seeking criticisms of their institutions, and they seem to be willing to pay money for them. But they pay very little attention to the proposals of this type of critic. This is an interesting American combination—asking for mordant criticism and then doing nothing about it.

The critique by Jencks and his Harvard colleagues is not bitter. Essentially, they say that the educational system does not do what some people think it does—offer economic opportunity to youth from low income families—and that only a major move toward socialism in the economic and political structure of the American society will do that job. I have already predicted a mild sociopolitical change toward a greater degree of socialism, but I do not see the school system as ineffective in the past or powerless in the present to enhance equality of opportunity. Hence it seems worthwhile to view changes in the educational system as having some important consequences in the intellectual, emotional, and economic life of students.

Questions to Be Asked about Schools in the 1985–1990 Period

My view of the future of education will be presented in relation to four periods of the human life cycle: ages three to nine, ten to fifteen, sixteen to twenty-two, and twenty-three to sixty-five. For each of these periods, the following questions about the educational system will be asked:

What does it do for the economically disadvantaged student?

How does it relate to the integration-pluralism issue?

What are its instrumental characteristics?

What are its expressive characteristics?

How does it relate to the goal of self-direction for the student?

How does it relate to student rights?

Education for Ages Three to Nine

It will be assumed that children need some kind of group educational experience as early as the fourth year of their lives. In families with two or more children born within five years, if the mother or father has time and interest to equip a room with playthings and to do some reading to the children and supervising, the children may as well spend ages three and four and even five at home. But few families will fit this criterion. There will probably be two broad types of preschool.

For children from low income homes, where the mother does not have the time, interest, or know-how to teach her children a variety of concepts and an extensive vocabulary, there will be publicly supported schools with teachers trained to foster cognitive development in children. These teachers will be sensitive to the social development of their pupils but will be aware that cognitive development is the principal objective.

For children from middle and upper income homes there will be a variety of nursery schools where the main emphasis is on the total personal-social development of the children; cognitive developmental exercises will be more or less incidental. Some of these will be child care centers, for children of working mothers, and will be open over a long day. Others will be half-day schools for children whose mothers are at home.

From the age of five or six, the primary grades will be taught in ways not much different from the range of rather open situations found in eclectic schools today. Children will be grouped loosely at their reading levels for reading instruction and at their arithmetic levels for arithmetic instruction. They will be grouped generally by age for the other learning activities of the school.

Teachers will be rather firmly in charge and will determine the activities of the class in an easy fashion. Conscious attention will be given to arranging attendance patterns to achieve a social and racial mix, but the children will usually attend a neighborhood school.

For children whose cognitive skills are clearly below the average for their ages, there will be a good deal of special teaching and tutoring. A major goal will be to prevent retardation of more than one year in reading or arithmetic.

Education for Ages Ten to Fifteen: Grades 5 to 10

The principal objective of the educational system during this age period will be to help the boy or girl to become a self-directed student. Students will be given progressively more free time for which they will be asked to take responsibility during the school day. They will do this under the supervision of the teacher, and with advice from the teacher, if this seems necessary. But the school will make a bona fide effort to help the pupil take a growing responsibility for the planning and conduct of his own education.

This effort will start somewhat as follows, in the fifth grade: Each pupil will have one hour per school day of time that is not scheduled for any class or study assignment. He will be responsible for making a plan—with the help of his teacher, if necessary—for his use of this time. He may work in the school library; or he may leave the school building for some learning project; or he may work in a science room, or a school kitchen, or a school garden, or in some other situation that promises a useful or pleasurable learning experience. Periodically, the student and his teacher will evaluate his project. The project will be changed when the student feels that he should change it. If he proves incapable of making good use of this free period, he may be asked to try it with the help of another teacher, who specializes in helping pupils who have difficulty with this task.

Experience will tell how this first step toward self-direction works for various kinds of pupils and various kinds of teachers. When this first step has been done successfully, a second step will be taken, perhaps involving two hours a day, or perhaps involving a half-day twice a week. By this time the pupil may be ready to work with other students on a group project, with or without help from teachers. Also, the school may offer the time of teachers of special subjects—such as music, dramatics, foreign language, and dance—who would work with self-chosen groups that ask for assistance. But students would not be required to work with other students in group projects.

By the eighth or ninth grade there will be a number of elective courses that are teacher-organized, and the student will be permitted to use some of his free time for these courses. If he does, he will be expected to attend regularly. And there will continue to be a required core of subjects which gets smaller as the student grows older. The student's choices of ways to use his free time may be instrumental or expressive. Both kinds of activity will be approved by the teacher or the principal. The school curriculum will contain a number of expressive activities—some elective and some a part of the required core.

Students from economically disadvantaged homes will be scheduled, as much as possible, with students from middle income homes. And racial integration will be favored by a number of procedures, including the busing of students to schools some distance from their homes. It will be a deliberate policy of the school district to promote integrated experience across social class and ethnic lines. By this time—1985–1990—the society will have made substantial progress toward residential integration. The inner city will have middle class residents widely distributed, and the suburbs will have working class residents in every suburban district, those suburban districts having been consolidated into regional districts with no fewer than ten or twelve thousand pupils.

There will also be a number of alternate schools or magnet schools designed to attract an integrated enrollment on a voluntary attendance basis. These will all receive at least some assistance from the public school funds, provided they follow some ground rules about acceptance of students from heterogeneous income and ethnic backgrounds. These schools will be valued by the community because they provide for the children of families who prefer life styles that may be deviate from the typical. But these schools will have values that are appreciated by the education authority or school board, which will have the authority to give such schools a measure of financial support. One recurrent and unsolved problem will be the question of approval for public support of schools which tend to be separatist, because they offer courses of ethnic studies or of the expressive arts which attract a special clientele. The society at large and the education authority will be watching this kind of situation, evaluating it, and coming to conclusions about the extent of pluralistic emphasis that is healthy.

During this age period, the educational authorities will deal in *1985 terms* with what will be known as *student rights.* That term refers to a controversy of the 1970s over the extent to which the pupil must be treated as an adult, with adult rights of privacy, free speech, and self-determination. During the 1970s, there were debates, seminars, and lawsuits over such issues as corporal punishment, the power to search pupils' lockers at school, censorship of student newspapers, the right of parents and students to examine the cumulative record made by the school concerning the student, the right of students to keep school information secret from their parents, and the right of school authorities to permit researchers to ask pupils personal questions and to make use of data in school records. These issues were focused on the age period from ten to fifteen, and a substantial body of administrative decisions and court rulings came into existence and into use. These dealt with the question of the proper functions of the school *in loco parentis*; of the relation of pupil self-determination to pupil age within this age period; and with the relation of the school system to the parents of school pupils.

By the end of this age period, most students are fifteen or sixteen years of age. This will be the end of the period of compulsory education, but the society will maintain supervision over all youth up to the age of twenty-one, under a policy which provides a variety of avenues to adulthood but insists that every youth must be making progress along some acceptable avenue of growth.

The fifteen- or sixteen-year-old, at the end of this period, will be expected to be at least up to the eighth grade level in reading and mathematics and may be placed in special classes or given special tutoring to help him reach this minimum level. It will be expected that all except possibly 3 percent of youth will be at or above this level; that 3 percent will be students who are definitely mentally handicapped.

Education for Ages Sixteen to Twenty-Two: Grades 11 to 16

The greatest overt change in the educational system over the next twenty years will probably take place in the lives of young people aged sixteen to twenty-two, the traditional years of senior high school and the four-year college. The conventional patterns of behavior in this age period have lost their value for most young people. The patterns of the first third of the century did not suit the second third, but young people stumbled through this period with the aid of wartime occupations and a booming job market that fizzled out at the close of the 1960s. The secondary school and college educators generally were surprised and bewildered by the student protest that erupted in 1968 and by the collapse of the job market for college graduates in 1970.

The postindustrial society has little need for adolescents in the labor force and encourages them to stay in school until they reach twenty or twenty-one. But the senior high school and the college focus on learning from books, libraries, and laboratories and therefore are not attractive to young people who have not developed academic skills. The opportunities for growing up are too limited. Taking a job is closed off, schooling seems pointless to many, military service is anathema, and early marriage is less attractive for young women than it was earlier (Havighurst, Graham, and Eberly).[6] Unemployment in the sixteen-through twenty-year-old age group was at a peak in 1970, and teenage marriage rates for girls were down 28 percent between 1960 and 1970.

High school graduation and college entrance rates were at an all time high, as noted in Table 4. Eighty percent of an age cohort graduated from high school in 1971, and 50 percent entered college. Probably half of the young people felt comfortable with their situation. Perhaps half of the college entrants took to college life with the same zest that was prevalent among college students fifty years earlier. Perhaps half of the high school dropouts and new graduates who looked for work found jobs through which they could gain maturity. Some of the girls married at age eighteen or nineteen and enjoyed homemaking. But it was clear from what they did and what they said that a considerable group did not feel that they were really growing toward

**TABLE 4.   HIGHEST EDUCATIONAL LEVEL REACHED BY
YOUNG PEOPLE IN 1971 (percentages)**

	MALE			FEMALE		
	Total	White	Black	Total	White	Black
High school dropout	20	18	35	19	18	34
High school graduate	26	24	40	38	37	48
College, 1 to 3 years	30	32	14	24	25	10
College graduate	25	26	11	19	20	8

SOURCE: U.S. Bureau of the Census, Series P-20. No. 224 (March 1972).

maturity through these experiences. They were not discovering or working out an *identity* for themselves. They did not feel that they were in charge of their lives—they did not know *who* they were. Furthermore, they were not acquiring a set of values, or an ideology (to use Erik Erikson's term)—"a coherent body of shared images, ideas, and ideals, which provides for the participants a coherent if systematically simplified overall orientation in space and time, in means and ends (Erikson, 1959)."[4]

The pervasive change in values that is sweeping through the contemporary American society affects some young people enough to make them dissatisfied with the experience they get in school and college or in the work place. Some seek new experience and excitement through smoking marijuana, hitchhiking through Europe, going to rock music festivals, joining motorcycle gangs, and expressing sexual freedom. Some set aside their studies in order to work out a new ideology through the civil rights or antiwar movements, the Eugene McCarthy or George McGovern campaigns. The ecology movement captures the hearts and minds of others, who join the "Club of Rome," read *The Limits to Growth* (Meadows, 1972)[9] and work for zero economic growth to prevent a world collapse which they see ahead in their own lifetimes unless they succeed in halting the rush toward ecological suicide. Some work for a better deal for disadvantaged minority groups, including women, and some work for gay liberation. These young members of the counterculture want the schools and colleges to aid them, or at least not to hinder them in their search for new life styles.

Then there is another group, mainly high school dropouts or unwilling riders on the school and college bandwagon. They lack the academic skills and interests to keep up and would be more comfortable with steady jobs—which they cannot find.

It looks as though something like 30 percent of American youth aged sixteen to twenty-two find school and college unsatisfactory and do not find any satisfactory alternative. What does the American society propose to do about this situation?

Simple expansion of the educational establishment. Spokesmen of the educational establishment, as late as 1971, predicted that the increasing enrollments of the 1950s and 1960s would continue. Thus, the very able and dynamic Carnegie Commission on Higher Education, in its report entitled *New Students and New Places* (1971, p. 8), could say:

Higher education in the United States until about 1940 was largely for the elite; from 1940 to 1970, we moved to mass higher education; and, from 1970 to 2000, we will move to universal-access higher education—opening it to more elements of society than ever before. We do not anticipate a further move to universal higher education in the sense of universal attendance; in fact, we consider this undesirable and believe that public and private policy should both avoid channeling all youth into higher education and create attractive alternatives to higher education. But we clearly are moving from mass to universal-access higher education.[2]

However, a year later, in 1972, the commission was stressing the fact that declining birth rates of the 1960s would produce smaller cohorts of college age in the 1980s and therefore would cause a decline in college enrollments between 1982 and 1987. Nevertheless the commission announced, in its *Report on The More Effective Use of Resources*, that it expected enrollment rates *as a percentage of the age group* to continue to rise in the 1970s and 1980s. My guess is that this will not happen. My estimates in Table 3 indicate that 52 percent of the age cohort will be entering college or another postsecondary institution in the 1980s, which is only 3 percent above the 1971 rate shown in Table 4.

The Carnegie Commission also predicts that college attendance will be spread out by the students over a wider span of years with periods of absence. In *New Students and New Places*, the commission says:

Along with the continuation of recent trends, we anticipate a new type of development as perhaps the predominant characteristic of the last three decades of the present century—a movement away from participation in formal institutional higher education in the years immediately following high school toward a more free-flowing pattern of participation spread over a broader span of years, perhaps well into middle age and beyond. Students will be encouraged to gain some work experience for several years after high school or after one or two years of college and return to college later, perhaps on a part-time basis, with, it is hoped, more clearly formulated career goals and a better understanding of what additional advanced education might contribute both to the achievement of career goals and to each individual's cultural development.[2]

I agree with this prediction, and I believe this process will hold down the total college enrollment to a stable percentage of the numbers in the eighteen to twenty-one age group, although these numbers will vary somewhat due to variations of the birth rate.

What Young People Will Do: New Alternatives. In predicting the shape of the educational structure for young people in the sixteen to twenty-two age range, we should take account of the fact that they will be an active force. Whereas the younger groups will have to put up with what the society provides for them, this group can take things into their own hands.

It looks as though roughly half of the young people will follow the conventional patterns of the mid-century, choosing one of three:

1. attending a conventional college and going from there into a job or into postgraduate training for a profession;

2. dropping off the school and college bandwagon and taking a stable job when they get a good chance; or

3. marrying, keeping house, and starting a family.

The others will find alternatives. The most important constructive alternative will be some form of *instrumental service* that has value to the society and to the individual. This was foreseen by President Kennedy when he established the Peace Corps and VISTA. The idea has been expanded, in the early 1970s, and named *Action-Learning* or *Service-Learning*. It has also been extended down in age level to the senior high school by the National Committee on Secondary Education. The committee made a bold proposal for a nationwide program of action-learning that would become part of the regular high school and community college curriculum, with academic credit toward graduation (Havighurst, Graham, and Eberly, 1972).[6] This proposal looks toward the creation of four million action-learning slots, each taking part of the time of a youth (up to half-time) in the areas of: educational services (tutoring, teacher aides); health services (health aides in hospitals and community health centers); social services (day care aides, settlement house aides, community center aides); environmental services (conservation aides, pollution prevention aides, park development aides); other public services (library aides, recreation aides, public housing aides). Some form of payment will be worked out for those who give a major share of their time to this work, probably through an expanded work-study program of the Neighborhood Youth Corps type.

National service. The proposal for a year or two of required national service will be opened for discussion and debate in the mid-seventies, and will be related to the action-learning concept. All young people of both sexes may be required to serve for a year or two in a national service corps, with options for domestic conservation service, military service, foreign peace corps, urban renewal service, and so on.

Broad objectives. The general objectives of these alternatives are clear. They are to give young people more options for healthy growth during the sixteen to twenty-two age period, and at the same time to serve the social goals of: social integration (youth from all economic and ethnic groups sharing instrumental service); world order (a variety of forms of foreign service); self-direction (a variety of constructive options which young people can work out for themselves).

In addition, the movement toward recruitment of young people from disadvantaged economic and ethnic groups for college education and professional training will be stepped up. As Table 3 indicates, the proportions of Black and Spanish surname youth who graduate from college and who pursue professional training in graduate school will increase substantially. The period around 1985 will see a more open, democratic situation for young people, in which they can do their thing and at the same time take a constructive part in the renewal of society.

Education for the Adult Stretch of the Human Life Span: Ages Twenty-Three to Seventy-Five

The age of twenty-two to twenty-three is taken as a break-point between education as a *preparation* for adult life and education as a *part* of adult life. This will be understood and acted on by most young people by 1985. By that time they will come to see the period from twenty to twenty-two as a time in which they get started on a career in the labor force, or get married and start keeping house, or finish four years of college and look for a job that does not require special postcollege training. Those who go on with formal postgraduate work do so with the intention of preparing for a job that requires a special postgraduate program of study.

This group of postgraduate students numbered about 7 percent of an age cohort in 1970, and gradually moved up to about 10 percent in 1985, or 40 percent of the college graduates. They will go on for one to seven or eight years of graduate work, seeking the MA, MS, PhD, EdD, or one of the professional school degrees: bachelor of laws, doctor of jurisprudence, bachelor of theology, doctor of medicine, dentistry, osteopathy, optometry, podiatry, veterinary medicine, or a degree in business administration. These degrees are nearly all required credentials for some jobs or licenses to practice. There is not likely to be an oversupply of people working for these degrees for any length of time, because enrollment in the courses is generally restricted, and students as well as admissions officers are sensitive to the supply and demand factor.

The principal difference between 1985 and now is that a substantial amount of federal government money will be allocated to opportunity grants and loans at low interest rates to young people from families below the median of family income. This means that the society is positively committed to keeping open the avenue of success and advancement in the professions to all young people who have the abilities and the ambition to make this arduous ascent.

Adult education. Between 1970 and 1985 there will be a substantial but not sensational growth in the field of adult education, which will have two separate goals. One is the goal of career education, with educational programs designed to keep all kinds of skilled and professional workers up-to-date in their developing careers. This is a clear necessity, and it will be met partly by employers setting up in-service training programs for skilled workers, technicians, and classroom teachers. For people in the more complex careers, there will be continuing education courses operated by universities and by professional societies.

The other goal is one of flexibility of career, maximizing options for change and development. I expect that increasing numbers of people will change their jobs in their forties and fifties, either because they are curious about other work categories, or because they have reached a point of low satisfaction with their work and would like to make a change. Thus we see universities and professional organizations becoming more interested in enabling students past forty years of age to renew their life styles. At the same time I expect a growth in the expressive activities fostered by our affluent society. More people will be looking for interesting and exciting or amusing things to do in their growing amount of spare time. This will probably support an expanded program in the performing and graphic arts, especially dramatics, dance, painting, and music.

THE FUTURE OF DETERMINING CONDITIONS OF THE EDUCATIONAL SYSTEM

There are three socio-politico-economic factors which bear effectively on the educational system, although they might be overlooked in a too narrowly focused study of educational futures. These are:

1. teachers—categories of teachers, organizations of teachers, supply of teachers;
2. the financing of education; and
3. the governance of the educational system.

These factors are obviously changing, but the end results of these changes are not at all obvious. Simple extrapolation of present day trends would almost certainly lead to error, except in the case of financing of education. Because I am not prepared to predict the situation as of 1985 with respect to the first and third forces, I can only do some guessing about alternative futures.

Teachers

Teacher power has grown enormously since 1950. The American Federation of Teachers (The Teachers Union) has become the collective bargaining agent in several large cities, and the National Education Association has responded by taking on collective bargaining roles whenever possible. Also, the NEA has deliberately separated itself from close association with superintendents and school principals. Teachers have become much more militant, about their salaries and about such educational policy matters as integration of students and teaching staff, class size, annual school calendar, and use of teacher aides.

There is now an oversupply of licensed teachers, and this will grow greater during the next ten years. Furthermore, large numbers of teacher aides have been trained in recent years, and some of them have become good enough to take the place of inferior persons with teaching licenses. The influence of this situation on teachers' salaries is not likely to lead to higher salaries, although tight organization may enable teachers to hold their recent gains.

It seems likely that alternate schools or open schools may be favorably affected by the existence of large numbers of young and unemployed teachers. If ways are found to support many schools outside of the public school network, the oversupply of teachers may make it easy to staff such schools and thus to maintain a great deal of schooling outside of the mainstream.

A prediction of greater teacher unrest seems justified. The oversupply of licensed teachers will contribute to conflict within the teaching profession. Those with seniority and tenure will be wary of what they may perceive as attempts by younger and unemployed teachers to militate for change within the teachers' organizations and to work for the expansion of alternate schools where new teachers will be welcomed. To some extent, the younger and unemployed teachers will be radicalized by their exclusion from the main body of tenured teachers. Their influence will be felt both within the profession and in the wider civic-political arena.

Financing Education

The future seems quite certain with respect to the placement of *responsibility* for paying the cost of education, but uncertain with respect to the *amount* of money that will be allocated.

The trend is clearly toward assumption by the federal government of a greater proportion of the cost of education. This trend was established during the 1960s, both in higher education and in elementary and secondary education. The federal government now pays 12 percent of the total national education bill. The states carry 40 percent of the cost, and the local community school districts and the private educational corporations (through endowments and gifts) carry a diminishing proportion. The proportion of the gross national product devoted to education has risen since 1950 from 3.5 to 8.1 percent. It is likely to stabilize at a level slightly higher than the present level; but there will probably be a substantial redistribution of funds among the various age levels.

The movement toward expansion of the *service* roles in the labor force will tend to favor education, through greater provision of public funds for low paid service positions such as teacher aides, foster grandparents, and retired senior volunteers.

An element of uncertainty is the possible use of public funds to facilitate private educational programs. To date this has proceeded with remarkable momentum in the field of higher education—through low interest loans to colleges for dormitories, through grants for science buildings, and through opportunity grants to students to help them pay tuition costs. But assistance to private elementary and secondary schools is more questionable, in view of constitutional issues over the separation of church and state, and in view of the use of some private schools as a device for avoiding racial integration. Probably some ways will be found to assist private schools with public funds, because of the popularity of such a policy with various groups of the public, and because of the economy (for the public purse) that goes with payment by parents of a substantial part of the cost of their children's education in a private school. This will encourage diversity of educational methods to facilitate the development of small experimental schools and alternative schools. The trend toward expressive forms of education will be facilitated by the allocation of public funds to private schools.

Governance of the Educational System

By *governance* I mean the making of decisions about broad policy questions *and* the making of decisions about finer details, such as the content and methods of the curriculum, the appointment of school principals, the assignment of teachers, the discipline of students, and the transportation of students.

Here we have two opposing trends. First, there is the trend to bigness. School systems and universities have grown larger, on the average. There are more and more large school districts, due to the growth of cities. The opposing trend has a variety of sources. One source is the continued existence of small towns, which are not likely to disappear. These have stable enrollments, including the former one-room schools which have been replaced by consolidated schools. Another source is the small private college and private schools. These are likely to grow in numbers with the greater interest in varieties of experience and expressive activity and the decreased emphasis on career training within the traditional avenues of career development.

Another opposing force is the movement toward decentralization of big city school systems, which is an offshoot of the pluralism of the 1960s. This tends to place more decisions in the hands of people involved in smaller units of the educational system—down to individual schools. Still another force opposed to bigness is the self-satisfaction of many middle-sized suburban school systems. They have succeeded, during the past twenty years, in avoiding some of the ills of the big city. Their school systems are large enough to be efficient. And they do not wish to become involved with the social and educational problems of the central cities on whose fringes they lie.

These are all strong forces, and none is likely to pass out of existence. Consequently, I foresee a set of compromises which may work toward a more satisfactory balance of the tendencies that have been mentioned, without any broad and simple resolution of the issues.

There are two socially desirable goals to be sought. One is the general welfare of a significantly large element of the society. A significantly large unit of the American society appears to be a *standard metropolitan statistical area*, which accounts for about 70 percent of the population. The remainder of the country may be organized into regional districts—each consisting of a set of rural or semirural counties with a diameter of approximately one-hundred miles—which are economically and geographically interrelated.

If a set of administrative education authorities were established on this pattern, each authority would have within its boundaries an approach to a cross-section of the society, in terms of family income, labor force, and educational institutions. Each authority could have a teacher training program, an educational television program, a special education program, a performing arts program, and at least one public college or university. And there would be no scandal such as a wealthy school district made up of owners, managers, and professional people with their children, with a contiguous poor district made up of the people who work for the people of the wealthy district. Educational opportunity could be maximized for the youth of poor families, and social understanding and democratic attitudes would be maximized for youth of rich families.

The other goal is the increase of local self-determination for schools or small groups of schools. This can be done through decentralization of responsibility without decentralization of legal authority. The central education authority can delegate responsibility for particular kinds of decisions to local school or district education advisory councils, without giving such units the power to make decisions on their own which are against the general welfare of the larger district. There must be some control over the separatist tendencies and limited educational and social vision of the residents of a small area—often segregated by race, income, religion, or other subcultural factors. The ill consequences of dividing up big cities into autonomous school districts with their own school boards are already evident and will become more obvious in the next few years. Consequently I foresee a movement toward defining and limiting the decision-making of these smaller districts.

These changes will not come easily. I foresee a period of at least ten years of controversy, experimentation, and compromise, until eventually a rational solution is worked out for the governance of the educational system through a basic governmental unit of the modern society.

REFERENCES

1. Bane, Mary Jo, and Jencks, Christopher. "The Schools and Equal Opportunity." *Saturday Review of Education*, September 16, 1972.

2. Carnegie Commission on Higher Education. Reports and Recommendations. New York: McGraw-Hill.

   New Students and New Places: Policies for the Future Growth and Development of American Higher Education. October 1971. Used with permission.

   Institutional Aid: Federal Support to Colleges and Universities. February 1972.

   The More Effective Use of Resources: An Imperative for Higher Education. June 1972.

3. Eberly, Donald J. *The Estimated Effect of a National Service Program on Public Service Manpower Needs, Youth Employment, College Attendance, and Marriage Rates.* Mimeographed. New York, N.Y.: Russell Sage Foundation, 1970.

4. Erikson, Erik H. *Identity and the Life Cycle: Psychological Issues.* Vol. 1, No. 1, p. 157. New York: International Universities Press, 1959.

5. Harman, Willis W. "Contemporary Social Forces and Alternative Futures." *Journal of Research and Development in Education* 2 (Summer 1969):67–89.

6. Havighurst, Robert J.; Graham, Richard A.; and Eberly, Donald J. "American Youth in the Mid-Seventies." *Bulletin of the National Association of Secondary School Principals.* 56 (November 1972).

7. Illich, Ivan. *Deschooling Society.* New York: Harper and Row, 1971.

8. Jencks, Christopher, et al. *Inequality: A Reassessment of the Effect of Family and Schooling in America.* New York: Basic Books, 1972.

9. Meadows, D. H., et al. *The Limits to Growth.* London: Earth Island, Ltd., 1972.

10. Rossman, Michael. *On Learning and Social Change.* New York: Random House, 1972. Previewed in *Saturday Review,* August 19, 1972. pp. 27–33.

Nat
Hentoff

Nat Hentoff

Novelist, jazz critic, educational reformer, free-lance writer, Mr. Hentoff is an associate professor at New York University's Graduate School of Education. His columns and articles on education appear in numerous professional and lay periodicals, including a regular column on learning for The New Yorker. *One of his many notable books,* Our Children Are Dying, *helped focus national attention on the plight of urban schools.*

the future
of education:
basic
considerations

The temptation, I find, in accepting soothsaying
invitations is to selectively arrange the future so that
the odds appear to be in favor, with help from friends
and fate, of what I devoutly wish will happen. Unless,
that is, one is a doomsayer. My own bent is toward
hopefulness, if not always optimism, and yet I cannot
examine the auguries for education from 1975 to 2000
without emphasizing my great misgivings about present
directions in the politics of education.

I am assuming that most contributors to this
volume will be urging diverse alternatives to the ways
in which we learn and teach now. My concern is that
many education futurists tend to ignore the prickly fact
that the key to change in any field is whether those
opposed to present practices have the *power* to do
more than write books or construct (attractive) models
of what the majority out there ought to be doing.

For example, although I consider Ivan Illich a
seer—with the reminder that seers can produce effects
quite different from their intentions—I do not see
deschooling involving more than a very small percentage
of children within the next twenty-five years. Considering
how weak the political constituency is for educational
vouchers—a desideratum which I feel would facilitate
many alternative learning routes, including deschooling—

I do not understand how the Illich learning networks, or "webs," are going to connect more than a relatively few youngsters for some time to come, and most of those are already self-starters anyway.

Let me put it this way. Consider Ivan Illich, or one of his disciples, telling a Black, Puerto Rican, or Chicano parent who is fighting for community control of the local school that this parent has really missed the point. The schools aren't worth fighting about. O.K., the parent may respond for the sake of argument, here are my three children. I don't want them to grow up into welfare dependency (and no guaranteed annual income passed by any Congress in this century is going to be enough). And I don't want them to live in the limbo of the marginally employed. So, what are you offering them in place of school?

Well, Illich or his disciple would probably be resourceful enough to place those three children in some kind of self-motivating, skill-acquiring match with someone who has some reason to want to teach them what they want to know. But what would Illich or his disciple do with three million kids? Or ten million? I'll make it easy—fifty thousand.

Granted that funding for deschooling could be a lot less than what is spent on schools now; but where on earth, let alone in America, is even enough seed money going to come from? I mean seed money for large numbers of children. So far as I can foresee—and that's what I'm supposed to be doing here—deschooling is going to be an elitist trip for a long time to come, even for those token poor sprung thereby from what John Holt calls "the great glass box" in which nearly all kids are now contained.

No, the schools are not going to dissolve by the year 2000. Many, as you'll probably read elsewhere in this volume, are going to assume new shapes (smaller, without walls, each child hooked into all kinds of technology—including maybe surveillance devices, I might add). But that's not what I'm going to write about. No matter what transmutations (and some transmogrification) take place, the key is still going to be who has the *power*. The power to hire and fire teachers; the power to define people as teachers who haven't a single credit in "education"; the power to alter, subvert, jettison curriculum; the power to share power.

If I am right that we are still going to have plenty of schools by the year 2000—however "opened," plugged in, extended out into the real world—we are also going to have plenty of teachers. Unionized teachers. I consider it extraordinarily naive to explore the future of education without keeping in mind that for at least the next twenty-five years, most kids are still going to be attending public schools; and that increasingly, control of these schools is being taken by organized teachers. Consider, for example, that the only way in which to fundamentally break the monopoly of public education for those children and parents who can afford no other is public funding for educational vouchers. Even if the Supreme Court were eventually to declare compulsory schooling unconstitutional—and don't let the Amish decision get your hopes up because it was most narrowly drawn—where but from public funds would the money come for those who nonetheless wanted to learn something somewhere? Confronted with rapidly growing teacher union power, what legislature—state or federal—is going to make the educational voucher pervasive learning currency?

I reemphasize that the public schools are not going to wither away by 2000; most kids will still be in them, or connected with them in one way or another. Long before 2000, moreover, there is a considerable likelihood that, despite current reluctance by the National Education Association, there will be one big national teachers' union—a fusion of the NEA and the American Federation of Teachers, from prekindergarten through graduate school. For reasons that entirely escape me, Myron Lieberman, director of the Teacher Leadership Program of the City University of New York, actually looks forward to such a fusion. ("The Union Merger Movement/Will 3,500,000 Teachers Put It All Together?", *Saturday Review*, June 24, 1972.) But his figures, if not his reasoning, are persuasive. Well before 2000, a massive teachers' union could include:

2,100,000	regular classroom teachers
750,000	faculty in higher education, public and private
300,000	paraprofessionals in public schools
224,000	nonpublic elementary and secondary teachers
150,000	miscellaneous (U.S. Office of Education, state departments of education, nonprofit educational organizations, and so on)

No matter what suggestions and prescriptions for educational change that you read elsewhere in this book, the reality of teacher power has to be taken into account.

A significant figure in the rise of teacher unionism is Albert Shanker, head of New York City's United Federation of Teachers (the largest single local union of any kind in the country) and also in charge of the New York state amalgamation of NEA and AFT affiliates (now the largest single state organization of public employees in the United

States). When and if there is one big national teachers' union, Albert Shanker is likely to be its godfather.

As an illustration of the kind of role model this maximum leader of teachers presents to children in the public schools of a nation trying to be a democracy, there is Shanker's statement to a *New York Times* reporter (June 26, 1972): "It isn't important what I think or how I feel. Building an institution—that's important."

That particular institution is indeed being built; and its goal, as Robert Braun documents in *Teachers and Power* (Simon and Schuster), is "the reduction of the minutest detail of daily school operations to (union) contract language so that any change must have union blessing." Braun, education editor of the *Newark Star-Ledger*, has focused on the American Federation of Teachers in his book, but the NEA is moving in the same direction; and an eventually merged national union will certainly grasp for as total control of the schools as it can get. In that context, then, minischools, schools without walls, multilane bridges between the school and the actual world of work—any change you can name—could be dependent on union approval, on union criteria of staffing and the accountability of that staff.

In a letter to me in June of 1972, John Holt noted:

Albert Shanker knows that the future of the schools is not going to be written in the classrooms but in the courts and the legislatures. He understands, better than most school reformers, that schools are an arm of the State (not the fifty states, but the State). He understands that if he can forge the proper alliances with legislatures and other unions, he doesn't have to worry about what all the school reformers and angry parents in the world say. The Teachers' Union will determine what happens in the school.

Holt continued:

I would bet a substantial sum of money that within the next ten years or so the Teachers' Union will be the most regressive and repressive force in all U.S. education—unless those of us who care about humane education have done something to limit the power of the schools over children . . . Radicals working within the system, as they like to say, are going to have Mr. Shanker to deal with, not just those superintendents and school boards. But with this difference—the time may not be far away when the union, by blacklisting teachers or kicking them out of the union, can prevent a recalcitrant teacher from getting a job anywhere. There will be a union-prescribed orthodoxy in education. Those who oppose it will be out. There will be no more question of parents changing what happens in schools by electing a reform-minded school board. The union will establish the position that the school boards have nothing to say about what goes on in classrooms. The union determines that, and writes it into all teacher contracts. Albert Shanker, or some counterpart, will be the boss of U.S. education.

Holt believes that the only way to prevent this freezing of learning is to

take quick steps to limit the power of schools to compel attendance, to limit
choices, and to control the future lives of students. That, to a large degree,
is what the deschooling business is all about. Either we break the schools'
monopoly on learning and the legitimizing of learning, or we are going to
that hitherto rather diffuse monopoly controlled by a few shrewd and determined men . . . What is at stake here is political and legal and economic
power, and, as I say, we had better make damn sure that the power of the
schools and of teachers is limited—and the place to do that is not in school
buildings, but in the political arena.

As I've noted, although Holt and I agree on the identity of
this primary threat to changes in education advocated in this or any
other book, I do not believe deschooling to be politically feasible. Nor
do I believe that even if deschooling for large numbers of children
were possible, it would help to empower the poor in any significant
political way. Individuals in separate orbits are difficult to organize.

I do agree that the way to redistribute schooling power is in
the political arena. And that means organizing parents and children
to provide an effective counterforce to teachers' unions and unre-
sponsive school administrations. After all, oughtn't the public schools
be *publicly* controlled?

The way it is now, both children and parents are, for the most,
powerless in "their" schools. Consider, for instance, that for all the
writing and some action in recent years concerning the humanizing
of education, corporal punishment continues to exist, often ferociously,
in many schools throughout the country. In my research on this issue
for the American Civil Liberties Union, I have discovered not only the
broad extent of this way of beating democracy into children but also
the intensive support it receives from organized teachers as well as
from many superintendents and boards of education. Now *that's* something to keep in mind in a book focusing on enlarging the possibilities
of learning in the last quarter of this century. We have yet to leave
behind the paddle and the stick.

In an NEA-conducted national survey in 1970, 57 percent of
its teacher-members approved paddling. Most AFT locals are no less
zealous in fighting for the retention of corporal punishment. The courts
so far have been resistant to ACLU suits aimed at declaring child-beat-
ing in the schools unconstitutional. I think that, in time, the ACLU
may win some victories in this area; but if the courts are so slow to
move against such egregious abuse of power by teachers and adminis-

trators, what chance is there—in legislatures and in courts—to effect the other limitations of school powers that John Holt calls for?

I have heard from parents in many states—parents who do not want their children beaten but who, lacking the money to place their kids in private schools, feel helpless to intervene. This in 1973!

Or consider the increasing practice of using psychoactive drugs on allegedly hyperkinetic children in the public schools. I will not argue here whether there is an actual, clearly diagnosable condition which can be legitimately called hyperkinesis or minimal brain dysfunction, but I will state unequivocally, on the basis of considerable research, that careless, indiscriminate drugging of children—particularly "difficult" inner-city kids—is very much on the rise. (As of 1972, between 200,000 and 300,000 children in public schools had been officially placed on various drugs, usually amphetamines which help them to "concentrate" and thereby cease "bothering" the teacher.)

Those pediatric neurologists who claim that the efficacy of these drugs can be proved, nonetheless admit that careful, extensive testing is required prior to the most tentative diagnosis of hyperactivity. They add that close observation of the child must be maintained while he is on medication. However, there is irrefutable evidence that in more and more cases, these drugs are routinely administered after minimal testing and observation of the child and with no follow-up at all. Nor is there any consideration of whether it is the learning environment rather than the child that ought to be changed.

In this book about the future of education, I submit that there is a real possibility that by the year 2000, much more sophisticated and pervasive drugging of the young in school will be the order-keeping norm in much of American education. Certainly the one big national teachers' union is not likely to be in opposition to making classrooms—structured or open—more "peaceful."

On this issue too, I have heard from parents in many states who feel desperately impotent when they are instructed by school personnel to place their children on drugs or face the suspension of the children from school. As with corporal punishment, this is a clear violation of civil liberties; and yet it is going to be difficult for abused children and their parents to cope with what one dissident psychiatrist calls the Educational-Psychiatric-Psychological Establishment.

My basic point throughout this essay is that the forces for dehumanizing schools—now and for the next quarter-century—ought not to be underestimated by those who consider themselves liberators of learning. Arthur Pearl, for instance, has written a useful, though largely neglected book, specifying changes that can and should be made in education. (*The Atrocity of Education*, New Critics Press/E.

P. Dutton). He believes, as I expect all the contributors to this book do, that "the primary goal of education in a technologically advanced society is to enable every citizen to exercise autonomy in an interdependent world." But nowhere in his book, or in many other volumes on the future of education, is there sufficient realization that—with regard to the politics of education—speculative essays and a model learning situation here and there are no match for those with power in the public schools, where the real battle has to be fought.

There is no dearth of theories, and actual programs, for enabling children and teachers (veteran instructors as well as apprentices) to learn how to be both autonomous and responsible to each other. But the spirits of many children will continue to be mutilated in our schools, no matter how many "innovations" are introduced, until each school, with or without walls, is itself autonomous—a democratic polity in which everyone involved shares in rights, responsibilities, and governance.

Schools—or learning situations, if you will—cannot nurture autonomy if they are hooked into systems and if decision making is the unappealable prerogative of any one source—school board, administration, or teachers' union. No amount of electronic technology, relevant curriculum, or new teacher-preparation programs can substitute for an authentic, independent community of learning. Education for the future—in a society which still intends to become democratic—should begin in an autonomous school in which the full constitutional rights of all its members are respected and—if the school works—are exercised.

To me this seems, on the face of it, a most modest proposal. But when you realize how rare such a learning situation is in this country—all the more rare in the public schools—the work that has to be done to democratize learning in a little more than a quarter of a century (according to the prospectus of this book) is enormous.

It's not going to be done by teachers' unions, although autonomous groups of teachers may join together for this purpose—in alliance with students and parents. If there is to be any real, basic transformation of schools from great glass boxes to places where learning to learn is as natural a part of living as slaking thirst, it's going to happen through a political coalition of students, parents, and deinstitutionalized teachers in one specific community. And then another and another and another. But what if, as is often the case, no real community exists outside the school from which to draw strength? Then the school has to be the initiating community.

In such a school, or learning situation, in which autonomy and mutual accountability were intertwined, it would be as impossible for a child to be beaten or forced on to controlling medication as it is now to fire a teacher for incompetence or inhumanity in a tightly unionized school system.

And in such a school, if any one child were "failing," the whole school would accept *its* responsibility—not the child's—for that failure and adapt *itself* to that particular child's needs.

If this sounds fanciful or naive or romantic to you, then read on in this book about the future of education and be assured that another collection of articles on this theme will be commissioned in the year 2000 to try to find out why all those new programs and computers and video cassettes and multipurpose buildings and no-buildings didn't work either.

Theodore
W. Hipple

Theodore W. Hipple

A professor in the Department of Secondary Education at the University of Florida, Dr. Hipple received his Ph.D. in education from the University of Illinois. Active in writing and convention work for the National Council of Teachers of English, he includes among his publications Teaching English in Secondary Schools *and* Secondary School Teaching: Problems and Methods. *He also serves as general editor for the Goodyear Publishing Company's series in education. (Dr. Hipple was the developer and editor of this volume.)*

some (specific and not-so-specific) notions about the (distant and not-so-distant) future of education

Reflections about the future of education must
inevitably be filtered through a variety of lenses. One is
reminded of a common toy, a kaleidoscope. When he
turns it, the pieces fall into place and form an attractive
and clearly outlined pattern, a mosaic with its own
structure and content. Yet let him turn it ever so
slightly more and a new pattern emerges, one equally
attractive, equally distinct, but markedly different.
Another spin produces another pattern. And no matter
how often a kaleidoscope is spun, it never repeats an
earlier design. The combinations and permutations are
not only infinite but also fleeting, and they cannot be
recaptured.

So is it with attempts to see what education is
all about. If one looks through the lens marked dollars,
and concentrates on the economic aspects of
education—on the need for funding, the sources of that
funding, and the ways in which that funding will be
dispersed—he may be unable to focus concurrently on
the important relationships between education and the
society that it shapes and serves. Similarly, examinations
of educational philosophy and purpose, apart from
practice, create limited images. Looking at how
teachers teach, apart from how pupils learn, reveals an
incomplete picture. The instant one alters his perspective,

or turns the kaleidoscope, what he sees shifts. There are simply too many interacting variables. It seems impossible to capture the whole.

If this is true about the present state of education, how much more complicated is the situation when one confronts the task of describing education in the future? As Toffler and others have adequately, but by no means exhaustively, demonstrated, change is the order of the day, not only in things and in people but in change itself. To predict the future of anything is risky, a task beset with the conviction that one is more likely to be wrong than right, to be conservatively short of the mark or radically beyond it. When prediction deals with a field as complicated as education, the issue is even more beclouded. Perhaps one should forget all about it, live—as the posters have it—for this day only, and concentrate on lowering his golf score or improving his tennis serve.

But one is human, by his nature curious about the future, and by his humanity anxious to have some voice, however small, in its form and its substance. Given the impossibility of examining at one and the same time the whole of education, either now or in the future, one may be best advised to fall back on that salvation of the predictor, the list. An eclectic approach, an itemization and discussion of many somewhat disparate aspects of education, may produce as many rights as wrongs. Such a scheme, it must be confessed, avoids the all-the-eggs-in-one-basket risk and may, therefore, be construed by some readers as a cop-out, a failure of nerve. Yet it offers in compensation the likelihood that readers, able to plug in and out as their interests dictate, will find some aspects of the list sufficiently palatable to command their support. These same readers might reject out of hand the one fully developed idea, and all, therefore, would have been written in vain. This distinction about reader reaction is important because it is the readers, taken as a group, who will ultimately shape the future of education. No one man, through his charisma or his way with words or the substance of his ideas, can by himself make much difference or have much effect except as he is able to impose his thinking on a large number of people.

But enough of apologia and on to the lists (pun intended). What follows are my notions about the future of education—what I think will happen, and what I believe ought to happen. Before I begin, however, my compulsion for a logical ordering of things demands that I treat briefly of two significant questions: Will education change? Should education change?

No compelling evidence supports the conviction that education will change in substantive ways. There will be—indeed there already are—changes in some tangential aspects. Ranch house buildings will continue to replace the early gothic four-story structures of yesteryear. Teachers will write on green blackboards with yellow chalk. Computers will keep better track of student's transcripts and test data. But the substantive matters—the ways teachers teach (and are themselves taught), the ways students are presumed to learn or not learn, the purposes society has for its schools, the curricula presented in them—these may change very little.

This is a bold and depressing assertion, but some evidence for it may be found in the past. As I write these words, the Vietnam prisoners of war are much in the news. They are returning home now, some of them after an infamously isolated captivity of almost a decade. The popular media have devoted considerable attention to the changes these men will have to cope with: the altered family patterns, as the nuclear family now sometimes includes two or three extra resident adults not sanctioned by traditional marriage vows; the x-rated movies, in which things the returning prisoners doubtlessly dreamed of are now served up graphically every Friday night at the local drive-in; and women's liberation. The list could go and on, but these few examples suffice. One area conspicuously absent from the media presentations has been education. Apparently—and mere observation supports the contention—the schools have changed so little that no returning POW will be shocked or even surprised by them. Or conjure up an example involving a greater time span. Suppose a modern Rip Van Winkle had dozed off twenty or thirty or even forty years ago. He would be completely nonplussed by many of the aspects of life that contemporary Americans take for granted. But not by the schools and what goes on in them. Rip could sit in on a fifth grade class or one in sophomore English, and within a few days he would be completely caught up.

Those who insist that schools have changed may charge me with myopia and cite such examples as the new math or the new science. I would argue that, for the most part, these are old wine in new bottles. It is still the teachers, with their ubiquitous textbooks, who determine what will be taught—some even ingenuously proclaim that this is what will be learned—and how it will be taught. (All but a few of them seem unfortunately inarticulate about why it should be taught.) Matters like attention to individual differences or individualized instruction are far more often mouthed in college classrooms than practiced there or in the public schools. Students are still expected to be docile, to act as passive recipients of the wisdom, passed down as if from on high, of their betters and mentors. Superintendents, principals, and their proliferating administrative assistants still reign supreme and still seem more concerned with order and control than with learning and humanity. The lay public still expects the schools to do all things for all people—at minimal costs. Stated goals for schools so far outstrip actual practices that the gulf between the two sometimes seems beyond bridging. The following quote from Royce Van Norman of Johns Hopkins University is apt:

Is it not ironical that in a planned society of controlled workers given compulsory assignments, where religious expression is suppressed, the press controlled, and all media of communication censored, where a puppet government is encouraged but denied any real authority, where great attention is given to efficiency and character reports, and attendance at cultural assemblies is compulsory, where it is avowed that all will be administered to each according to his needs and performance required from each according to his abilities, and where those who flee are tracked down, returned, and punished for trying to escape—in short, in the milieu of the typical large American secondary school—we attempt to teach "the democratic system"?

The question of whether education will change is still very much an open one. Yet there may be seen in current movements in education some anomalies—one cannot yet call them trends—that permit anticipations of change. The misnamed *free schools* springing up here and there have provided substantially different kinds of education for many of their students. Parents in some communities are demanding and getting a greater share of the decision-making authority for their local schools. Students, too, want a piece of this action and in some places they are matching the wish with service on administrative advisory boards. Teachers are banding together into organizations to fight for their own welfare. Books that call for an end to compulsory schooling or for a deschooled society now regularly make the best-seller list and are, presumably, read now by butchers and bakers as well as college professors. Accountability measures have been created in many districts in response to community pressures that schools not only say what they are trying to do but also demonstrate that they are doing it. There is, in contemporary education, ferment on a grand scale, with unprecedented numbers and kinds of people expressing an unprecedented concern about education. Such attention renders unconvincing the argument that the lack of any change in the future of education will result from the inactivity that has been characteristic of the past. Indeed, such ferment is itself a change, as well as a harbinger of things to come.

In large part this ferment addresses itself to the second question I raised as an issue to be handled prior to the listing of my notions about the future of education: Should education be changed? It should. Indeed, it must. Perhaps the best documentation of the ills of contemporary education and, by inference, of the need for change is Charles E. Silberman's *Crisis in the Classroom.*

After quoting Erik Erikson's assertion that "The most deadly of all possible sins is the mutilation of a child's spirit," Silberman writes as follows:

It is not possible to spend any prolonged period visiting public school classrooms without being appalled by the mutilation visible everywhere— mutilation of spontaneity, of joy in learning, of pleasure in creating, of sense of self. The public schools . . . are the kind of institution one cannot really dislike until one gets to know them well. Because adults take the schools so much for granted, they fail to appreciate what grim, joyless places most American schools are, how oppressive and petty are the rules by which they are governed, how intellectually sterile and esthetically barren the atmosphere, what an appalling lack of civility obtains on the part of teachers and principals, what contempt they unconsciously display for children as children.

And it need not be! Public schools *can* be organized to facilitate joy in learning and esthetic expression and to develop character—in the rural and urban slums no less than in the prosperous suburbs. . . .

What makes change possible, moreover, is that what is mostly wrong with the public schools is due not to venality or indifference or stupidity, but to mindlessness. To be sure, teaching has its share of sadists and clods, of insecure and angry men and women who hate their students for their openness, their exuberance, their color or their affluence. But by and large, teachers, principals, and superintendents are decent, intelligent, and caring people who try to do their best by their lights. If they make a botch of it, and an uncomfortably large number do, it is because it simply never occurs to more than a handful to ask *why* they are doing what they are doing—to think seriously or deeply about the purposes or consequences of education.*

One could also quote to much the same effect, albeit with less eloquence, from the numerous first-person accounts about educational experiences—those by John Holt or James Herndon or Jonathon Kozol or Esther Rothmann. Like Silberman, these educators are not only deeply concerned about the present state of the schools—they are also professionally committed to the idea that schools must change.

The anomalies mentioned above—the alternative schools, the thrust for power made by teachers, parents, and students, and the demands for accountability—suggest still further the contemporary malaise in education and the need for change. It may be putting the matter too simplistically to assert that the schools face the choice of making substantive changes or closing up shop, but never before in the history of education have its critics been so numerous and so outspoken. And not simply those critics who write books or articles for the popular press, but also those housewives, professional men and women, and blue collar workers who sense, sometimes not even consciously, that something is wrong with the fabric of education, that neither are the

*Reprinted by permission of the publisher from Charles E. Silberman, *Crisis in the Classroom* (New York: Random House, Inc., 1970), pp. 10–11. © 1970 Charles E. Silberman.

schools meeting the noble expectations held for them nor are they even achieving the minimal demands made upon them.

That the schools will change, then, is a fairly safe prediction. The direction of change and its scope are far less certain. My notions about that change—some of them radical, some cautious, some mandatory, some wistfully hoped for—comprise the remainder of this article.

1. Financing of public education will be enlarged and its base broadened. Presently most of the burden for school support falls to local districts and to state boards of education. In the future the share from the state is likely to increase proportionately in an attempt to curb the inequities that presently exist. For example, an affluent suburb may spend upward of $1,000 per pupil, while a center city school may have only $500 per pupil to spend. The minimum foundation program (the guarantee by the state of a minimal level of funding for each school child) now in effect in most states will be substantially increased.

Additionally, the burden assumed by the federal government will be significantly greater than it presently is. In a society as mobile as ours, it is nationally self-defeating to permit an inferior education to occur anywhere in the country if lack of money is the root cause of the inferiority. The federal government has the resources to support education in a grand manner. What is presently lacking is a system of priorities with educational spending at or near the top. Societal demands for increased spending can reorder the present commitments.

Increased funds will lead to numerous benefits for pupils. Perhaps the most significant will be an increase in the number of teachers employed—the pupil-teacher ratio will be narrowed considerably. Moreover, many of these additional teachers will be highly specialized, with expertise in areas such as remedial and developmental reading, counseling and guidance, and education of the gifted and the retarded. Supplies now woefully lacking in a distressingly large number of districts will become plentiful. (In one school I visited late last spring the teachers had run out of ditto paper in mid-April and had had to do without or purchase their own for the remainder of the year.) Physically unsafe or depressing buildings will be renovated or replaced. Money will be available for those activities now regarded as too expensive for all but the affluent districts: field trips to zoos or museums or factories or theaters; expanded extracurricular programs; in-school assembly performances; subjects like advanced science or foreign languages that attract few students; private, but school-supported, tutoring for students with unusual needs.

2. A concomitant of increased funding for education will be an increase in teacher's salaries. American society, virtually since its birth, has underpaid its civil servants, its policemen, its firemen, its

teachers. Teachers have experienced some gains in recent years, but even today any college graduate who goes into teaching faces a career with financial rewards that are significantly smaller than those in almost any of the numerous other fields his fellow graduates enter. I recently read that the federal government was proposing to subsidize any physician who agreed to go to a small, rural town for at least three years, so that his minimal salary would be $30,000 annually. The chances are the teachers in that town will be making less than a third of that figure. Admittedly physicians have had longer and more expensive training, but not by two-thirds. Admittedly, too, they render a service that has high visibility and satisfies immediate needs, unlike the teachers, who are simply there, and the benefits of whose work may not be evident for some years. But neither a society nor an individual can safely consider only the short-range goal, the need to cure cancer or to alleviate a stomachache. Both must also attend to their long-range needs, among which the education of youth deserves a high priority. People must accept the principle of delayed gratification, of paying today for what may not be realized until tomorrow.

If tomorrow's benefits are to be good ones, then society needs good teachers today. Good teachers are available now. More potentially good teachers can be attracted to education, provided that vocational choice offers an opportunity for monetary rewards comparable to those available in other occupations. No longer can we afford to say to teachers that we know we do not pay you very much, but then you work only nine months a year and you get tremendous personal satisfaction from what you do. We must, and I believe we will, come across with cold cash.

3. Alternative forms of education will continue to flourish, especially beyond elementary school. Presently most schools resemble each other, not only in their physical aspects but also—and more importantly—in what goes on inside them. The same goals are held at most schools, the same activities are used to achieve those goals, the same evaluative techniques (for schools and for pupils) are employed to measure that achievement. The principal exceptions to these generalizations are the free schools and the vocational schools.

It seems probable that, in the future, different types of schools will be established to achieve different goals or to achieve standard goals in different ways. In part, the American system of secondary education will begin to resemble the European tradition, in which, at age ten or twelve, the student has several alternatives open to him: vocational schools, academic schools, science and engineering centers, and the like. However, in many European countries the student is virtually forced by test scores and past achievements to attend one kind of school. In the United States students, acting in concert with their parents and the elementary school guidance team, will be able to choose the kinds of schools they wish to go to. For some, vocational training leading to skilled occupations will be available. Other students may opt for an academic center that will prepare them for college work. Still others may choose schools which focus on creative expression in art or music. Open schools, those with free-flowing, often spontaneous curricula, will be available for students who want the kind of experience these institutions provide. Modifications of the Philadelphia Parkway Plan, which utilized the whole city for its educational program, will become more common. Work-study combinations will be widespread.

Of course, these optional educational arrangements are more easily effected in urban settings than in rural areas or small towns, but even here the comprehensive high schools that tried, and failed, to do and be all things for all people will give way to as many options as the community is able to provide.

4. The school will be a community center as well as a user of community facilities to enhance its educational program. On the one hand, schools will be operated for longer hours each day; students will be able to select hours to fit schedules they and their families want. Additionally, these extra hours will be utilized to provide basic and enrichment courses for the adults of the community. Numerous school personnel have already realized the financial waste incurred in building for adult use those facilities—gymnasiums, auditoriums, athletic fields, meeting rooms—that are already available in the schools.

New schools will be built only after discussions with many other community planning agencies. In the future schools will be grouped together in clusters of several schools, probably serving grades kindergarten through twelve or fourteen. Within a school cluster may well be built the community library, the community parks, and the community swimming pool. Office buildings may be built near the school cluster so that those adults—music teachers and orthodontists, for example—whose work involves many children will be able to give piano lessons or straighten teeth during the students' free hours within the school day. Such planning and construction would avoid unnecessary duplication and would make the schools a part of the community, the community a part of the schools, in far closer ways than are now possible.

5. To permit students to use the community facilities constructed near the schools, it seems probable that the time students spend in actual classrooms will be shortened. Those students in alternative schools or in work-study programs will have such time readily avail-

able; those in more traditional academic programs will find their school days shortened. In secondary schools the employment of modular scheduling will increase. Students will have free time during the normal school day to pursue independent study projects, to go to the adjacent library or to one of the buildings near the school for music lessons or dental appointments, to meet students from another school in the educational cluster for a tutoring session, or simply to talk with friends. The freed time in a modular schedule is also designed to help students acquire the maturity and discipline that they will learn by being responsible for deciding how they will use their unscheduled time. Such decisions are rare for most secondary school youth in today's schools. Virtually every in-school minute is programmed in advance, and all sorts of punitive measures are set in motion if students are not where they are supposed to be when they are supposed to be.

Today's elementary school student usually attends school for approximately six hours a day, a length of time as often determined by the availability of transportation as by any educational considerations. If school buses are not available until 3:30 in the afternoon, then the children must remain in school until 3:30 P.M. Double sessions—with reduced in-school time—that have been experienced by thousands of children have not been shown to have been detrimental to their learning. It seems likely that tomorrow's schools will have shorter days. With students in school for fewer hours, teachers will have more time for lesson preparation, for cooperative planning, for needed relaxation. Those families who have come to think of the school as, among other things, a day-long babysitter, need not be concerned about the shortened day. Near the school cluster will be playgrounds and youth centers staffed with supervisory and instructional personnel employed jointly by the schools and the community. In these locations students will learn many of the things the schools now try but often fail to teach because of shortages of equipment or properly trained personnel: arts and crafts activities like sewing or carpentry; physical education activities like tennis or swimming; musical activities like singing or playing the guitar.

6. Some of the "teachers" at the nearby playgrounds and youth centers will be high school youth who are using their free time to work, on a paid basis, at the centers. Such a practice will be in keeping with a trend sure to become more common in the schools than it presently is: cross-age teaching. Consider the present day kindergarten teacher in upstate Wisconsin on a wintry day. Shortly before the end of school she must pause and dress her charges for their snowy trip home: thirty snowsuits to wrestle with, sixty boots, thirty scarves, fifty-nine mittens.

Yet when little Johnnie reaches home, undresses, and then decides he wants to go back outside and play, what happens? Johnnie's mother instructs Susan, his fifth grade sister, to dress him. One wonders why a few of the Susans of the fifth grade could not be dismissed ten minutes early each day to report to the kindergarten classes to help with the dressing of the students there.

Dressing little children is but one example, and a mundane one at that, of the great but relatively untapped potential the schools have for using older children to help younger ones. Students in advanced foreign language classes will provide assistance in the elementary school French lessons. Bright high schoolers will provide tutorial services not only for younger children but for their peers and will receive academic credit for doing so. Other students will staff the adjacent community/school facilities, supervising and instructing in activities that range from archery to needlepoint, gymnastics to folk singing.

Such participation in the education of others, so little used in the schools today, is truly at the heart of a system of education that promotes itself as an exemplar and a promoter of the democratic ideal. Helping others ought to be a keystone of our social fabric. Tomorrow's schools will train students to accept this responsibility and—because these students will be using their talents in ways they select—to delight in it. Moreover, the use of older students as assistants and instructors will permit certificated teachers to use their time more wisely once they are freed of time-consuming, routine duties that could as easily be handled by reasonably alert ninth graders.

7. The curricula of the schools—that which is taught in them and which students are presumed to learn—will change in the last quarter of the twentieth century, but perhaps not as radically as some educational seers have suggested. The schools will remain in the business of training in the three Rs. Although it is undeniable that a person can lead a moderately successful adult life—get married and raise a family, hold a job, entertain himself via television, participate in government by voting—without literacy, such a regimen cannot be encouraged. Adult life will continue to demand and reward literacy, and society will continue to expect the schools to provide that literacy for its citizens. Indeed, to the basic skills of reading, writing, and arithmetic will be added those related to the new technology, especially computers. It is highly probable that all citizens in future years will be trained in elementary uses of computers and of data retrieval systems. Community centers will house such instruments for use by the general populace.

Much of the content presently being taught in the schools will be replaced by content useful in problem solving. That is, students will not study content for the sake of acquiring the facts of that content (for example, the population of Houston), but will instead use content to help them solve problems or understand issues of their own or their teachers' design. For illustration, consider a problem that sixth graders could conceivably wrestle with: What kinds of difficulties would colonists on the moon encounter? To arrive at answers, students would have to learn about and apply their knowledge of such different fields as space travel, moon ecology, and governmental formation. They may well solicit information from science, civics, sociology, and even history.

Problem solving, then, will be a common method of instruction. Typically, the problems will demand the intermeshing of the intelligence and efforts of several students, possibly even the entire class. Cooperation among students will replace the competition that is stressed now, and will help produce adults who are skilled in the give-and-take required for successful corporate activity. There will be spin-off activities as students individually pursue interests they develop as they work at resolving problems.

Another dimension of the curriculum of the future is that it will focus on values and attitudes. In the past schools have largely avoided controversial issues that might have, at their source, different sets of operative values: the relationships between loyalty to self, family, and friends and loyalty to government, for one example; the role of a society with regard to its indigent, for another. These were issues which the schools have felt they could never win. Always they have risked alienating people whose views differed from the positions the schools were believed to be espousing—even when the schools were attempting to be neutral and to explore all sides fairly and without bias. A simple, perhaps even spur-of-the-moment classroom discussion of a subject like abortion could be so misconstrued, when reported in community homes, that it could earn the wrath of the pros, the antis, and even of the neutrals who felt the schools should keep hands off "topics like that."

Well, topics like that are going to be common classroom fodder in the decades ahead, not in order to permit the school or its teachers to promulgate a particular point of view but in order to allow the kind of classroom interchange that leads to value identification and clarification. Students will be asking questions like these: What are my values on this particular issue and how strongly do I cherish them? What forces (for example, family, peers, media) have shaped my values? How are they changing? Am I content with them? Do they conflict with values I espouse about related issues? The school will not be trying to persuade its students to a particular point of view. Rather, it will try to help each student discover what his point of view is, how it was acquired, whether it ought to be modified, and, if so, how it can be modified.

It is, of course, ingenuous to assume that overt or covert attempts at indoctrination will not occur. Despite a teacher's attempts to be neutral and impartial, he will be construed by some of his students as leaning in one direction or another and subsequently approved or disapproved for that presumed leaning. Then, too, there will be teachers who believe that their role is to shape their students' beliefs in the right (that is, in the teachers') ways. Just as some teachers yearly fail to teach reading well, so also will some teachers fail to handle value clarification activities responsibly.

8. Curricula that focus on problem solving and on value clarification activities will call for new instructional strategies. Classroom discussions, small group work, and independent study projects will replace the teacher's lecture as the standard teaching tactic. There will be more questions than answers, more asking than telling. Already these kinds of activities are being called for in textbooks on teaching methods and in education classes at the universities, where, it must be confessed, they are even more rarely practiced than in the elementary and secondary schools.

Techniques of evaluating student performance will change, too. The standard five-point, A to F grading scheme will give way to satisfactory-unsatisfactory or pass-fail systems, and these broad classifications will be determined more on process than on product. If, for example, a student pursues the solution of a problem by formulating hypotheses, gathering data, examining alternatives, and developing strategies, his work will be considered satisfactory even if his solution is not at all feasible—or even if he does not arrive at a solution. His knowledge of the process, of the approaches he should take, will be important. As he progresses to the upper grades, workable solutions will assume more importance; but even there, achievement will be measured by process, as the schools attempt to produce students who, as adults, will be able to look for solutions to problems they encounter. Similarly, value clarification studies cannot be graded on what values a student has or arrives at, but, rather, on his serious and sincere attempt to seek clarification for the values he holds.

Schools will continue to make reports to parents, but those reports will be anecdotal in nature. Face-to-face communication between teacher and parent will be readily available via the picture-telephones and will be used regularly to apprise parents of their children's progress. In part, the benefits of keeping Johnny's parents abreast of what and how he is doing (and of how they can help) will be reflected in greater parental understanding of and support for the schools. The greater number of counselors and other trained specialists made available through increased financial support will also participate in student evaluation through their work with students, with teachers, and with parents. Evaluation will be based less on what a student has done, more on what he can next do. Growth, in a total gestalt sense, will be more crucial than achievement.

There will be no failure in the usual sense that the schools have employed this term. Students will not be retained in a grade, in part because there will not be conventional age groupings. Rather, there will be, within limits, ability levels; those on a particular ability level will work on problems and value-related issues appropriate to that level. The relative difficulty of the problems and issues will be a derivative of the students' abilities, not a function of a previously established curriculum. Some students will proceed through problems faster than others, but no disapprobation, in the form of F grades or yearly retention, will obtain for the slower ones. They will be seen simply as taking longer. Perhaps they will ultimately leave school having covered far less than some of their age mates, but they will leave with the important conviction that what they covered they succeeded at. On the principle that success begets success, these people, who would be labeled failures in contemporary education, will face adult life and its challenges with positive self-images born of their success in school. So far as possible, schooling will be a positive experience for all.

Technology will also change the ways in which teachers teach and students learn. Sophisticated teaching machines with sophisticated instructional programs will handle much of the skills work the schools will still be doing. They will teach some students to read; they will help some with calculus assignments; and they will play chess or word games with others. Computers will be readily available for a variety of uses: immediate printouts on a student's past performances on specific kinds of standardized tests, records of the number of minutes of student talk compared with the minutes of teacher talk, combining of previously established materials into new arrangements to fit new instructional goals. Libraries of cassettes and videotapes will support the teachers' lessons and the students' quests for specific information. Schools will be built with movable walls to accommodate a variety of instructional settings. (A number of these items I am listing as "innovative" are already utilized in a few schools. They are not accessible, however, to the great majority of the nation's teachers and pupils.)

9. The notions I have so far suggested have dealt mainly with elementary and secondary school youth, with those students who are presently expected to be enrolled in school between the ages of six

and eighteen. (And they will continue to be expected to be enrolled during those years. The pleas of some of the critics of education for an end to compulsory schooling will be, in practice, ignored.) But it is also important to attend to the future of education for younger children, for college age youth, and for adults.

Education of the young child is just now coming into its own in terms of parental demand and governmental support for it. Day care centers and nursery schools will probably continue to expand and flourish, and not simply, as now, mostly in the private school sector. Instead, they will become an important part of the public school system. Compulsory schooling will begin, as now, around the age of five or six, but all districts will offer preschool educational facilities for as many of their constituents as wish to take advantage of them. Custodial day care will be available for infants, with actual educational programs geared to children from two to three years of age upward also accessible to any in the district who want it. In part, these early childhood centers will be staffed by older children on released time from their schools.

Colleges and universities, save for the few Benningtons and Antiochs, are notoriously conservative. Any predictions about their rates and kinds of changes must be tempered with recognition of their institutional reluctance to alter the status quo. Yet some kinds of alterations do seem in the offing. For one, many colleges and universities, even state supported ones, will, of necessity, have to become more specialized. The duplication of services cannot continue, especially in programs with relatively few students or with extraordinarily high costs of implementation (for example, nuclear science laboratories). State systems may be organized to avoid unnecessary duplication. In such a scheme advanced graduate work in, say, foreign languages would be available at only one of the cooperating schools, with advanced engineering or medical education available at another. Some universities will concentrate almost exclusively on graduate education; others almost exclusively on undergraduate education. The multiversity so common today will be on the wane.

Small private colleges will continue to have a difficult time making ends meet and will have to (1) close down, (2) become highly specialized and try to attract students on the basis of the excellence of their relatively few programs, (3) become part of the state system (as some previously private schools have done in Texas and New York), or (4) be given public funds. In a time of rapidly escalating costs and declining enrollments, it seems unlikely that much support can be expected for the fourth alternative. Public funds given to private schools would reduce funds available for existing state institutions, which are faced with the same spiraling expenditures and reduced student bodies. Probably alternatives two and three will come nearer the mark.

Provisions will be made in all colleges for students to shorten or lengthen the number of years required to earn a degree. Institutional restraints that now make acceleration all but impossible will have been removed for those students able intellectually and financially to earn a BA in two or three years. For those who wish to plug in and out of college, time statutes will be removed.

It seems highly probable that junior and community colleges will continue to expand, so that most states will offer the easily accessible additional education now available in only a few states (California, Florida, New York, Illinois). Some of the new structures will be built within or near the educational clusters referred to earlier. Junior college students in need of remedial help in skills areas will attend classes in the nearby secondary schools. Advanced secondary school youth will be able to spend part of their time on junior college campuses to take courses that are not available in their high schools or that, if available, are unnecessary and avoidable duplications. Junior colleges will continue to attempt to fulfill the three functions they are typically charged with now: (1) preparation for advanced work in a senior college, (2) occupational training for vocations that do not require BA degrees or better, and (3) enrichment courses for the total adult community.

This last function is presently the least important in most junior colleges. In the future it may well become the dominant purpose of the junior college. Already educators are speaking of the desirability of schooling as a lifelong process. Adults of the future, faced with greater amounts of leisure time as the four-day work week becomes a reality for many workers, will consider schooling among their options for leisure time activities. The number of adults who watch such programs as "Sunrise Semester" on television attests to the desire of many people to continue their education beyond their formal schooling. Junior colleges will accommodate these desires and will offer courses to meet any demands their constituencies have.

10. Problems not yet mentioned in this paper will continue to plague education. Some of them will be the age-old and still contemporary problems; some of them will be new, the result of the changes described above.

Probably still with us twenty-five years from now will be the problems associated with urban education, especially inner-city education. The existence of a problem, someone has said, does not imply the existence of a solution. Very possibly no good solutions exist for the many problems that comprise the urban education can of worms.

Despite the building of a few inner-city luxury apartments to attract affluent suburbanites back to the city, the proportion of poor Blacks living in the core areas of most cities continues to increase. Schools in such areas are not in compliance with civil rights education. Nor will they become so unless massive and, in some cases, lengthy cross-busing patterns are established. Because these patterns would be inter-district, encompassing impoverished urban areas and opulent suburbs, the problems that would be encountered are not handled by legislative enactments alone. It is conceivable, for example, that cross-busing be-tween downtown Detroit and Grosse Point would result in the establish-ment of numerous private schools catering only to affluent Whites (such schools are justifiably called "segregation academies" in the south) and the proportion of Black students in the public schools would remain almost as high as it is in the inner-city schools now. The one difference would be that the core city Blacks would be bused a sizable distance from their homes to attend still largely segregated schools. Money is not the only issue separating the cities and the ring of suburbs sur-rounding them. Attitudes about the efficacy of education differ. In White suburbia, school is seen as a concomitant of upward social mobility. Better schooling leads to better jobs. In the Black central city, the color of one's skin somewhat mitigates the benefits presumed to be derivable from education. Why work hard to succeed at school if you still cannot get a job because you are Black?

Those who have read on in this section expecting that sooner or later they would come across some solution are doomed to be disap-pointed. Urban education is one of those problems discussed at the beginning of this chapter. Different solutions seem feasible from dif-ferent perspectives. A shift in the kaleidoscope creates a new problem which demands a new solution. Yet it is virtually impossible for one man or one commission to have sufficient breadth of vision to encom-pass all the problems at once, to synthesize them, and to propose solu-tions. Perhaps the best we can hope for is a vast improvement in the *quality* of education offered in the inner cities of America. Such an improvement, however, is going to require expenditures of an unprece-dented order, perhaps even a quadrupling of presently allotted funds to enable inner city schools to be refurbished or rebuilt and to be staffed with the very best in personnel and equipment.

A related problem—although one not confined to the inner cit-ies—that the schools are facing and will continue to face is racial in-tegration. So long as the schools are the only societal institution charged with integrating the races, these schools will be in trouble. Presently churches, housing patterns, even employment criteria can openly or covertly maintain a separation of the races. Not until these agencies can be brought into line can we hope for any substantive accomplishment in the schools. What the schools are doing now, especially in the South, is both noble and beneficial, but its effects, although promising, are far short of what could be expected if there were a society-wide attack on segregation.

Numerous other problems exist now and will persist into the future: disagreements about educational purposes, about measures schools use for punishment, about the methods most likely to succeed in teaching, about optimum class size, about spending priorities within the schools and within the larger society as it decrees how and how much it will pay for education, about governance of the schools. These problems are far more easily written about than solved. Yet it is to the credit of educators, used here as a global term to include virtually everyone interested in education, that they are trying, first, to recognize and define the problems, and then to solve them.

11. One is always tempted to save the best until last, to come on strong at the finish. I do not. What I have to say here is more wish than expectation. It seems to me that the chief weakness in contemporary education may not lie within the institution itself, but within the expectations held for it by the larger society. That is, education has always been "for" something, has always been seen as a means to an end and never as a valid, pleasant end in itself. People do things, including going to school, to achieve purposes important to them; they will always do so. But we have so concentrated on education for something else—a better job, a house in the suburbs, a chicken in the pot— that we have virtually ignored the fact that for most citizens formal schooling occupies a major portion of their day for *about 20 percent of their lives.* That's a long time to spend preparing for something else.

My desire, then, is that professional educators realize that, even as they are preparing students for that inevitable next step, they are also demanding a lot of the students' time. Our attempts to make that time pleasurable, to make of school a joyous experience for all participants, to cause students to tingle with the excitement of learning—learning done for the here and now and only incidentally for the future—may indeed enable education to be better tomorrow than it is today or was yesterday.

Ivan
Illich

Ivan Illich

Born in Vienna, Dr. Illich earned a Ph.D. in history at the University of Salzburg after an earlier study of theology and philosophy at Gregorian University in Rome. From 1956 to 1960 he served as vice-rector of Catholic University of Puerto Rico, after which time he was a co-founder of the Center for Intercultural Documentation in Cuernavaca, Mexico. There he directs seminars on "Institutional Alternatives in a Technological Society." Among his far-reaching publications is the controversial best seller, Deschooling Society.

the breakdown of schools: a problem or a symptom?

Schools are in crisis and so are the people who attend them. The former is a crisis in a political institution; the latter is a crisis of political attitudes. This second crisis, the crisis of personal growth, can be dealt with only if understood as distinct from, though related to, the crisis of school.

Schools have lost their unquestioned claim to educational legitimacy. Most of their critics still demand a painful and radical reform of the school, but a quickly expanding minority will not stand for anything short of the prohibition of compulsory attendance and the disqualification of academic certificates. The controversy between partisans of renewal and partisans of disestablishment will soon come to a head.

The breakdown of schools, because it affects all members of the society, will become a fascinating and consuming preoccupation of the public forum. As attention focuses on the schools, however, we can be easily distracted from a much deeper concern: the manner in which learning would be viewed in a deschooled society. Would people continue to treat learning as a commodity—a commodity which could be more efficiently produced and consumed by greater numbers of people if new institutional arrangements were established? Or would we set up only those

139

institutional arrangements which protect the autonomy of the learner—
his private initiative to decide what he will learn and his inalienable
right to learn what he likes rather than what is useful to somebody
else? We must choose between more efficient education of people fit
for an increasingly efficient society—and a new society in which education ceases to be the task of some special agency.

All over the world schools are organized enterprises designed
to reproduce the established order, whether this order is called revolutionary, conservative, or evolutionary. Everywhere the loss of pedagogical credibility and the resistance to schools provides a fundamental
option: Should this crisis be dealt with as a problem which can and
must be solved by substituting new devices for school and readjusting
the existing power structure to fit these devices? Or should this crisis
force a society to face the structural contradictions inherent in the
politics and economics of any society which reproduces itself through
the industrial process?

The problem-solving approach to deschooling could serve as
a means to tighten the alliance between the military, the industrial
sector, and the therapeutic service industries. Deschooling, as a merely
administrative program, could be the accommodation which would
permit the present political structure to survive into the era of late
twentieth century technology.

On the other hand, the crisis of the schools could be understood
as a breakdown of the most important, respected, noncontroversial
sector of society, the branch which employs 60 of the 140 million full-
time institutionally active Americans as either pupils or teachers.

In the United States and Canada, huge investments in schooling
only serve to make institutional contradictions more evident. Experts
warn us: Charles Silberman's report to the Carnegie Commission, published as *Crisis In the Classroom*, has become a bestseller. It appeals
to a large public because of its well-documented indictment of the
system—in the light of which his attempts to save the schools by mani-
curing their most obvious faults palls to insignificance. The Wright
Commission in Ontario had to report to its government sponsors that
postsecondary education is inevitably and without remedy taxing the
poor disproportionately for an education which will always be enjoyed
mainly by the rich. Experience confirms these warnings: Students and
teachers drop out; free schools come and go. Political control of schools
replaces bond issues on the platforms of school board candidates and—
as happened in Berkeley—advocates of grass-roots control are elected
to the board.

On March 8, 1971 Chief Justice Warren E. Burger delivered
the unanimous opinion of the Court in the case of *Griggs et al v. Duke*

Power Co. Interpreting the intent of Congress in the equal opportunities
section of the 1964 Civil Rights Act, the Burger court ruled that any
school degree or any test given prospective employees must "measure
the man for the job" and not "the man in the abstract." The burden
for proving that educational requirements are a "reasonable measure
of job performance" rests with the employer. In this decision, the court
ruled only on the use of tests and diplomas as means of racial discrimination, but the logic of the chief justice's argument applies to any use
of educational pedigree as a prerequisite for employment. "The Great
Training Robbery," so effectively exposed by Ivar Berg, must now face
challenge from a congeries of pupils, employers, and taxpayers.

In poor countries schools rationalize economic lag. The majority of citizens are excluded from the scarce modern means of production and consumption but yearn to enter the economy by way of
the school door. The legitimization of hierarchical distribution of privilege and power has shifted from lineage, inheritance, the favor of king
or pope, and ruthlessness on the market or on the battlefield to a more
subtle form of capitalism: the hierarchical but liberal institution of
compulsory schooling which permits the well-schooled to impute to
the lagging consumer of knowledge the guilt for holding a certificate
of lower denomination. Yet this rationalization of inequality can never
square with the facts, and populist regimes find it increasingly difficult
to hide the conflict between rhetoric and reality.

Upon seizing power, the military junta in Peru immediately
decided to suspend further expenditures on free public schools. They
reasoned that because a third of the public budget could not provide
one full year of decent schooling for all, the available tax receipts would
be better spent on a type of educational resources which make schools
more nearly accessible to all citizens. The educational reform commission appointed by the junta could not fully carry out this decision
because of pressures from the school teachers of the APRA, the Communists, and the Cardinal Archbishop of Lima. Now there will be two
competing systems of public education in a country that cannot afford
one. The resulting contradictions will confirm the original judgment
of the junta.

For ten years Castro's Cuba has devoted great energies to
rapid-growth, popular education, relying on available manpower, without the usual respect for professional credentials. The initial spectacular successes of this campaign, especially in diminishing illiteracy, have
been cited as evidence for the claim that the slow growth rate of other
Latin American school systems is due to corruption, militarism, and
a capitalist market economy. Yet, now the hidden curriculum of hierarchical schooling is catching up to Fidel and his attempt to school-

produce the New Man. Even when students spend half the year in the cane fields and fully subscribe to Fidelismo, the school trains each year a crop of knowledge consumers ready to move on to new levels of consumption. Also, Castro faces evidence that the school system will never turn out enough certified technical manpower. Those licensed graduates who do get the new jobs destroy, by their conservatism, the results obtained by noncertified cadres who muddled into their positions through on-the-job training. Teachers just cannot be blamed for the failures of a revolutionary government which insists on the institutional capitalization of manpower through a hidden curriculum guaranteed to produce a universal bourgeoisie.

This crisis is epochal. We are witnessing the end of the age of schooling. School has lost the power, which reigned supreme during the first half of this century, to blind its participants to the divergence between the egalitarian myth which its rhetoric serves and the rationalization of a stratified society which its certificates produce. The current collapse of schools is a sign of disaffection with the industrial mode of production. The dropout manifests consumer resistance, which rises faster in the service industry than in the market for manufactured goods. The loss of legitimacy of the schooling process as a means of determining competence, as a measure of social value, and as an agent of equality threatens all political systems which rely on schools as the means of reproducing themselves.

School is the initiation ritual to a society which is oriented toward the progressive consumption of increasingly less tangible and more expensive services; a society which relies on worldwide standards; large-scale and long-term planning; constant obsolescence through the built-in ethos of never-ending improvements: the constant translation of new needs into specific demands for the consumption of new satisfactions. This society is proving itself unworkable.

Because the crisis in schooling is symptomatic of a deeper crisis of modern industrial society, it is important that the critics of schooling avoid superficial solutions. Inadequate analysis of the nature of schooling only postpones the facing of deeper issues. Worse still, superficial reforms can ease present tensions, only to promote a smooth transition from antiquated industrial forms to a postindustrial society which would lack even the saving graces of the present system.

Most school criticism is pedagogical, political, or technological. The criticism of the educator is leveled at what is taught and how it is taught. The curriculum is outdated, so we have courses on African culture, on North American imperialism, on women's liberation, on food and nutrition. Passive learning is old-fashioned, so we have increased student participation, both in the classroom and in the planning of curriculum. School buildings are ugly, so we have new learning environments. There is concern for the development of human sensitivity, so group therapy methods are imported into the classroom.

Another important set of critics is involved with the politics of urban school administration. They feel that the poor could run their schools better than a centralized bureaucracy which is oblivious to the problems of the dispossessed. Black parents are enlisted to replace White teachers in motivating their children to make time and find the will to learn.

Still other critics emphasize that schools make inefficient use of modern technology. They would either electrify the classroom or replace schools with computerized learning centers. If these critics follow McLuhan, they would replace blackboards and textbooks with multimedia happenings. If they follow Skinner, they would compete with the classical teacher and sell economy packages of measurable behavioral modifications to cost-conscious school boards.

The pedagogical, the political, and the technological critics of the school system do not call the institution itself into question. Nor do they recognize the most important effects of schooling. I believe that all these critics miss the point, because they fail to attend to what I have elsewhere called the ritual aspects of schooling—what I here propose to call the hidden curriculum, the structure underlying what has been called the certification effect. Others have used this phrase to refer to the environmental curriculum of the ghetto street or the suburban lawn, which the teacher's curriculum either reinforces or vainly attempts to replace. I am using the term hidden curriculum to refer to the structure of schooling as opposed to what happens in school, in the same way that linguists distinguish between the structure of a language and the use which the speaker makes of it.

THE HIDDEN CURRICULUM

The traditional hidden curriculum of school demands that people of a particular age assemble in groups of about thirty under the authority of a professional teacher for from five hundred to a thousand hours a year. It does not matter if the teacher is authoritarian so long as it is the teacher's authority that counts; it does not matter if all meetings occur in the same place so long as they are somehow understood as attendance. The hidden curriculum of school requires—whether by law or by fact—that a citizen accumulate a minimum quantum of school years in order to obtain his civil rights.

The hidden curriculum of school has been legislated in all the nations from Afghanistan to Zambia. It is common to the United States and the Soviet Union, to rich nations and poor, to electoral and dictatorial regimes. Whatever ideologies and techniques are explicitly transmitted in their school systems, all these nations assume that political and economic development depend on further investment in schooling.

The hidden curriculum teaches all children that economically valuable knowledge is the result of professional teaching and that social entitlements depend on the rank achieved in a bureaucratic process. The hidden curriculum transforms the explicit curriculum into a commodity and makes its acquisition the securest form of wealth. Knowledge certificates—unlike property rights, corporate stock, or family inheritance—are free from challenge. They withstand sudden changes of fortune. They convert into guaranteed privilege. That high accumulation of knowledge should convert to high personal consumption might be challenged in North Vietnam or Cuba, but school is universally accepted as the avenue to greater power, to increased legitimacy as a producer, and to further learning resources.

For all its vices school cannot be simply and rashly eliminated: in the present situation it performs some important negative functions. The hidden curriculum, unconsciously accepted by the liberal pedagogues, frustrates conscious liberal aims because it is inherently inconsistent with them. But it also prevents the takeover of education by the programmed instruction of behavioral technologists. While the hidden curriculum makes social role depend on the process of acquiring knowledge, thus legitimizing stratification, it also ties the learning process to full-time attendance, thus illegitimizing the educational entrepreneur. If the school continues to lose its educational and political legitimacy while knowledge is still conceived as a commodity, we will certainly face the emergence of a therapeutic Big Brother.

The translation of the need for learning into the demand for schooling and the conversion of the quality of growing up into the price tag of a professional treatment changes *knowledge* from a term which designates intimacy, intercourse, and life experience into one which designates professionally packaged products, marketable entitlements, and abstract values. Schools have fostered this translation; they might not be its most effective agents. The new media people might be able to distribute knowledge packages more rationally, more efficiently, and more intimately; many of them would like nothing better than to eliminate school administrators who are out of touch with the latest technology.

Personal knowledge is unpredictable and surprising with respect to both occurrence and outcome, whereas official knowledge must be anticipated and directed to measurable goals. Personal knowledge is always incomplete, because there are always further questions to be asked. Official knowledge is always unfinished, because there are always newer packages to consume. The progress of personal knowledge is governed by intrinsic rules of inquiry. The acquisition of official knowledge is measured by compliance with extrinsic rules of attendance. Personal knowledge is confident even though incomplete because it obeys its own restlessness. Official knowledge rests uneasy because its current value depends on institutional acceptance. Official knowledge only can solve puzzles within the present framework—only personal knowledge can lead to investigation which aims at change.

Schools are by no means the only institutions which pretend to translate knowledge, understanding, and wisdom into behavioral traits, the measurement of which is the key to prestige and power. Nor are schools the first institutions used to convert knowledge to power. The Chinese mandarin system, for example, was for centuries a stable and effective educational system in the service of a class whose privilege depended on the acquisition of official, scholastic knowledge. About 2200 B.C., the emperor of China is said to have examined his officials every third year. After three examinations, he either promoted them or dismissed them forever from the service. A thousand years later, in 1115, the first Chan emperor established formal general tests for office: music, archery, horsemanship, writing, and arithmetic. One in every hundred who presented himself for competition with his peers—and not for competition against some abstract standard—was promoted through the three degrees of "budding geniuses," "promoted scholars," and those who were "Ready for Office." The selection ratios of the exams to three successive levels were so small that the tests themselves would not have had to be very valid in order to be useful. Promotion to a scholarly rank did not provide entitlement to any of the coveted jobs: it provided a ticket for a public lottery at which offices were distributed by lot among the mandarins. No schools, much less universities, developed in China until she had to begin waging war with European powers. Voltaire and many of his contemporaries praised the Chinese system of promotion through learning acquired. The first civil service examinations in Europe and the United States used the Chinese system, directly or indirectly, as a model. Civil service testing was introduced by the revolution in 1791 in France, only to be abolished by Napoleon. The English civil service system began as a selection for service in India by men familiar with the Chinese system. Congressman Thomas Jenckes, one of the fathers of the U.S. Civil Service, sold his program to Congress in 1868 by praising the Chinese system.

For a while, public schools parlayed the consumption of knowledge into the exercise of privilege and power in a society where this function coincided with the legitimate aspirations of those members of the lower middle classes for whom schools provided access to the classical professions. Now that the discriminatory effects of the use of schooling for social screening have become more apparent, a new mandarin system becomes an appealing alternative to many people. Christopher Jencks, misread by uncritical followers, could easily turn tuition vouchers into identification tags of the new mandarins. It becomes equally tempting to use modern techniques for seducing individuals to the self-motivated acquisition of packaged learning. This can be done without the protection of schools in a society already trained to conceive of valuable learning as a commodity, rather than as an act of total participation by an individual in his culture.

AN EXPANSION OF THE CONCEPT OF ALIENATION

Since the nineteenth century, we have become accustomed to the claim that man in a capitalist economy is alienated from his labor: that he cannot enjoy it, and that he is robbed of its fruits by those who own the tools of production. Most countries which appeal to Marxist ideology have had only limited success in changing this exploitation, and then usually by shifting its benefits from the owners to the New Class and from the living generation to the members of the future nation state.

Socialist failures can be explained away by ascribing them to bad readings of Marx and Engels or to inadequacies of the original theory. Then again, blame can be transferred to war, blockade, or invasion. Or failure can be interpreted in terms of inherited sociological conditions, such as a particular type of rural–urban balance. Whatever the argument, however, Marxist orthodoxies and revisionist heresies and value-free rebuttals now put up smoke screens against independent analysis.

The concept of alienation cannot help us understand the present crisis unless it is applied not only to the purposeful and productive use of human endeavor but also to the use made of men as the recipients of professional treatments. Language reflects this alienation when it translates these verbs into substantives, which make it possible to say that "I have" leisure, learning, transportation, rather than that "I do" enjoy, learn, move, or communicate. An expanded understanding of alienation would enable us to see that in a service-centered economy man is estranged from what he can *do* as well as from what he can *make*, that he has delivered his mind and heart over to therapeutic treatment even more completely than he has sold away the fruits of his labor.

Schools have alienated man from his learning. He does not enjoy going to school; if he is poor he does not get the reputed benefits; if he does all that is asked of him, he finds his security constantly threatened by more recent graduates; if he is sensitive, he feels deep conflicts between what is and what is supposed to be. He does not trust his own judgment, and even if he resents the judgment of the educator, he is condemned to accept it and to believe that he cannot change reality.

The mutation of the concept of revolution cannot occur, however, without a rejection of the hidden curriculum of schooling and the correlative attitude toward knowledge, for it is this curriculum and this attitude which turn out disciplined consumers of bureaucratic instructions ready to consume other kinds of services and treatments which they are told are good for them. The converging crisis of ritual schooling and of acquisitive knowledge raises the deeper issue of the tolerability of life in an alienated society. If we formulate principles for alternative institutional arrangements and an alternative emphasis in the conception of learning, we will also be suggesting principles for a radically alternative political and economic organization.

Just as the structure of one's native language can be grasped only after you have begun to feel at ease in another tongue, so the fact that the hidden curriculum of schooling has moved out of the blind spot of social analysis indicates that alternative forms of social initiation are beginning to emerge and are permitting some of us to see things from a new perspective. Today, it is relatively easy to get wide agreement on the fact that gratuitous, compulsory schooling is contrary to the political self-interest of an enlightened majority. School has become pedagogically indefensible as an instrument of universal education. It no longer fits the needs of the seductive salesmen of programmed learning. Proponents of recorded, filmed, and computerized instruction used to court the schoolmen as business prospects; now they are itching to do the job on their own.

As more and more of the sectors of society become dissatisfied with school and conscious of its hidden curriculum, increasingly large concessions are made to translate their demands into needs which can be served by the system—and which thus can disarm their dissent. I here describe some of these attempts under the general label of *cooptation*.

As the hidden curriculum moves out of the darkness and into the twilight of our awareness, phrases such as the "deschooling of society" and the "disestablishment of schools" become instant slogans. I do not think these phrases were used before last year. This year [1971] they have become, in some circles, the badge and criterion of the new orthodoxy. Recently I talked by amplified telephone to students in a seminar on deschooling at the Ohio State University College of Education. Everett Reimer's book on deschooling became a popular college text even before it was commercially published. Unless the radical critics of school are not only ready to embrace the deschooling slogan but also prepared to reject the current view that learning and growing up can be adequately explained as a process of programming, and the current vision of social justice based on it—more obligatory consumption for everybody—we may face the charge of having provoked the last of the missed revolutions.

The current crisis has made it easy to attack schools. Schools, after all, are authoritarian and rigid. They do produce both conformity and conflict. They do discriminate against the poor and disengage the privileged. These are not new facts, but it used to be a mark of some boldness to point them out. Now it takes a good deal of courage to defend schools. It has become fashionable to poke fun at alma mater, to take a potshot at the former sacred cow.

Once the vulnerability of schools has been exposed, it also becomes easy to suggest remedies for the most outrageous abuses. The authoritarian rule of the classroom is not intrinsic to the notion of an extended confinement of children in schools. Free schools are practical alternatives; they can often be run more cheaply than ordinary schools. Accountability already belongs to educational rhetoric, and so community control and performance contracting have become attractive and respectable political goals. Everyone wants education to be relevant to real life, so critics talk freely about pushing back the classroom walls to the borders of our culture. Not only are alternatives more widely advocated, they are often at least partially implemented. Experimental schools are financed by school boards; the hiring of certified teachers is decentralized; high school credit is given for apprenticeship and college credit for travel; computer games are given a trial run.

Most of the changes have some good effects. The experimental schools have fewer truants; parents have a greater feeling of participation in the decentralized districts; children who have been introduced to real jobs do become more competent. Yet all these alternatives operate within predictable limits, because they leave the hidden structure of schools intact. Free schools which lead to further free schools in an unbroken chain of attendance produce the mirage of freedom. Attendance as the result of seduction inculcates the need for specialized treatment more persuasively than reluctant attendance enforced by truant officers. Free school graduates are easily rendered impotent for life in a society which bears little resemblance to the protected gardens in which they have been cultivated. Community control of the lower levels of a system turns local school board members into pimps for the professional hookers who control the upper levels. Learning by doing is not worth much if doing has to be defined as socially valuable learning by professional educators or by law. The global village will be a global schoolhouse if teachers hold all the plugs. It would be distinguishable in name only from a global madhouse run by social therapists or a global prison run by corporation wardens.

In a general way I have pointed out the dangers of a rash, uncritical disestablishment of school. More concretely, these dangers are exemplified by various kinds of cooption which change the hidden curriculum without changing the basic concept of learning and of knowledge and their relationship to the freedom of the individual in society. The rash and uncritical disestablishment of school could lead to a free-for-all in the production and consumption of more vulgar learning, acquired for immediate utility or eventual prestige. The discrediting of school-produced complex curricular packages would be an empty victory if there were no simultaneous disavowal of the very idea that knowledge is more valuable because it comes in certified packages and is acquired from some mythological knowledge-stock controlled by professional guardians. I believe that only actual participation constitutes socially valuable learning, a participation by the learner in every stage of the learning process, including not only a free choice of what is to be learned and how it is to be learned, but also a free determination by each learner of his own reason for living and learning—the part that his knowledge is to play in his life.

Social control in an apparently deschooled society could be more subtle and more numbing than in the present society, where many people at least experience a feeling of release on the last day of school. More intimate forms of manipulation are already common, as the amount learned through the media exceeds the amount learned through personal contact in and out of school. Teaching from programmed information always hides reality behind a screen.

Let me illustrate the paralyzing effects of programmed information by a perhaps shocking example. The tolerance of the American people to United States atrocities in Vietnam is much higher than the tolerance of the German people to German atrocities on the front, in occupied territories, and in extermination camps during World War

II. It was a political crime for Germans to discuss the atrocities committed by Germans. The presentation of United States atrocities on network television is considered an educational service. Certainly the population of the United States is much better informed about the crimes committed by its troops in a colonial war than were the Germans about the crimes committed by its SS within the territory of the Reich. To get information on atrocities in Germany, you had to take a great risk; in the United States, the same information is channeled into your living room. This does not mean, however, that the Germans were any less aware that their government was engaged in cruel and massive crime than are contemporary Americans. In fact, it can be argued that the Germans were *more* aware, precisely because they were not psychically overwhelmed with packaged information about killing and torture, because they were not drugged into accepting that everything is possible, because they were not vaccinated against reality by having it fed to them as decomposed bits on a screen.

The consumer of precooked knowledge learns to react to knowledge he has acquired rather than to the reality from which a team of experts have abstracted it. If access to reality is always controlled by a therapist and if the learner accepts this control as natural, his entire world view becomes hygienic and neutral: he becomes politically impotent. He becomes impotent to know in the sense of the Hebrew word "jdh," which means intercourse penetrating the nakedness of being and reality. He becomes politically impotent because reality for which he can accept responsibility is hidden for him under the scales of assorted information he has accumulated.

The uncritical disestablishment of school could also lead to new performance criteria for preferential employment and promotion and most importantly for privileged access to tools. Our present scale of general ability, competence, and trustworthiness for role assignment is calibrated by tolerance to high doses of schooling. It is established by teachers and is accepted by many as rational and benevolent. New devices could be developed, and new rationales found, both more insidious than school grading and equally effective to justify social stratification and the accumulation of privilege and power.

Participation in military, bureaucratic, or political activities or status in a party could provide a pedigree just as transferable to other institutions as the pedigree of grandparents in an aristocratic society, standing within the Church in medieval society, or age at graduation in a schooled society. General tests of attitudes, intelligence, or mechanical ability could be standardized according to other criteria than those of the schoolmaster. They could reflect the ideal levels of professional treatment espoused by psychiatrist, ideologue, or bureaucrat. Academic criteria are already suspect. The Center for Urban Studies of Columbia University has shown that there is less correlation between specialized education and job performance in specialized fields than there is between specialized education and the resulting income, prestige, and administrative power. Nonacademic criteria are already proposed. From the urban ghettos in the United States to the villages of China, revolutionary groups try to prove that ideology and militancy are types of learning which convert more suitably into political and economic power than scholastic curricula. Unless we guarantee that job-relevance is the only acceptable criterion for employment, promotion, or access to tools, thus ruling out not only schools but all other ritual screening, then deschooling means driving out the devil with Beelzebub.

The search for a radical alternative to the school system itself will be of little avail unless it finds expression in precise political demands: the demand for the disestablishment of school in the broadest sense and the correlative guarantee of freedom for education. This will require legal protections, a political program, and principles for the construction of institutional arrangements that are the inverse of school. Schools cannot be disestablished without the total prohibition of legislated attendance, the proscription of any discrimination on the basis of prior attendance, and the transfer of control over tax funds from benevolent institutions to the individual person. Even these actions, however, do not guarantee freedom of education unless they are accompanied by the positive recognition of each person's independence in the face of school and of any other device designed to compel specific behavioral change or to measure man in the abstract rather than to measure man for a concrete job.

TOUCHSTONE FOR REVOLUTION

Deschooling makes strange bedfellows. The ambiguity inherent in the breakdown of schooling is manifested by the unholy alliance of groups which can identify their vested interests with the disestablishment of school: students, teachers, employers, opportunistic politicians, taxpayers, and Supreme Court justices. But this alliance becomes unholy, this bedfellowship more than strange, if it is based only on the recognition that schools are inefficient tools for the production and consumption of education and that some other form of mutual exploitation would be more satisfactory.

The insurmountable problems of inefficiency, consumer resistance, and political scandal which the school system can no longer hide could be solved by more rational, attractive, and specific learning packages, the diversification of educational procedures and a cloud-like dispersal of production centers. A new educational lobby could even now be organized on behalf of more effective training for jobs and social roles, more job-related measurements, and more benevolently cooperative acculturation. The hidden curriculum of schooling could be transmuted into the unseen mask of a therapeutic culture.

We can disestablish schools, or we can deschool culture. We can resolve provisionally some of the administrative problems of the knowledge industry, or we can spell out the goals of political revolution in terms of educational postulates. The acid test of our response to the present crisis is our pinpointing of the responsibility for teaching and learning.

Schools have made teachers into administrators of programs of manpower capitalization through directed, planned, behavioral changes. In a schooled society, the ministrations of professional teachers become a first necessity which hooks pupils into unending consumption and dependence. Schools have made learning a specialized activity. Deschooling will only be a displacement of responsibility to other kinds of administration so long as teaching and learning remain sacred activities separate and estranged from fulfilling life. If schools were disestablished for the purpose of more efficient delivery of knowledge to more people, the alienation of men through client relationships with the new knowledge industry would only become global. Deschooling must be the secularization of teaching and learning. It must involve a return of control over what is learned and how it is learned to persons, and not a transfer of control to another, a more amorphous set of institutions and their perhaps less obvious representatives. The learner must be guaranteed his freedom without guaranteeing to society what learning he will acquire and hold as his own. Each man must be guaranteed privacy in learning, with the hope that he will assume the obligation of helping others to grow into uniqueness. Whoever takes the risk of teaching others must assume responsibility for the results, as must the student who exposes himself to the influence of a teacher; neither should shift guilt to sheltering institutions or laws. A deschooled society must reassert the joy of conscious living over the capitalization of manpower.

The touchstone of mutation in education is the honest recognition that most people learn most of the time when they do what they enjoy doing. Most people are capable of personal, intimate intercourse with others unless they are stupefied by inhuman work or snowed under by treatment with programs. Once this is admitted, we will understand that to increase learning opportunities means to facilitate communication between the learner and his world, between the learner and his fellows, between the learner and those who can point him toward traditions and methods tested by their experience. Once we take hold of the simple insight that personal knowledge is always unpredictable but never unconnected, we will undertake the real task of setting up institutional arrangements which guarantee the freedom necessary for independent inquiry. We will multiply the roads, bridges, and windows to learning opportunities and make sure that they are opened at the learner's bidding.

THREE RADICAL DEMANDS

Any dialogue about knowledge is really a dialogue about the individual in society. An analysis of the present crisis of school leads us, then, to talk about the social structure necessary to facilitate learning, to encourage independence and interrelationship, and to overcome alienation. This kind of discourse is outside the usual range of educational concern. It leads, in fact, to the enunciation of specific political goals. These goals can be most sharply defined by distinguishing three general types of intercourse in which a person must engage if he would grow up.

Get at the facts, get access to the tools, and bear the responsibility for the limits within which either can be used. If a person is to grow up he needs, first, access to things, places, processes, events, and records. To guarantee such access is primarily a matter of unlocking the privileged storerooms to which they are presently consigned.

The poor child and the rich child are different partly because what is a secret for one is patent to the other. By turning knowledge into a commodity, we have learned to deal with it as with private property. The principle of private property is now used as the major rationale for declaring some facts off-limits to people without the proper pedigree. The first goal of a political program aimed at rendering the world educational is the abolition of the right to reserve access necessary for the purpose of teaching or learning. The right of private preserve is now claimed by individuals, but it is most effectively exercised and protected by corporations, bureaucracies, and nation states. In fact, the abolition of this right is not consistent with the continuation of either the political or the professional structure of any modern nation. The end of property protection would mean the abolition of most professional secrets and the consequent removal of the rationale for professional exploitation. This means more than merely improving the distribution of teaching materials or providing financial entitlements for the purchase of educational objects. The abolition of secrets clearly transcends conventional proposals for educational reform, yet it is precisely from an educational point of view that the necessity of stating this broad—and perhaps unattainable—political goal is most clearly seen.

The learner also needs access to persons who can teach him the tricks of their trades or the rudiments of their skills. For the interested learner, it does not take much time to learn how to perform most skills or to play most roles. The best teacher of a skill is usually someone who is engaged in its useful exercise. We tend to forget these things in a society where professional teachers monopolize initiation into all fields and disqualify unauthorized teaching in the community. An important political goal, then, is to provide incentives for the sharing of acquired skills.

The demand that skills be shared implies, of course, a much more radical vision of a desirable future. Access to skills is not only restricted by the monopoly of schools and unions over licensing. There is also the fact that the exercise of skills is tied to the use of scarce tools. Scientific knowledge is overwhelmingly incorporated into tools that are highly specialized and that must be used within complex structures set up for the efficient production of goods and services for which demand becomes general while supply remains scarce. Only a privileged few get the results of sophisticated medical research, and only a privileged few get to be doctors. A small minority will travel on supersonic airplanes and only a few pilots will know how to fly them.

The simplest way to state the alternatives to this trend toward specialization of needs and their satisfaction is in educational terms. It is a question of the desirable use of scientific knowledge. To facilitate more equal access to the benefits of science and to decrease alienation and unemployment, we must favor the incorporation of scientific knowledge into tools or components within the reach of a great majority of people. These tools would allow most people to develop their skills. Any peasant girl could learn how to diagnose and treat almost all the infections which occur in rural Mexico, if she were introduced to the use of techniques which are now available but which were undreamt of by doctors a couple of generations ago. In poor countries most people still build their own houses, often using mud or the covering of oil barrels. Now, we want to give them low-cost, prepackaged housing—thus modernizing them into regarding housing as a commodity rather than an activity. We would better provide them with cement mixers. Certainly the tools used in learning—and in most scientific research—have become so cheap that they could be made available to anyone: books, audio and video tapes, and the simple scientific in-

struments used to learn those basic skills which form the basis for
the supposedly advanced skill required of the very few who might
have to operate an electron microscope.

Insight into the conditions necessary for wider acquisition and
use of skills permits us to define a fundamental characteristic of postindustrial socialism. It is of no use—indeed it is fraudulent—to promote
public ownership of the tools of production in an industrial, bureaucratic society. Factories, highways, and heavy duty trucks can be symbolically *owned* by all the people, as the Gross National Product and
the gross national education are pursued in their name. But the specialized means of producing scarce goods and services cannot be *used*
by the majority of people. Only tools which are cheap and simple
enough to be accessible and usable by all people, tools which permit
temporary association of those who want to use them for a specific
occasion, tools which allow specific goals to emerge during their use—
only such tools foster the recuperation of work and leisure now alienated through an industrial mode of production.

The development and wide dispersal of simple and durable
tools would discredit the special privileges now given to technocrats.
The growth of science would not be jeopardized, but the progress of
complex scientific technology at the service of technocratic privilege
would become scandalous. This style of progress is now justified in
the name of developing a necessary infrastructure. A new style of research would reveal this infrastructure as the foundation of privilege.

To recognize, from an educational point of view, the priority
of guaranteeing access to tools and components whose simplicity and
durability permits their use in a wide variety of creative enterprises
is to simultaneously indicate the solution to the problem of unemployment. In an industrial society, unemployment is experienced as the
sad inactivity of a man for whom there is nothing to make, while he
has unlearned what to do. Because there is little really useful work,
the problem is usually "solved" by creating more jobs in service industries like the military, public administration, education, or social work.
Educational considerations oblige us to recommend the substitution,
of the present mode of industrial production which depends on a
growing market for increasingly complex and obsolescent goods, by
a mode of postindustrial production which depends on the demand
for tools or components which are labor-intensive and repair-intensive,
and whose complexity is strictly limited.

Science will be kept artificially arcane as long as its results
are incorporated into technology at the service of professionals. If it
were used to render possible a style of life in which each man can
enjoy housing himself, healing himself, educating, moving, and enter-

taining himself, then scientists would try much harder to retranslate the discoveries made in a secret language into the normal language of everyday life.

The level of education in any society can be gauged by the degree of effective access each of the members has to the facts and tools which—within this society—affect his life. We have seen that such access requires a radical denial of the right to secrecy of facts and complexity of tools on which contemporary technocracies found their privilege, which they, in turn, render immune by interpreting its use as a service to the majority. A satisfactory level of education in a techno-logical society imposes important constraints on the use to which scien-tific knowledge is put. In fact, a technological society which provides conditions for men to recuperate personally (and not institutionally) the sense of potency to learn and to produce, which gives meaning to life depends on restrictions which must be imposed on the tech-nocrat who now controls both services and manufacture. Only an en-lightened and powerful majority can impose such constraints.

If access to facts and use of tools constitute the two most obvious freedoms needed to provide educational opportunity, the abili-ty to convoke peers to a meeting constitutes the one freedom through which the learning by an individual is translated into political pro-cess—and political process in turn becomes conscious personal growth. Data and skills which an individual might have acquired are shaped into exploratory, creative, open-ended, and personal meaning only when they are used in dialectic encounter. And this requires the guaran-teed freedom for every individual to state, each day, the class of issue which he wants to discuss, the class of creative use of a skill in which he seeks a match—to make this bid known—and, within reason, to find the circumstances to meet with peers who join his class. The right of free speech, free press, and free assembly traditionally meant this freedom. Modern electronics, photo-offset, and computer techniques in principle have provided the hardware which can provide this free-dom with a range undreamed of in the century of enlightenment. Un-fortunately, the scientific know-how has been used mainly to increase the power and decrease the number of funnels through which the bureaucrats of education, politics, and information channel their quick-frozen TV dinners. But the same technology could be used to make peer-matching, meeting, and printing as available as the private conversation over the telephone is now.

On the other hand, it should be clear that only through the definition of what constitutes a desirable society—arrived at in the meet-ing of those who are both dispossessed and also disabused of the dream that constantly increasing quanta of consumption can provide them with the joy they seek out of life—can the inversion of institutional arrangement here drafted be put into effect, and with it, a technological society which values occupation, intensive work, and leisure over alienation through goods and services.

Max
Rafferty

Max Rafferty

Graduated from UCLA in 1938, Dr. Rafferty began teaching in 1940 and has been an active educator since that time. He has served as teacher, coach, principal, district superintendent, and, from 1963–1971, gained national renown as the superintendent of public instruction for the state of California. It was during this latter period that his book, Suffer Little Children, *became one of the all-time best sellers in education. Currently he is dean of the School of Education at Troy State College in Alabama and author of a nationally syndicated column that focuses primarily on educational issues of today and tomorrow.*

american education: 1975-2000

Aside from the perhaps legendary figures of Mother
Shipton and old Nostradamus, the most uncannily
accurate prophet since Biblical days just has to be the
late H. G. Wells. Long before any of them were even a
gleam in their creators' eyes, Wells was accurately
predicting the invention of the airplane, the
development of the tank, the explosion of the first
atomic bomb, the use of poison gas, and the discovery
of the laser.

On a somewhat more modest scale,
meteorologists can forecast future weather for as much
as a week ahead, although most of them carry
umbrellas to picnics just like the rest of us. And of
course there are always the economists, who for three
years running have been predicting a runaway boom on
the American industrial front which presumably will get
here sooner or later.

So you see it's possible to foretell the future, at
least in some areas and within relatively narrow frames
of reference. Education, however, has always been
another breed of cats altogether, defying all predictions
of meaningful change for the simple reason that it just
never changed very much. Describing the look of things
up ahead on the school front for the next thirty years
has always been like charting the course of an Alpine

glacier during the same period of time: infinitely slow, completely pre-dictable, and very, very dull.

There are some indications that this immemorial state of affairs may now be changing. But before I try to anticipate what lies ahead for education, it will be necessary to do two things: (1) define education, and (2) dispose of some false premises which have grown up around it in recent years like so many tares and thistles.

If you will grant me my own definition, namely that education is learning to use the intellectual tools which the human race, over the centuries, has found to be indispensable in the pursuit of truth, then it follows that the following assumptions about education—though widely held for more than a generation now—are as preposterous as a Russian peace plan:

PHONY ASSUMPTION # 1: That the schools exist to adjust pupils to their environment, or to make pupils accepted easily, comfortably, and happily by their peer group, or to enable them to practice together-ness, or to promote on-going, forward-looking relevance. Schools exist to do none of these things; they exist to make pupils learned. Period.

PHONY ASSUMPTION #2: That in education there are no posi-tive and eternal verities, no absolutes—everything is relative. If this should by some remote and unlikely chance turn out to be true, then we teachers would be automatically unemployed, just as a minister of the gospel would be out of work if God indeed should turn out to be dead.

PHONY ASSUMPTION #3: That the school curriculum should be based on the immediate interests and the felt needs of the pupils. A child's "felt needs" differ both widely and wildly from child to child and from year to year, indeed almost from day to day. A curriculum built upon such shifting sands would be a fragile edifice indeed.

These first three phonies are, I regret to say, the philosophical underpinnings of modern American education, and they go a long way toward explaining why the schools of the future are going to have to give John Dewey's pragmatism, utilitarianism, or what-have-you the old heave-ho if they are not to be engulfed in a deepening pool of bland, unctuous, cloying, sentimental slop.

Try a few more of the education establishment's phonies on for size:

PHONY ASSUMPTION #4: That a big school is better than a small one. Not necessarily. Not any more than a big man is necessarily better than a small man. Or a big mistake better than a little mistake, for that matter. It all depends on the school.

PHONY ASSUMPTION #5: That a teacher with ten years' experience is better than a teacher with only one and therefore should be paid more. Nope. One of my profession's oldest chestnuts is that a teacher may simply have had one year's experience over again ten times.

PHONY ASSUMPTION #6: That an athlete is usually a dummy. This is an insufferable manifestation of smug superiority emanating from some of our self-styled intellectuals. In all the high schools where I ever worked, the athletes had a higher collective grade point average than did the nonathletes.

PHONY ASSUMPTION #7: That memorizing things in school is hopelessly stultifying. The multiplication tables may be a little square, I suppose, but children must learn to memorize them anyway. And they must memorize key dates, names, and events in history, the letters of the alphabet, the continents of old earth, and the planets of the solar system, especially these days. And ability to call trippingly to the tongue certain passages of great poetry and prose can certainly brighten up an otherwise humdrum and even dreary mortal safari through this vale of tears. Memorization in school is a must. Today we don't ask pupils to do enough of it.

PHONY ASSUMPTION #8: That school dress and personal appearance codes are outrageous, tyrannical, and even unconstitutional. The theory here is that school is a place which society subsidizes expensively so that every kid can turn on, blow his mind, and do his own thing. Sorry. It isn't. And society doesn't. School is a place where teachers try to establish a climate conducive to organized, systematic, and disciplined learning. Anything which interferes with a scholarly atmosphere is inimical to good education, and should be tossed out on its exhibitionistic ear. Hence school dress codes. And personal appearance standards. And disciplinary rules. And a lot of other things.

PHONY ASSUMPTION #9: That school policy should be set by the students and/or faculty. This concept is patently and outrageously undemocratic. Any public, tax-supported institution must be run by those who pay the taxes, not by those who benefit from them. This means that public schools and colleges have to have their policies set by representatives responsible to all the people, not by stray groups of students and instructors responsible to nobody on God's earth except themselves alone. The latter should be heard, true enough, if only because they are the ones most directly and immediately affected by the policies adopted. But welcoming their participation in the policy-making process doesn't mean abandoning the whole shebang to them, lock, stock, and barrel. In any democratic society, you simply cannot turn the institutions over to the inmates.

PHONY ASSUMPTION #10: That report cards are meaningless status symbols, catering to an unhealthy parental craving to experience vicarious success at the expense of their children. Tommyrot. Report cards are precisely what their name implies; they inform parents how their children are doing in school. Like any other school tool—including books, maps, or tests—report cards are subject to abuse at the hands of a stupid teacher or to misinterpretation by an hysterical parent. But the fact that a valuable tool is capable of being misused is no reason to revile the tool itself, nor to relegate it to the junk pile.

PHONY ASSUMPTION #11: That modern technology and the welfare state are producing better education than the schools did a generation ago. Enters now from the wings one Prof. Sir Cyril Burt, who in 1970 completed a study showing that English school children in 1914 scored higher in every category of scholastic achievement than did their counterparts of 1965. And on the same tests, too.

Here's the way the generation gap shaped up:

	1914	1965
Reading	101.4	96.7
Spelling	102.8	94.6
Arithmetic	103.2	95.5

Oh, I know. The argument has always been: "But back in those days, the less able didn't stay in school very long. So the ones who took the tests were a select group compared to the school children of today. It's a rigged comparison."

Sorry. It won't wash, as the English say.

The youngsters tested in 1914 were just ten years old; so were the ones tested in 1965. And while I'm sure a lot of teenagers weren't going to school in pre-World War I Britain, I'm equally sure they were enrolled when they were ten. I'm almost as sure, incidentally, that American test figures would show similar results, if we had them.

How now, fellow educators? After a half-century of new ideas, new techniques, new psychologies of learning, why should the horse-and-buggy kids of Grandma's day show up so well, and our own progressive, permissive swingers show up so sorrily?

It's even worse than the cold statistics show. Hear Sir Cyril further: "A comparison of essays written by average school children in 1914 and fifty years later reveals yet more obvious signs of decline."

Bear in mind that the England of those dim, dead days before the guns of August ushered in our current century of wars and wickedness was a land of startling extremes: stately homes and ghastly slums, magnificence and squalor, the very rich and the abysmally poor. Where does this leave the educational environmentalists, who swear so confidently and so copiously that culturally deprived children cannot learn as much or as well as their less disadvantaged peers? Surely the welfare state which Britain has become since 1945 has less abject poverty than did the Britain of a half-century ago. Surely, too, the English youngsters of 1914 had less food, less medical care, less of everything than do their grandchildren. Yet they could read, spell, and cipher today's crop of well-fed scholars right off the map.

How to explain it?

In part, it's a failure of will and nerve. School in those days was a hair-raisingly competitive proposition. It was survival of the fittest, root hog or die. No one expected to enjoy himself in class. It was more like going to the dentist; you knew it was going to hurt, but you also knew the alternative was a whole lot worse. So you went and you endured and you gritted your teeth. And you learned.

Today, school is expected to be amusing and sparkling and fitted accommodatingly to the "felt needs" of each individual. It counsels and it psychoanalyzes and it entertains its pupils, but even as it does all these delightful things it educates them ever less effectively in the use of the intellectual tools which it was originally created to burnish and to hone and to hand down from one generation to the next.

There's a little more to it than mere slackened application, though. Somewhere along the long line since 1914, between the blaze of wars and the dry rot of depressions, we lost sight of the real nature of education. It's not fun and games. It's not intended to entertain or to divert. It's far too important to be watered down and gussied up and made palatable for a generation which prefers a placebo to a physic, even as all generations would have chosen to their disaster had their elders been stupid enough to give them a choice.

We and our English cousins have shortchanged the children during the past fifty years. I wonder. What will the same tests show in the year 2000?

PHONY ASSUMPTION #12: That tomorrow's school problems can be solved by more permissiveness. As one who has spent his life simultaneously loving education and criticizing it, I'm more than a little miffed at the recent Carnegie Corporation study report which portrays American public schools as a cross between Sing Sing and a General Motors assembly line. Aside from the execrable grammar involved in the phrase, I don't object one whit to telling it like it is. I do object more than somewhat to the indiscriminate use of pejorative adjectives such as "oppressive," "grim," and "joyless" to describe our educational system as a whole, thus telling it like it certainly is not.

According to the report's author, Charles Silberman, the schools are regimented, the curriculum is banal, the teachers are slaves, and the pupils are being "educated for docility." That last crack sent my eyebrows clear up to my receding hairline. Our youngsters today are many things; docile they aren't.

However, let's go on. Mr. Silberman recommends a radical restructuring of the classroom along more "informal" lines so that the student will be free to use his own interests as a starting point for his education. Above all, he must avoid any kind of "domination" by the teacher.

Sound familiar? It should. The disciples of John Dewey were spreading whole layers of this kind of guff all over the country back in the thirties, like so much malignant margarine. The entire fabric of "life adjustment" education is shot through with this bland, infuriating assumption that the child knows more than the adult, the pupil more than the teacher.

There's more. In the elementary schools, it seems, much of what is taught "isn't worth knowing as a child, let alone as an adult, and little will be remembered." Like the ability to read, Mr. Silberman? The multiplication tables, perhaps? The United States Constitution? Punctuation and sentence structure? How to spell?

Quite a few adults manage to remember these things, and even to regard them as pretty important.

What does Mr. Silberman recommend in place of this nation-wide educational disaster area his report limns so luridly?

Well, for one thing, he wants to abolish lesson plans. Each child should be allowed to go at his own pace, select his own subject matter, and structure the curriculum in terms of his own personal "interests." "The child," he states, "is the principal agent in his own education and mental development." So let him organize his own education.

Good grief! This is the sort of permissive pap I was being fed back in 1939, when I was first training to be a teacher. It was swallowed hook, line and sinker by enough schools and teachers to produce a generation composed of entirely too many quasi illiterates. We broke with this "do as you please" philosophy after we looked up during the late fifties and found Sputnik I beeping merrily all over our American skyspace. Now Mr. Silberman wants to resurrect it and breathe new life into its ancient flab.

Children have interests appropriate to their stages of development: bubble gum and dolls at one stage, dune buggies and Tom Jones records at another. But we teachers are paid to prepare them for life in the extraordinarily complicated world of the twenty-first century, and units in gum-chewing, doll-dressing, and jalopy-driving are not precisely what the parents of those children had in mind when they paid us their hard-earned tax dollars to share our knowledge with their offspring.

School in the days beyond tomorrow should be interesting, granted. It should also be important. And the things it teaches should be those which adults have found to be indispensable, not things which they found enjoyable at the age of ten and then discarded at the age of twelve.

The trouble with gearing a curriculum to the interests of children is precisely that: they *are* children. But education is for life.

Having disposed of the phony assumptions which have kept my profession bottled up in port so long for all the world like a semantic minefield, I've now cleared my decks for action and am ready to advance my predictions along the whole line of battle. Each is supported by its own auxiliary vessels of argument and reinforced by its independent squadron of supporting developments summoned fresh from the teeming shipyards of current educational happenings. Let us then consider the armada well launched into the mysterious future and the combat fairly joined.

>   PREDICTION A: *The oversupply of teachers will get worse and will have perfectly splendid spin-offs.*

In 1940, I was one of 220 eager beavers who qualified for high school teaching credentials at UCLA. About 20 of us got jobs. I had haunted the university's placement office for months. Finally the director took pity on me and offered me a job nobody else wanted.

"Where is it?" I asked gratefully.

"Trona, California," he replied.

"Where in blazes is that?"

"Search me. Let's look on the map."

I quickly discovered that when I said "blazes" I was righter than I knew. Trona turned out to be thirty miles from Death Valley as the crow flies, except that no crow in his right mind would have flown over that cauldron without an atmospheric reentry heat shield. The thermometer got stuck above 110 degrees for weeks on end, once in a while bubbling up to a balmy and salubrious 120. A huge chemical plant spewed odorous potash fumes all over the lunarlike landscape where nothing grew except a certain kind of salt tree imported from the Great Australian Desert.

The job itself left something to be desired, though certainly not in the way of variety. I was expected to teach seven periods per day, each period in a different field of preparation. After school I coached football and track for a couple of hours to keep myself from the clutching hands of sloth. Even with the teacher surplus now building up, a wet-behind-the-ears graduate of one of today's mod and swinging teachers' colleges, confronted with an offer like that, would send for the little men with the white coats and the butterfly nets.

I took it, and was darned glad to get it. It paid me the magnificent sum of $1,750 a year. I've never regretted it. In many ways, it was the best job I ever had.

Now, after more than three decades, the pendulum has swung back to 1940. What's causing the current glut in the teacher market? Two things:

First, the American birthrate started swooning and collapsing all over the charts back in 1964. Right now it's the lowest ever. Demographic projections indicate that the slump in number of warm bodies has hit the elementary schools during the early seventies, will drain the high schools by the end of the decade, and will hit the colleges and universities like a blockbuster around 1980.

Second, there was a big push in 1967–1968 and since toward "public service" career preparation—things like VISTA, the Peace Corps, ecology, welfare work, and of course teaching. This has switched tens of thousands of college graduates from careers in business and science to careers of do-goodism, vocations which don't produce fallouts of wars, napalm-brewing, and air pollution. *Result:* a lot more people than usual artificially propelled into teaching, and a resultant buyers' market in education of colossal proportions.

There's no indication that this state of affairs is going to change much in the foreseeable future. And there are a lot of implications emerging from this unexpected phenomenon, all of them good.

One is that we're not going to need many new schools for a while.

Another is the beckoning invitation to lower class sizes, with all which this implies in the way of increased attention to the needs of individual pupils.

Still a third is the opportunity, unique since Depression days, to exercise more selectivity in the hiring of new teachers. An administrator who adds to his faculty headaches from now on by employing either lethargic bores or wild-eyed, obscenity-spouting activists will deserve exactly what he gets.

PREDICTION B: There will be better education in the big cities without forced busing.

Mandated busing is one of the real wild hares of our time. Our descendants are going to think we were out of our minds when they study this aberration in their history classes. Mind you, there is no question about the need to equalize educational opportunities, especially for Blacks. But busing fails to take one stark, inescapable fact of life into consideration: in huge, sprawling areas of de facto segregation such as New York, Chicago, and Los Angeles, busing cannot possibly work. When a ghetto extends for miles and miles in all directions, there simply is no logistically or financially conceivable way to transport or to redistribute the millions of Black and White youngsters who would have to be shipped all over the map to attain any kind of ethnic balance in the schools.

The future's solution to this problem?

1. Compensatory education will be provided wherever and whenever we find children who need it. And if this means spending more money on better equipment and smaller class sizes for Black children, that's the way it's going to be.

2. Every state in the union during the next twenty years will adopt a policy which requires the best school buildings and supplies to be placed in the slums and ghettoes.

3. Slum school teachers will be paid more—a lot more—to stay and teach in slum schools. Too often, the finest, most inspirational instructors dodge assignment to the schools where the need for their services is greatest. You can't blame them. They don't like to be mugged and robbed and placed in sordid surroundings any better than the rest of us. But it is absolutely vital that our best teachers, not our worst, be placed in these schools. And the only way to get them to stay put is to make it worth their while.

What happens to racial integration of the schools, you ask? It will occur when whole cities and neighborhoods are integrated naturally, and not before. As far as real education is concerned, racial balance is happily irrelevant, no matter what Coleman and others have said. A school with decent facilities, reasonable class sizes, good materials, and excellent teachers is a school where children will learn. And I don't care if those children are all Negroes, Caucasians, Eskimos, or Berbers.

PREDICTION C: The frequency of teacher strikes will decline to zero.

In every state, teacher strikes are unprofessional and immoral; unprofessional because teaching is a self-proclaimed learned profession, and members of learned professions don't strike; immoral because leaving classrooms unsupervised and pupils uninstructed for prolonged periods of time hurts children who cannot defend themselves.

In most states, teacher strikes are illegal as well. This serves to point up the recent bankruptcy of the educational establishment as contained in a statement by Robert Chapin, general counsel for the National Education Association: "We don't view a strike as a planned strategy. Usually it's something teachers are forced to do. Sometimes you can make progress by testing what you think are unjust laws."

A fascinating philosophy, Mr. Chapin. Suppose I get the idea that the existing homicide laws are "unjust." Should I "test" them by murdering someone? Like an NEA general counsel, for instance?

Any school child above the age of ten knows that if he considers a law to be unjust, his proper recourse is to work to get it changed, not to go out and break it. I'm not even going to comment on the idiocy of the statement about teachers (or anyone else) being "forced" to strike. If our successors during the eighties and the nineties aren't smart enough to figure this one out, there probably won't be any society around to support schools for teachers to picket.

But it won't be illegality or immorality or unprofessionalism that will blow the whistle on teacher strikes. It will be the fact that such strikes are counterproductive. Allow me to quote from an article in a major national publication, published in February of 1971:

"Teacher strikes are backfiring, no longer serve their intended purpose, say private reports being sent from AFL-CIO headquarters to teachers' unions. Officials at the American Federation of Teachers tell local groups that strikes 'have done more harm than good.' "

And that's why, by the time the year 2000 has rolled around, teacher strikes will be as extinct as the dodo and the passenger pigeon. A final quote on this topic, this one from East St. Louis teacher union boss Donald Miller, just after his strikers trooped back into their classrooms after a twelve-week walkout:

"The new contract certainly is no great improvement over the one we had last year. However, at least we're hired back, and I think that's a victory in itself."

Oh brother! Using reasoning like this, Napoleon actually won at Waterloo. After all, he did get out of the battle alive, and received a free sea voyage to St. Helena into the bargain.

PREDICTION D: Mandated statewide use of standardized tests will be universal.

During the 1960s, California adopted regulations requiring the annual testing of all public school children in certain grades. The tests were in reading, mathematics, and English usage. The first year the tests were given, the city of Los Angeles ended up low man on a twenty-city totem poll in regard to how well its children knew how to read.

The test results didn't exactly come as a surprise to those of us who had been begging Los Angeles to junk its obviously inadequate reading techniques and start teaching phonics to its first graders as soon as they arrived in school. Neither were we surprised by the initial reaction to the horrendous test scores. Everybody denounced the tests. This is precisely comparable to the hospital patient with a high fever who denounces the doctor's thermometer.

Fortunately, Reaction No. 2 was more interesting. Feeling the heat from the newspaper headlines, Los Angeles promptly invested in several thousand so-called "phonics kits" and distributed them to all its elementary teachers, along with no-nonsense orders that they had to be used. *Result:* The next year, the test scores went up, and the next year they went up even higher.

The important thing, however, is that mandated standardized testing in the fundamentals did three things:

1. It raised the curtain and showed how bad things were.

2. It generated irresistible demand for reform.

3. It pointed the way to make results better in the future.

For years beyond counting, the leaders of my profession have been dosing the laity with anesthetic bromides like these:

"Teaching good citizenship is more important than teaching mere subject matter."

and

"Competence in reading as in other subjects will spring naturally from the felt needs of the child, and when the proper maturation level of the individual has been reached."

and

"A teacher's effectiveness can never be measured by objective testing in the so-called fundamentals."

Poppycock.

Every one of the above platitudes is demonstrably false.

First, subject matter—especially reading—is far and away the most important thing the schools exist to teach. Good citizenship springs from familiarity with our nation's history, from knowledge of its government, from at least a nodding acquaintance with great literature, and from a lively interest in current happenings. None of these wellsprings of good citizenship, you will notice, can be tapped by the nonreader.

Second, competence in reading does *not* spring spontaneously from the felt needs of the child. It springs from an efficient, inspirational teacher and from interesting, challenging books, both dedicated to the proposition that learning the letters of the alphabet, the sounds of those letters, and how to combine them into syllables is the best possible way to teach anyone how to read.

Third, bosh to the comfortable theory that good teaching is so ethereal and intangible a commodity that it can't be measured objectively. Right now, and probably on into the next century, an effective elementary teacher will be one who sees that the children in her class learn to read easily and fluently before she ships them on to the next grade. In other words, if she's effective, her kids will learn to read.

Standardized testing has its weaknesses. But the future will use it the way California used it—to measure its progress in curricular areas which lend themselves to measurement. And what's wrong with that?

PREDICTION E: More and better vocational education is in the cards, and for a lot more children than are getting it now.

Never in any nation's history has there been such a hue and cry after vocational education as the one in which we have been engaged—with indifferent results—since the middle sixties. The Youth Corps and the Job Corps have been nosing into every likely copse and thicket, quivering with eagerness at even the slightest hint of short-cut methodology stirring within and pointing rigidly whenever a bashful new technique whirred unexpectedly from covert.

The beaters and gunbearers of the Economic Opportunities Act were flushing the countryside in all directions, seeking not only the elusive quarry of trainable and willing unemployees, but also the game bags labeled "job rehabilitation" in which to bear the spoils of the chase triumphantly back to the nearest vocational training center.

The whole power of Uncle Sam was unleashed during a period of full employment to get into the hands of unskilled labor the tools and the skills needed to transform it into skilled labor. Now the unemployment rate has risen and the bloom is off the boom. Yet the problem underlying vocational education is still essentially the same.

We are still being told that the aircraft industry is crying for all sorts of strange and esoteric mechanical abilities, and that the schools are going to have to install in the future everything from micro-millimetric measuring devices to nuclear reactors in order to train the highly specialized technicians needed to service both the Air Age of today and the Space Age of tomorrow. The same claims are being made for an increasing segment of both light and heavy industry.

There's no doubt that this is basically true. In the decades ahead, and regardless of how the historical ball bounces, we're going to need more and better trained experts in many industrial fields, and it's perfectly true that this will mean more complex and expensive vocational courses in the schools. But important as this is, it isn't the real problem.

For every exotic job opportunity involving advance knowledge of slide rules and electronic transistors there are now, and will continue to be at least through the mid-eighties, twenty job opportunities which will involve nothing of the sort.

Want to know the kind of qualifications these jobs require? Here they are:

1. Ability to read without lip-moving and without a glazing of the eyeballs whenever a word of more than two syllables comes along.

2. Proficiency in making simple change out of a cash drawer, which in turn requires certain minimum essentials in adding and subtracting.

3. Moderately acceptable vocal speech patterns—that is, the ability to conduct a conversation with a customer, with relatively few gross grammatical errors, and with absolutely no reliance upon such ineffable verbal crutches as "Blast off, weirdo!" and "De cat ha just split."

4. Willingness to shut up, take orders, and work hard.

5. Cheerfulness, helpfulness, and a civil tongue in one's head.

I submit that all five of these qualifications will be in uncommonly short supply during the years ahead, even with a major emphasis on supplying them. I submit further that the schools are in excellent posture to supply all five. And I'm willing to bet that in the vast majority of jobs available tomorrow and twenty years from tomorrow the applicant who has mastered all five is not only going to get hired; he's going to stay hired.

The proprietor of a combination garage and gas station cornered me the other day after a meeting, backed me into a corner, and prodded me on the chest with a meaty and slightly discolored forefinger.

"I hire a lot of kids just out of high school," he began, breathing heavily. "And I have to fire a lot of them pretty quick. Not because they don't know how to operate the equipment. Heck, I can teach them that in a day or two."

"Oh, no," he went on. "It's because they don't know how to work. They lean on a broom or a grease gun for ten minutes, and they want a coffee break. Leave 'em unsupervised for five minutes, and they're over in the corner rapping about last Saturday's rumble or next Friday's rock festival. Dock 'em when they come in late, and they think you're one of the bad guys in the black hats."

He eyed me despairingly.

"Why don't you school fellows forget about how to operate the lathe and how to set the band saw rigging and all that until you've taught these kids the right *attitudes*? If they've got that, we can give 'em the rest, right on the job."

I told him I'd do my best to spread the word. As he walked away, he looked back over his shoulder.

"And while you're at it, try to talk 'em into shaving, getting a haircut, and throwing away the sandals. I've got no objection to some character going around looking like Peter the Hermit but I'm hanged if he's going to work in my place."

This is what the vocational education instructor of the future is going to have to teach first: attitudes.

PREDICTION F: Ethnic studies will be as important in the cur-
riculum as etruscan tomb-carving, and no more so.

The most futile "cause" of the Sixties has turned out to be the ethnic studies hassle. Remember five years ago when all the bedlam and brute force were used to compel colleges to institute classes in black history, brown culture, and the like? Well, here's what happened in the biggest state of the union, and in the biggest city of that state.

Los Angeles Valley College, under pressure from militants whose abundant hair fairly bristled with outraged indignation, launched an elaborate program of ethnically oriented courses in 1968–1969. The rioters and cop-cursers, who had done their best to turn California campuses into bloody battlefields, won their fight. Their demands were met in full.

So what happened? Valley College gave an ethnic party, but nobody came. Half the bitterly fought-for classes didn't even open a year later. *Reason:* hardly anyone wanted to take them, apparently. The Mexican-American courses attracted exactly four eager students. Black studies enrollments told the same deflating story, particularly in regard to Afro-American literature, a class in which only three students registered.

The same surprise on a somewhat less spectacular scale occurred at Los Angeles' California State College, which had a sizable enrollment of 21,000, of which 2,310 were Negroes and Mexican-Americans. All of Cal State's ethnic courses lumped together drew 500 students, about 2.5 percent of the total student body.

Let me stress here that there's nothing at all wrong with establishing college courses in the culture and history of our racial minority groups. But there's a lot wrong with letting immature kids unilaterally change the entire curriculum of an institution of higher learning, with all the time, money, and energy which this requires. For results, you need look no farther than Los Angeles.

Hopefully, our grandchildren in A.D. 2000 will have learned from our sad and somewhat sappy experience.

PREDICTION G: Merit pay for teachers and modification of tenure laws are coming up around the bend of the time stream.

Long before the year 2000 comes along, if we are still refusing in this country to pay good teachers more money than we pay poor teachers, then public education will be permanently becalmed in a Sargasso Sea of insipidity. And unless we drastically reorganize the state laws governing lifelong, ironclad tenure for teachers to permit firing the senile, the stupid, and the subversive, public education is going to be a dead duck. We are the only profession which refuses steadfastly to police its own ranks and to weed out its loafers, its incompetents, and its loose nuts. Because the future cannot coexist with this nonsense, the nonsense will cease to exist.

Merit pay and tenure revision are in the wings getting ready to come onstage into the spotlight because they have to be; there is no alternative.

PREDICTION H: Better textbooks are already on the way.

This is an easy prophecy to venture. Today's elementary readers are demonstrably better than were their predecessors of ten years back. Remember Dick and Jane and Tom and Susan and Spot and all the driveling milksops of the early sixties? The new readers are better; our grandchildren's will be still better. Excerpts from the great children's classics—hero tales from American history, stories from Greek and Roman mythology—these are the ingredients which save children's reading from being stale and which make it savory.

Aside from the brain-numbing effect upon the youngsters of the old primers, consider what years of having to deal with the paltry vocabularies and the dry-rot repetitiveness may do to the unfortunate teacher. There is a story, perhaps but not necessarily apocryphal, of the first grade teacher who had saved up enough of her small salary to buy a gleaming new compact car. The first night she had it, she parked it in front of her apartment, and a large truck inadvertently squashed it like a beetle. Wakened by the crash of metal and the tinkling of broken glass, poor Miss Guggenslocker turned on the porch light, stood there helplessly wringing her hands, and in words conditioned by a decade of first grade readers sobbed: "Oh! Oh! Oh! Look! Look! Look! Damn! Damn! Damn!"

Science texts are so much better than the ones I had when I was a boy that I can hardly wait to see what the next few years will bring. There is still vast room for improvement, however, in the history and other social science texts, many of which show an almost creepy resemblance in both content and style to a UNESCO fund-raising appeal or to an ACLU brief.

PREDICTION I: Both a longer school year and school day seem in the cards.

It's pretty safe to assume that there will be a longer school year before long. Three months off each summer no longer makes sense. But there is even greater justification for a longer school day, if only because the humanities are gradually being shoved out of big-city high schools and junior high schools by the shortening of the school day which occurred for financial reasons during the past ten years.

Unless there is a seven- or eight-period day in secondary schools, such valuable subjects as art, music, and home economics are going to continue to be muscled aside by "must courses" such as math, science, English, and history. I just can't believe that America in the final quarter of the twentieth century is going to let this happen, especially when we are being bombarded from all sides by forecasts of shorter work weeks and increasing leisure time. Unless education can somehow take up the slack that seems to be accumulating, we're going to see all this extra time occupied in watching television daytime serials and nighttime wrestling, and this I positively refuse to contemplate.

PREDICTION J: More student participation in school administration will be occurring.

This is particularly true in the area of teacher evaluation, where thoughtful and constructive student rating of instructors is both practicable and appropriate.

The trend, however, is apparent in school policy making as well. In California in 1968, students began serving on local school boards and even on the state board of education. Alabama recently added student representatives to every one of its college and university governing boards. Stimulated by the recent constitutional amendment giving eighteen-year-olds the right to vote, this trend will continue and probably accelerate.

PREDICTION K: More part-time students and off-campus courses.

Both higher and secondary education are starting to branch out. Prospects are for more correspondence courses, televised home "extension" classes, and college offshoots out in Podunk, so that adults especially can benefit from lifelong learning. Nothing in all education's cloudy crystal ball shines more brightly than this almost certain development.

PREDICTION L: School and teacher accountability will be demanded.

Before the end of this century—hopefully before the end of this decade—we will challenge successfully the arrogant assumption that educators should not be held responsible for the product they turn out. The best way I know to establish the principle of accountability is to rate teachers at least in part on how much subject matter and how many effective skills they have been able to impart to their pupils as shown on the standardized tests advocated under Prediction D.

At this juncture, I can hear the dismal wails and piteous ululations emanating from the educational establishment, sobbing that such regimented goings-on will dehumanize the instructional process, to say nothing of ignoring such valuable intangibles as good citizenship, artistic appreciation, and—inevitably—relevance.

No matter. Such evaluation will certainly show how well Teacher is doing in the fields being evaluated. Right now, I'll settle for that.

PREDICTION M: There will be a change in the selection and training of school administrators.

For some time we've been operating on the theory that a good teacher will automatically make a good principal or superintendent. As Gershwin said about something else altogether, "It ain't necessarily so."

Long before the next decade has run its course, we will be recruiting school superintendents and business managers from the business world rather than from the academic community, and we will be giving them prolonged on-the-job intern training. It's about time.

These, then, allowing for a reasonable margin of error, are what will be happeing in education during the years ahead. There are also a few things which will *not* be happening.

For example, American children will not become mere wards of an all-powerful state, with the schools taking over the traditional functions of the home. That trend has been running now since World War II; it's about due to reverse itself.

Teachers are not going to be replaced by machines. It's certainly true that these electronic gadgets light up, whir, click, and buzz enticingly, none of which the human teacher can do without considerable difficulty. It's also true that one of the ultimate realities in education is the interplay of the personality of the teacher with that of the pupil, and a machine, no matter how impressive its memory banks, has no more personality than a tin can. A machine can certainly help a teacher test, drill, and present material. But it cannot—nor will it ever—really teach.

Finally, schools and classrooms will not be museum pieces in the year 2000. They'll still be around and recognizable, if only because children need to be with each other during an important part of their lives. More, they need the motivation to learn and to study which cannot be provided in the average home and which only a teacher-classroom milieu can supply.

As I said at the beginning, education has always moved more like a glacier than like a prairie fire. In the long haul, this is probably a good thing; most of us would not like prairie-fire education very much even if there were some way it could be made available. Actually education is a bridge on which perhaps we may be able to meet our successors halfway.

But more than anything else, education is a great mirror, reflecting always the strengths and the weaknesses, the follies and the frailties which add up to the nation which supports and populates the schools, and which first called them into being on this continent. Those of us whose life work calls upon us to look deeply and regularly into that gleaming surface find it fascinating, almost hypnotic. A crowded, swarming, colorful caravan unrolls before us every day—as old Omar said, "A moving row of magic shadow-shapes that come and go." America, drawing now toward the end of the thunderous, cataclysmic twentieth century, passes in review, in all its baffling profusion, its tumult and its shouting, in the persons of its children.

Unlike the more conventional looking glass, however, the mirror which is education takes unto itself two additional and somewhat unorthodox dimensions.

First, it reflects not only the faces of people and the appearance of things, but also the semblance of ideas themselves. They troop like armed battalions across the shining surface, and even as they pass they war with one another.

Is it to be education as the pursuit of truth for truth's own sake, or is it to be the easy, comfortable adjustment of the child to his environment? Shall it be schooling to impart the accumulated and

well-weighed wisdom of the ages to the citizens of the future, or schooling to impose unilaterally and tyrannically upon a malleable and cap-
tive daily audience a particular socioeconomic or political dogma? Are
we to have instruction or indoctrination? Pedagogy or demagoguery?

And even as we try to winnow from among the struggling,
grappling mirror images a true depiction of the future, the great glass
shifts and changes into its second strange dimension: the depiction
in its glowing, enigmatic depths of what Wells called the Shape of
Things to Come, seen darkly perhaps and teeming with uncertainties,
but nonetheless and in the long run certainly.

Like the children of Hamlin town so long ago, following an
inscrutable Piper into an unimaginable world, a strange, enchanted
land of mixed beauty and balefulness, our younglings have set their
feet upon a path which leads to a universe where a million—that
number which has loomed so large to us—will be a very small number
indeed, whether in terms of dollars, or of miles, or of human beings;
a society where hard, monotonous physical labor will be as quaint
and forgotten as are slavery and witch burning; a mind-boggling com-
monwealth not of nations alone, nor even of continents, but of whole
planets, flung in ordered profusion across the spangled immensity of
the night sky.

Mothers' and fathers' breaths have always caught, and their
brows have furrowed, as the little ones went off so wide-eyed to school
on that first day of all September days. In the Seventies, the Eighties,
the Nineties, the breath-catching and the brow-furrowing will be doubly
warranted. For upon the schools and upon the teachers, upon the books
and the lessons and the tapes and the films, above all upon the educational way of thinking about life embodied in the schools' philosophy,
today as in no other day, hang all the keys to the future and the survival
of our children's America as a land of freedom and a bastion of democracy in a world which becomes a little less free, a little less democratic
with each passing year.

A mirror faithfully gives back the shadow, not the substance.
By itself, it is helpless to remedy old evils, to redress the ills of days
gone by, to straighten the passageway which stretches ahead, with all
its promise and peril. Used properly and with due regard for its built-in
limitations, the mirror tells its user the simple truth. It enables him to
tally the good against the evil. It arms him against surprise. It warns
him against approaching danger. It is incapable of flattery. It counsels
wisely and well.

Even so is education, now and in the days ahead. We who
wield it and who love it can use it as we choose. We can employ it
for the great purposes of life and learning, as the mirror in the laborato-

ry picks up the light waves which confirm some towering experiment, or we can utilize it for causes as vain and as foolish as the aimless focusing of the sun dance on some garden wall.

Education is not magic. It works with what is given to it. In the years ahead, it will be as it was in the days of Plato and of Aristotle— as it will be in the time of our remote descendants.

Yesterday, today, or tomorrow, the faces which look out hopefully or fearfully from its gleaming, passionless surface are always our own.

Charles
Weingartner

Charles Weingartner

Dr. Weingartner formerly taught at Queens College and is now a professor of education at the University of South Florida. Known widely among English teachers for his provocative work in semantics, he received national professional and lay public attention for his best-selling books, Teaching as a Subversive Activity *and* The Soft Revolution *(both co-authored with Neil Postman).*

schools
and
the future

Charles Kettering said that he was interested in the
future because that was where he was going to spend
the rest of his life. Most people are interested in the
future, if not for the same reason that Kettering gave,
then because of a pervasive—and possibly
primitive--feeling of anxiety produced by uncertainty.
Part of the price that humans pay for the ability to
invent and manipulate symbols is expressed in the
ability to transport oneself, psychically, in time. The
most common form this takes is worrying about
possible dangers and disasters in the future. Humans
can, and 'do, symbolically (that is, verbally) invent
threats to their physical, psychic, financial, and
emotional survival. The uncertainty that is an inevitable
part of most futures seems to be intolerable to most
people. Hence any procedure or ritual that purports to
reveal the future is endowed with high value, no matter
how improbable or implausible it might be. Even in the
second decade of the nuclear space age, Americans
spend about as much money on various attempts to
predict the future—from horoscopes to tea leaf or palm

reading, to phrenology or tarot cards—as they do on any other speculative venture, such as medical treatment. It seems as if *any* estimate of the future, no matter how arrived at, is more desirable than uncertainty.

The need for the illusion of security produced by *any* prediction permitting the illusion of certainty is so great, and has such a long history in human affairs, that it is a wonder that futurology has been the providence of mystics and magicians, even up to the present, rather than becoming a respectable intellectual or academic concern. This may be a product of the fact that intellectual and scholarly traditions developed in an environment characterized by such a slow process of change that the illusion of certainty derived from a redundant pattern from the past was inevitable. Precedent is the prime source for judging the good and the beautiful in most human groups. It is a very primitive approach, and one that is under much stress in a time when change is occurring at a completely unprecedented rate. Indeed, future shock would not be possible were it not for this tendency to look to the past for guidelines as to what should be done in the present and future. As if the past were any more determinable than the future! Yet, even the idea that the present is unknowable because of technologically produced complexity and rapidity of change is brushed aside as sophomoric. Perhaps the idea is intolerable because it is so obvious. History has always been someone's arbitrarily and ethnocentrically selective recapitulation of a story that fulfilled the biases and assumptions of the storyteller. Whether depicted in the Bible or the Odyssey or Beowulf or some other tribal epic such as MacArthur's history of the war in the Pacific, the past turns out to be a fictional narrative based on some fragments of an unknowable event.

All of this is simply a prologue to the point that I wish to make about predicting the future. Whatever futures we can invent are no more implausible, finally, than any of the pasts we invent. Academicians disparage, by and large, any estimates of the future merely because they are in the habit of looking backward rather than forward. Inventions of possible futures are no more, and no less, potentially useful or useless than are inventions of possible pasts. There is, however, one difference. We can affect what happens in the future. We cannot affect what happened in the past, even if we could somehow determine what actually happened.

Having said that much, I can now embark on some speculations about possible futures for the schools. Experts, we must note, have had, until now, really terrible records as predictors of the future. One of the reasons for this disappointing degree of inaccuracy has already been alluded to: it is our habit as a society to define someone as an expert who has accumulated a larger quantity of trivia from the past than have most other people. This condition is commonly called scholarship. It is curious indeed that the shamans of a technological civilization should be those who have memorized more prescientific trivia than those who have not. But, as Billy Pilgrim says, so it goes.

What I am doing, of course, is disqualifying myself as an expert on the future—or anything else, for that matter. Beyond this, I wish to make the uncongenial and unassailable point that my prognostications are as good as anybody else's. I am then a Visigoth to the Byzantines who are devoted to protecting some vision of the past that could just as easily have been—and quite probably was—quite different from the conventionally held one.

There is one point that has impressed me in my ruminations about predictions, and that is that they have been characteristically myopic because of a tendency to assume that the future will be merely an analogic extension of some imagined past or present. The joker in the deck seems always to have been the emergence or development of something or other that no one would think of who proceeds logically. The world, in sum, does not proceed like an Aristotelian syllogism. The damndest things keep happening. It is infuriating to anyone suffering from the quaint notion that the universe is rational.

Arthur C. Clarke, author of *2001*, gives an example of this point in his book *Profiles of the Future*, Rev. Ed. (New York: Harper & Row, pp. 16–17, 1971):

One can only prepare for the unpredictable by trying to keep an open and unprejudiced mind—a feat which is extremely difficult to achieve, even with the best will in the world. Indeed, a completely open mind would be an empty one, and freedom from all prejudices and preconceptions is an unattainable ideal. Yet there is one form of mental exercise that can provide good basic training for would be prophets: Anyone who wishes to cope with the future should travel back in imagination a single lifetime—say to 1900—and ask himself just how much of today's technology would be, not merely incredible, but *incomprehensible* to the keenest scientific brains of that time.

1900 is a good round date to choose because it was just about then that all hell started to break loose in science. As James B. Conant has put it:

Somewhere about 1900 science took a *totally* unexpected turn. There had previously been several revolutionary theories and more than one epoch-making discovery in the history of science, but what occurred between 1900 and say, 1930 was something different; it was a failure of a general prediction about what might be confidently expected from experimentation.

P. W. Bridgman has put it even more strongly:

The physicist has passed through an intellectual crisis forced by the discovery of experimental facts of a sort which he had not previously envisaged, and which he would not even have thought possible.

The collapse of "classical" science actually began with Roentgen's discovery of x-rays in 1895; here was the first clear indication, in a form that everyone could appreciate that the commonsense picture of the universe was not sensible after all. X-rays—the very name reflects the bafflement of scientists and laymen alike—could travel through solid matter, like light through a sheet of glass. No one had ever imagined or predicted such a thing; that one would be able to peer into the interior of the human body—and thereby revolutionize medicine and surgery—was something that the most daring prophet had never suggested.

This need to keep an "open and unprejudiced mind" in order to deal with the unexpected, the unpredictable, and the illogical is itself a suggestion for a future mission for education. This mission is the need to deal with subjects less from an abstract, expert point of view (for the purpose of preparing more experts) and more from a personal and general point of view—in response to the question: "What difference does this subject make to me, here and now as well as in the future?" Students, by and large, are not specialists in any of the traditional school subjects (even after considerable coursework, I might add). Although that lack of specialization is conventionally regarded as undesirable, I am suggesting that there might be some largely unnoticed advantages available. Edmund Carpenter notes, in *They Became What They Beheld* (Ballantine Books, 1971): "Specialists don't welcome discovery: they welcome only new proofs of what they already know. Discovery is unrepeatable. All specialists understand that discoveries are fatal to the stockpile of their unclassified data. Discovery makes the field of the specialist obsolete."

My point here is that everyone is equally inexpert or unspecialized in making estimates of probable futures, and that, paradoxically, those who are not limited by the bounds of some fancied expertise or specialty are freer to discover more probabilities than those who are committed to verifying estimates permitted by whichever closed system of knowledge they are expert in.

As I thought about some perspective that might help me discover probable futures for the schools, it occurred to me to use two contrasting metaphors. The central metaphors we use in talking about anything determine what we can say about it. I will start with a metaphor that is almost familiar. The most common role of the schools is assumed to be that of teaching subjects—with a nominal increase in the degrees of specialization of each as students go up the curriculum. The most common form of this activity is regarded as imparting subject matter, which imposes the burden on the teacher of getting his subject across or of *communicating it to students*. So I will look at the school first as a medium of communication. This approach will permit me to discover, or see, a probable future role for schools that other metaphors (and their subsequent perspectives) might not.

Having selected the perspective of the school as a medium of communication, I must then choose some generalization about communication that permits me to make some judgments about the school in this role. The generalization that I have selected is still apparently (and curiously) an exotic one despite wide publicity given to it by Marshall McLuhan. The generalization is: Two media of communication cannot exist at the same time if they are trying to do the same thing. That is, if more than one medium of communication exists at a given time to fulfill a particular function for a particular audience, the one that does it best (that is, with the least expenditure of time, effort, and money) will survive, and the others will not.

They will not survive, that is, in an open market, or one in which they depend on support from an audience that has the freedom to choose between or among different media. A medium can survive, however, no matter how anachronistic it may become because of developments in media of communication, *if* it is subsidized by some patron who, for whatever reasons, is interested in its survival.

The most recent, and obvious, example of this generalization operating in an open market is provided by the change in movies after the appearance of television. As soon as television began to fulfill the function that movies had fulfilled for about forty years—but in a way that was easier and more economical for the audience—the movies were in trouble. They were in trouble because the audience stayed home and watched television, instead of getting dressed, hiring a baby sitter, and driving to a movie house. Movies had to redefine themselves—to fulfill a function that television did not—in order to survive. They did, after various misbegotten efforts at gimmicks to attract audiences to the old thing, by becoming adult, that is, more realistic. Most people thought they had just become dirty. But that's the way reality is. Very different from the fantasy that movies had portrayed for forty years. As movies changed to fulfill a new role, they attracted a new audience. And with the new audience, they not only survived, they flourished. Movies even became cinema and film.

The school as a medium of communication, as a source of information, is bankrupt. There have been too many developments in electronic information-handling media for schools to make any sense in this role. Back in 1955, McLuhan noted that schools were, largely as a result of the emergence of television, the subsequent transmogrification of film, and the almost simultaneous emergence of the long-playing record, "a place of detention rather than attention." Schools in this instance refers to all formal classroom arrangements from kindergarten through graduate school. The schools are still acting as if they are a primary source of information for students, as they once were, in another time and place so remote as to be virtually beyond the recall of those who experienced them and beyond the imagination of those who did not.

James Coleman (in *Psychology Today*, February, 1972) described this situation in a piece titled "The Children Have Outgrown the Schools." He put it this way:

When the child lived in a poverty of information, the family and the school shaped the child's cognitive world by the selectivity of information they imposed. As the environment has become rich in information, the child's cognitive world has begun to be shaped by neither family nor school, but by comic books, television, paperbacks, and the broad spectrum of newspapers and magazines that abound, from the *Chicago Tribune* to the *Berkeley Barb* and from *Reader's Digest* to *Ramparts*.

It strikes me as curious that Coleman omits the most potent medium of communication for adolescents and young adults, the long-playing record. The whole youth culture—and it is the first international subculture in the history of the human group—is a product of the folk heroes and heroines of the young, accessible primarily, or at least initially, via the long-playing record. Perhaps this serves to illustrate the invisibility of the most potent media of communication around us, even to someone sensitive to their effects.

The schools, then, are a kind of time machine. One enters them and is transported back in time to a preelectronic communication era, where print is dominant. And the perspective of print is itself backward, leading McLuhan to his "rear-view mirror" metaphor for conventional schooling. It is not that there is nothing of value to be learned from the past, especially the kinds of folklore and simple skills in which most of us are now illiterate as a result of technological progress. It is that the schools are psychopathically obsessed with trivia about (not even from) the past that have no application, either immediately or at some future point in time, to anybody or anything. It is this obsession that has led to the epithets about mindlessness and irrelevance as the primary characteristics of the schools.

The process of chronic humiliation and vilification of those who cannot or will not participate in this relentless trivia contest must be recognized as a crucial part of the invisible curriculum. What we have in today's schools is a publicly subsidized form of punitive detention that not only does not help students to learn anything of any practical value, but also cripples so many of them emotionally that their intellectual potential will never be realized. The cost to all of us in wasted and unrealized human potential is incalculable.

And all of this because the schools persist—largely as a result of inertia and apathy, even in the midst of change-induced crises—in attempting to fulfill an anachronistic function. It is anachronistic because we live in an information rich environment (and it is possible that the environment is at least as rich in misinformation as it is in information). Even if the schools' mission is defined as that of a medium for imparting information, their present conventional form makes no sense, either economically or educationally. There are a variety of ways to handle information much more economically and efficiently than by transporting students from their widely spaced homes to a single building called a school.

It is, perhaps, too obvious a fact that human institutions tend to persist long after they cease to fulfill the functions and purposes for which they were ostensibly formed. Institutions are like juggernauts without steering mechanisms, plowing along in no particular direction, incapable of being steered even should some passenger wish to make the attempt. They just keep rolling along unless and until someone, not a passenger, decides that they are dangerous and must be stopped. At this point, an obstacle of substance sufficient to stop a juggernaut can be put in place to stop or overturn it, and thus reduce the threat it poses to all who are not riding it.

The obstacle of substance sufficient to stop the juggernaut—the present conventional school system—is the lack of money. People cannot choose an alternative unless they are aware of its existence. And so most talk about the increasing difficulty of raising money to support the school system is based on the assumption that the schools should continue to look and act pretty much as they did thirty or sixty or more years ago. At some point the lack of funds may force an examination of this assumption, and then schools as they presently exist will be finished.

Some discoveries may result from the examination of this automatically and unconsciously held assumption. One of these discoveries could be that causing students to travel (even short distances) from their homes to a school in order to have information imparted at them has made little sense since the printed book appeared, to say nothing of the lunacy of it since film, radio, and television have been around. Moving students in large numbers from wherever they otherwise would be to a school so that they can get at information made some sense when the only way to get at information was through the spoken word. When there was only one person around who knew something that someone else wanted to know about, and there were no printed books in which his words were made visible, the only way to get at his words was to go where he was speaking them. As soon as it became possible to get at the words via another medium, the process of people traveling from scattered places in order to gather in one place to hear someone speak made no sense. Persisting in this after print has been available for four-hundred years and after radio and film have been available for sixty years is ludicrous. But it does not seem ludicrous as long as the underlying assumption is unconsciously held.

McLuhan has described in elaborate detail how growing up and living in a world of electronic media has affected not only children, but all of us. Media saturation has so affected the perceptual modes of most children that schools have operationally been put out of business already as far as learning is concerned. Schools simply cannot compete with other media of cmmunication when it comes to attracting and holding the attention of students. And I mean students of all ages, through graduate and professional school.

As the money crunch intensifies, the realization that the present common form of schooling is inefficient, uneconomical, and obsolete will increase. Finally, use will really be made of computer-based instruction. Programmed instruction with television, typewriters, film, audio and video tape, and computers married into an information access (teaching-learning) system is already being used for business, industry, military, and professional training. Such instruction is not only feasible, it is economical and efficient, when learning is the basic criterion for judging economy and efficiency. Why, when memorization is the least important intellectual ability (because there is simply too much to remember, and because the computer remembers better than any human being can), do the schools persist in basing all judgments of student progress on the ability to memorize fragments of unrelated content that comprise the curriculum?

The present forms and uses of educational television make about as much sense as using jet airplanes to collect and transport garbage. About the only thing that educational television does is to make a teacher audible and visible in the home in about the same role as the teacher fills in a classroom. This isn't a *use* of television. It is a gross *misuse* of television. If a teacher talking at students in a classroom is the most inefficient way for students to learn (and there is an endless amount of evidence to support this dismal conclusion), what basis is there for supposing that this mode will suddenly become efficient when it is moved from one room to another electronically?

There is some evidence, from conventional testing of recall, that teacher-talk via television is retained better than teacher-talk in the classroom, but this is such small gain as to scarcely warrant the use of the hardware required.

I have thought about ways to use newer media of communication for making information available, easily and inexpensively, to anybody who wants it when they want it, and I have come up with several possibilities, one of which I will mention here.

Conventional forms of schooling violate everything that is known about how human beings learn. Basically, in schools, everyone has to be there when the school is ready, and then everyone must learn what the school teaches when it teaches it, all together, at the same time, and in the same place. This is simply not the way human beings learn anything—anything, that is, that is ostensibly taught. How can the newer media make access to information easy, economical, and unlimited? How, in other words, can we redefine the school so that it fulfills its information-imparting function without alienating its nominal audience?

Electronic information systems move information to the person who wants it, wherever he is, when, as, and if he wants it. Electronic information systems turn the whole environment into a library of information with unlimited access. What form might a future school take if these capabilities were acted on? In making the following estimate, I combined some generally known facts:

1. The best time for anybody to learn anything is when they want to know it.

2. Everybody's motives for learning—anything—are different from everybody else's, for genetic, social, emotional, and other mysterious reasons.

3. The present school system does not do what it purports to exist to do.

4. The economic base for the schools is eroding.

5. The first effort at enabling ordinary people (as contrasted to wealthy people) to select the form of schooling they feel is best occurred in 1972 via a pilot form of the voucher system advocated by Christopher Jencks.

I decided that a school based on these elements should look and function pretty much the way present neighborhood laundromats do. Laundromats are open, or can be open, twenty-four hours a day. The machines work when you put coins in them. You put coins in them when you want to wash some clothes.

The future school we are talking about would consist of a series of teaching-learning stations that would permit access to anything that anyone wanted to learn (which would or could include all of the subjects presently included in common school curricula and a good deal more), whenever they wanted to try to learn it. The schools would be scattered about local neighborhoods and would be open twenty-four hours a day. If for example, someone who wanted to learn algebra couldn't sleep at 2 A.M. on Thursday, he could go do algebra to his heart's content. Not only could everybody who wanted to learn anything try to learn it whenever they wanted to, they could redo lessons as many times as necessary, without failing any tests or being subjected to ridicule or sarcasm from teachers or other students.

How do you get the teaching-learning system to provide the desired lessons? Insert the appropriate tokens, which would be distributed pretty much along the lines laid out for the voucher system. Tokens equivalent to what it now costs to provide a year's worth of conventional schooling could be issued to each student. Why not? Arrangements could be made for adults to have access to the new schools, too. Those are just clerical details, not matters of substance. The point is that anybody could go to school to learn whatever he wanted, whenever he wanted, for as long as he wanted. Another advantage of this kind of school is that, as with most programmed instruction, the pernicious use and effects of grades will be eliminated! Everyone who finishes a course will have an A in it. That's just the way programmed instruction works.

All of the tests are an integral part of each course. Tests are used not merely for grading but for diagnosing learner difficulty. Tests help the learner to concentrate on what he doesn't know, so that he is not subjected (no pun intended) to instruction that might not have anything to do with his particular learning difficulty—as happens in any ordinary classroom.

This kind of school system eliminates the need for school buses. It never gets tired, or sick, or pregnant, it doesn't shut down for the summer, and it doesn't need cost-of-living increments or retirement benefits. It just makes instruction available as, when, where, if, and however some student wants it. Although a system such as this is decried as being inhuman by those who don't understand it, it is actually more humane to the student than a conventional classroom. And it makes individual instruction possible to a greater degree than can be achieved in any conventional school or classroom.

All it will take to redefine the school as a medium of communication is the decision to do it. We already have the technical capability. There is nothing theoretical about it. We put men on the moon because the decision was made to do it. We have the economic and technological capability to make schools into whatever we decide to make them into. Which brings us to what some regard as a philosophical question, although it is basic to any serious decision affecting schools: What purpose should the schools attempt to fulfill that is vital to the society and that will not be fulfilled in any informed or organized way otherwise? What kind of people do we want our schools to help our youth to become? What kinds of attitudes, assumptions, beliefs, values, perceptions, decisions, and behaviors do we want the schools to help them to learn that they will probably not learn otherwise? One way to answer this question is to look at the problems that youth face now and will increasingly face in the future.

The redefinition of the school into a process of education responsive to real personal and social problems creates an opportunity to fulfill a crucial function that is largely ignored in present schools because of their preoccupation with covering subject matter. The first phase of redefinition suggested above will be viewed by many as a catastrophe. This is not only predictable, it is regrettable. The feeling of distress in response to such a major change in the form of school will prevent most of those affected from seeing the opportunity presented by the relegation of the least important and most inefficient task of the schools, that of imparting content, to electronic information-handling systems. The opportunity lies in the fact that teachers will finally be free of the dominance of cognitive concerns and will be able to work with students in the affective domain. Whether they will do so depends, however, on the decisions that are made about the purposes that we want our schools to fulfill and the degree to which teachers are capable of redefining their roles.

In order to outline what I perceive to be the potential opportunity implicit in the shift of primarily cognitive concerns to electronic systems, let me mention some present and possible future problems facing youth and society in general. As you will recognize, young adults, middle-aged, and older people are at least as affected by these problems as are youth. And so I suggest that we now shift exclusively to the term *student*, which would include anyone, at any age. In the first phase of the redefinition of the schools, the laundromat school eliminates access limits as to time, place, and achievement. There is no reason why it can't eliminate age limits for students, too. Why not include all age groups as potential students?

Present schools, I must repeat, are concerned solely with academic matters. The student remains invisible as long as the school's expectations and demands based on and derived from this concern are met. Students become visible only when they fail to meet these expectations and demands. And when they become visible, they are subjected to some form of penalty intended to make them invisible. If they do not acquiesce, they are thrown out or they drop out. In either case, the school feels relieved because such students are—again—invisible to it. The usual way the school presently responds to personal and emotional (that is, affective) problems of students is with punishment.

This single mode of response, as horrifying as it is, is a product of the way in which schools presently define themselves. Their operational procedures—the rules that control student movement, both physical and intellectual, as well as student appearance—resemble no other institutions in our culture as much as prisons and mental hospitals. Even religious and military institutions are more humane today than are most schools. And this is a source of unending difficulty, expense, and waste.

If we can define a hypothetical role for schools that is different from the present one, the possibility of our illuminating the opportunity presented by shifting the cognitive burden to an electronic system may be increased. A number of possible paradoxes and platitudes are embedded in this exploration, but this seems to be inevitable in any attempt to deal with basic human problems, especially in an age of redefinition (which is what we are all trying, somehow, to live in or through).

First, we have to state the obvious fact that intellect and emotion can be separated only verbally. They cannot in fact be separated within any real human being. Plato noted that "in order for education to accomplish its purpose, reason must have an adequate emotional base." The single base on which all healthy learning is built is a feeling of adequacy, competence, and consequent confidence in the learner. Anyone who feels inadequate and incompetent in the face of whatever is to be learned and bereft of confidence in his ability to learn cannot learn because he has judged himself as incapable. Each of us carries emotional—and so intellectual—wounds of this kind. Almost everyone has said at least once, "Oh, I am no good at that." Or, "I have never been able to learn that." Or, "I have always been dumb in that." What is odd about such statements is that they are made by people of verifiable academic intelligence and learning ability. People who are "good" in English, for example, are commonly "dumb" in mathematics. Engineers, who are "good" in mathematics (or at least in manipulating a slide rule) are commonly "dumb" in English. And so on. Whole areas of "dumbness" seem to pattern out along personality and professional lines. What are we to make of this? Are we dealing with a genetic condition? Although this possibility exists, the probability is that areas in which we think of ourselves as good are those in which we have not learned to think of ourselves as being bad or dumb. Yes, there are learned beliefs. The invisible curriculum is that which profoundly affects each of us emotionally, and in the process teaches us that we are dumb in one way or another. It might have been the expression on the face of a teacher (whom we desperately wanted to please) just at the moment when we made a mistake. No words are needed to teach us that we are dumb. A change in expression, or body tone, or even just a sigh of disappointment or disapproval—even just once, at one crucial moment—will produce the most durable kind of learning. Once we are taught that we are dumb or incompetent in something, we seem unable to forget it. Such experiences are so charged with emotional meaning that they are indelibly imprinted on the top layer of our memory. We never forget such emotionally charged learnings, and we are highly resistant to unlearning them.

The schools have an opportunity for a new and unprecedented role when they no longer need to have everyone cover the same content at the same time and be tested on it with the same test at the same time. It is another curiosity of present schools that they emphasize individuality only when students take tests. If schools are to *help* students to learn, to become better learners, schools must become supportive, rewarding environments rather than disparaging, punitive ones. People who do not feel good about themselves do not feel good about anything—except, perhaps, wreaking vengence for feeling so bad. If they are to help students to become better learners, better citizens, and better human beings, the first step schools must take in the second phase of redefinition is to define their primary mission as that of helping students to feel good about themselves.

The opportunity to fulfill this role is dependent on how the role and purpose of the schools is redefined. I would begin the process of redefinition with a look at the real problems young people (and adults) face in their present daily lives, as well as those that they will face in the future. What are some of the most critical of these problems?

The most pressing is that of learning how to cope with change. Change is the dominant fact of our times, yet present schooling largely ignores it. Present schooling looks relentlessly backward—toward some bowdlerized version of the past—and pretends that the present and future do not exist. Present schools have no tolerance for reality because it is so uncongenial. In a very real sense, present schools are breeding grounds for mental illness.

All students know that the real world lies outside the school, and that school has virtually nothing to do with it. Rather than helping students to deal, for example, with the reality of change, schooling is based on the assumptions of absolutes, fixed-states, and certainties— there is only one right answer for every question in every course in every curriculum. This condemns students to a search for a single right answer to every question and problem that they ever encounter. But this is not the way it is in the real world. Change requires everyone to think in terms of probabilities rather than absolutes, in terms of processes rather than fixed-states, in terms of contingencies rather than certainties. People become mentally ill, withdrawing into a personal fantasy-reality, when they feel incapable of dealing with a complex and changing reality. They invent their own reality where they can keep their absolutes and certainties intact. And mental illness is our number one health problem as a nation. More people suffer from mental illness than from all other illnesses combined! Present schools ignore this staggering problem. Schools of the future *must* respond to it by helping students to develop the kinds of attitudes and habits of mind that will enable them to deal with a changing and uncongenial reality instead of withdrawing from it because they feel incapable of coping with it. It makes little difference how well you score on a standardized test in reading or algebra or anything else if you lack the personal resources to deal with a rapidly changing environment.

Present schools fail to develop the inner resources of students in another pernicious way, by functioning more as totalitarian states than as democratic republics. We learn what we do. Students spend twelve or more years in an autocratic environment in which all responsibility for their actions is assumed by an authority other than themselves. They are denied access to the kinds of information they need to form decisions that affect their lives as students. When, suddenly, they leave school, they are ill equipped to begin functioning as responsible individuals capable of judging which information is best and how to use it for making intelligent, independent, individual decisions as participating members of a democratic society.

Schools of the future must use the real environment, with everything that is in it, as the basic ingredient in the curriculum. And they must use it as a vehicle for helping students to learn the emotional and intellectual skills they need to become contributing citizens in an increasingly complex and constantly changing society. I would suggest that the best final examination in such an educational venture would be the behavior of students in the real world and the degree to which they leave the environment better than they find it. The ultimate objective of education in the future must be improvement of the quality of life.

If the community was the basis for the curriculum and the mission of the schools was the education of students in the emotional and intellectual skills they need to improve the quality of the community and thus to improve the quality of life in the community, we would have, finally, the kind of relevance for which students and teachers have been searching. What could be more relevant than an education designed to improve the quality of life for each student as an individual and as a member of society?

I have already stated the emotional focus of such an education: to help each student feel better about himself. But emotions and intellect are inseparable. The complementary intellectual focus would be to help students become aware of how they think—that is, of how they talk to themselves about themselves, and about the problems that must be solved in the daily process of living.

All of our behavior, after all, is a result of the decisions and choices we make. Each decision, or choice, in turn consists of an answer we come up with in response to the endless questions and problems we face in our daily lives. If we are insensitive to the way in which we ask these questions, the way in which we state them—that is, to the processes that determine the kinds of answers we can come up with—then we have no way of controlling the usefulness of the answers. This means that we have, as a result, no way of controlling our own behavior. People need psychotherapy when their behavior becomes nonfunctional. Behavior becomes nonfunctional because of the answers people come up with that comprise the decisions and choices upon which they base their behavior. It is interesting to note that psychotherapy consists of a process in which the therapist poses questions that the patient seems incapable of thinking of. Many patients resent their therapists for "not giving any answers." The purpose of the therapy is to free patients from dependence on single, fixed, right answers and to help them learn how to ask sensible questions. Indeed, the point at which therapy is no longer necessary is the point at which the patient has learned how to ask the kinds of questions the therapist has been posing all along. *Sanity* can be defined as the ability to ask the most appropriate and sensible questions in any given situation. Although students spend a great deal of time in school dealing with questions, I know of no instance in which there is any education in *how to ask questions.*

In a book titled *The Crazy Ape* (New York: The Philosophical Library, 1970, p. 17), Nobel laureate Albert Szent-Gyorgi noted:

We live in a new cosmic world which man was not made for. His survival now depends on how well and how fast he can adapt himself to it, rebuilding all his ideas, all his social and economic and political structures. His existence depends on the question of whether he can adapt himself faster than the hostile forces can destroy him. At present, he is clearly losing out.

We are forced to face this situation with our caveman's brain, a brain that has not changed much since it was formed. We face it with our outdated thinking, institutions and methods, with political leaders who have their roots in the old world and think the only way to solve these formidable problems is by trickery and double-talk.

Which is to say that the intellectual focus of education in the future must be on how to stop thinking like a caveman. This is an entirely new educational mission that has never been attempted before. The primary, and only, concern of schooling to date has been to merely add new quantities of facts and information to the student's temporary inventory—to cover more and more knowledge. Knowledge of this kind does not appear to be very durable nor to have had much effect on improving the quality of life—nor did it ever have, even before technologically produced change got out of control.

At the moment, despite all of our schooling and all of our traditional institutions (and perhaps because of them), we are, as a society, in the midst of massive emotional depression and intellectual regression. These are both fallout effects of rapid change of great magnitude. The depression stems from a general feeling of meaninglessness, as many of the truths and absolutes of the older generation are increasingly seen as lies and delusions, even by portions of the older generation. This feeling of meaninglessness produces a feeling of rage at being unable to keep the old sources of meaning from disintegrating. This rage, when it is not directed at a specific, palpable outside enemy, is directed inward and becomes a kind of self-hatred that produces the feeling of depression. Many of the young, mostly naive and romantic and largely misinformed, being strangers to the land of the older values, see those values more clearly as either bankrupt or hypocritical. The frequently invoked generation gap is wider on a cosmetic level, however, than on a substantive one. Neither the young nor the old seem able to endow life with much meaning, and both age groups resort to chemical soporifics and anodynes as a result. Again the difference is only cosmetic. The old use chemicals that are licit and legal, and the young use those that are not. In both age groups, it is virtually impossible to find anyone, businessman or rock freak, housewife or groupie, that can get through the day—or night—without popping or snorting some kind of chemical. The older, straight generation is at least as in need of a chemically induced fantasy as an alternative to a meaningless and uncongenial reality as the younger, hip generation.

And these are not even counted among the mentally ill who are most commonly treated (such is the nature of medical progress) with chemical tranquilizers or energizers, downers or uppers (as the kids say) depending upon the condition of either the patient or the doctor, or both.

Although depression is not new in the human condition, the degree and frequency of depression that we have achieved as a society is as impressive testimony to the degree of progress we have made as there is. And the need to resort to new ethics to rationalize our dependence on chemically induced euphoria is perhaps best illustrated by William F. Buckley's recent indication that the time may have arrived for the decriminalization of the personal use of marijuana.

All of this is related to an emerging educational fact that consists of the discovery (see for detailed documentation, *The School We Have* by Shephard Ginandes, M.D., Delacorte Press, 1973) that drug-using adolescents become free of dependence upon drugs in direct ratio to their *learning to feel good about themselves*. Recent studies of conventional drug education programs (conducted pretty much in the form of conventional schooling, based on exhortation and misinformation) show that such programs *increase* drug experimentation. They do, as conventional schooling does, just the opposite of what they purport to do. The use of hard drugs is, after all, an act of self-destruction deriving from self-hatred. Just as we can love others only to the degree to which we love ourselves, we can hate others only to the degree to which we hate ourselves. Only the weak need to be cruel, as Leo Rosten has said.

Education in the future must address itself to these realities. Otherwise nothing else that it does address itself to will make any difference.

The epidemic depression we are suffering as a society is accompanied by, and perhaps even engenders, a pervasive intellectual regression. The most dramatic forms it takes among the young is an affinity for metaphysical explanations—as in the ubiquitous preoccupation with astrology—and for primitive, fundamentalist forms of religion—as in the fantastic spread of fanatic Jesus freaks. These interests, far from being at odds, are complementary, in the way that fascism and communism are. Fascism and communism are commonly thought to be opposites. But, in fact, they are both totalitarian. Rather than being thought of as polar opposites, they might better be thought of as two closely adjacent points on a circle. This is what makes it so easy for a Communist to become a Fascist and vice versa.

The need to regress into primitive, fundamentalist religions seems to be enhanced by the affinity of the young for rock music.

The fallout effects of change include the emergence of a mode of anti-intellectual thought that comprises the regresssion I am describing. This has probably occurred because change has produced enormous complexity—particularly in the form of the most serious problems we face. None of our problems is simple enough to permit us, if we are rational, to blame them on a single cause and so permit us to actually do something about solving them. One has to be an expert even just to state them. Faced with multiple causality and the need for contingency-based probable solutions, and lacking any intellectual or emotional training intended to develop the abilities to deal with such circumstances, the collective psyche of many of the young—already debilitated by varying degrees of drug tripping accompanied by varying degrees of guilt—fanatically searches for a single solution to all problems, easily, and quickly. The primitive chanting of the "one way" to the accompaniment of a rhythmic jabbing of the index finger skyward, all reinforced by the combined social sanctions that accompany any sympathetic invocation of the name Jesus, must indeed produce a kind of high in the chanters not unlike that induced by rock and drugs.

So we have the paradox of a giant step backward for man being greeted by primitive thinkers as a religious reawakening! The need to find some agent—supernatural or otherwise, but preferably supernatural—to act as the ultimate authority for everything and everybody is the original atavistic cop-out. The ultimate rejection of responsibility consists of the reification of a self-invented name to which responsibility for everything is assigned. Man does indeed make gods in the opposite of his image of himself. Incapable of accepting responsibility for his own acts, he invents a deity who is responsible for everything. This is not only the most ancient and primitive form of religion, it is the most contemporary! How can this be? As Szent-Gyorgi said, we are still using a caveman's brain, in large part because education has yet to take on the job of changing it. Educators, as a group, are no less troglodytic in their thinking than are most politicians, generals, and professional religionists.

If education is to serve any survival functions in the future, it will have to address itself to the need for a major shift in the way we use our brains—in the way we think. Einstein noted, following Hiroshima, that the atomic bomb changed everything except the way we think. Most of the problems we face as a society, and, indeed, as a race, are symptomatic of the fact that we do not know how to think. It has been true, for at least the last seventy years, that most of our "solutions" to problems actually intensify them. It may be that this is too obvious to warrant any serious attention. Which permits me to refer to one of the astute observations made by Oliver Wendell Holmes.

He said, "We need education in the obvious more than investigation of the obscure." By the "obvious" is most generally meant the routine. But here is another paradox. Although the routine is commonly thought of as obvious, it is operationally invisible. Most of us are totally insensitive to what usually happens. The usual is normal, and the normal is invisible until it isn't there any more. We do not notice most of what we have come to expect until it is no longer there. Clean air and water are examples.

I am not referring here to the usual logical or critical thinking that is occasionally stated as an objective in conventional schooling. I am referring to novel meaning— making styles. How might education begin to assume the role of sensitizing us to the ways in which we think? One of the most accessible ways would be to focus attention on how we talk and on the ways in which we make meanings that lead us to act. Examining, in very pragmatic terms, the effects of what we *do* can best determine the meanings we have made.

Life, after all, consists of one problem after the other. The quality of life in general, and of each of our lives in particular, is a direct result of how well we can solve these problems—that is, how well we can ask questions and make meanings that comprise the answers to these questions. How well we talk to ourselves, in other words. Conventional schooling ignores completely the need to educate students in how to ask questions, especially about the processes involved in the making of meaning.

There are a variety of approaches to the reeducation of the ways in which think. Although they all involve alternatives to conventional syllogistic logic, referred to by a variety of names, some are more language-sensitive than others. One approach, developed by Alfred Korzybski, is more language-centered than others, and was called by him a "non-Aristotelian" method of meaning making. Another approach, which is less consciously concerned with language but uses it, inevitably, as the basic vehicle for thought, was developed by Edward DeBono, who calls it "new think" or "lateral thinking." Lateral thinking, in DeBono's approach, is an alternative to vertical thinking, which is conventional, linear, syllogistic, Aristotelian thinking. Both Korzybski's and DeBono's approaches explicate the limits of conventional thinking and suggest ways to make a range of meanings that are not accessible via "old think."

When approaches such as these are combined with an inquiry or inductive style—that is, a question-asking teaching/learning style—a viable, verifiable means of consciously affecting patterns of thought becomes available. Even in the rare instances in which inquiry teaching can be found in current, conventional schooling, the purpose of it is

to cover one form or another of ordinary subject matter more effectively, rather than to sensitize students to the dynamics of alternative mean-
ing-making processes.

Education in the future must help students become aware of
how they make meanings—of how they ask questions that shape the
ways they make inferences and the ways they make decisions and
choices. This requires a parallel study of how their emotional state
and the nature of the symbol system in which they are encoding meanings affects the meanings that they can make.

This kind of education, although not concerned with subjects
in the usual sense, can make use of conventional subjects to illustrate
the relationship between meanings that can be and are made and the
point of view from which they develop. Facts—it turns out—don't mean
a thing. They don't mean a thing, that is, apart from the way in which
the facts are perceived and the way in which they are ordered, structured, and related. It is annoying to come to know that facts require
that different meanings be made of them when their relationship to
each other is changed. What Alvin Toffler named "future shock" is
one increasingly common response to the increasing phenomenon of
changing facts and changing truths.

Much contemporary change resides in the process of shifting
relationships among facts. This shifting relationship requires shifting
the meanings made of the facts. To cite just one relatively recent example, when the relationship·between fish and Friday was changed for
Roman Catholics, many of them responded by charging that the Vati-
can had been infiltrated by Communists. Most primitive thinkers require that things stay the same. The only way they can deal with change
that affects them personally is to attribute it to the perversity of some
evil agent—like a Communist or a devil.

The pope, as a matter of fact, attributed many of the problems
afflicting contemporary Western civilization to the efforts of the devil
as recently as November of 1972. There is little prospect of human
beings solving the critical problems that beset them here and now if
they think the problems are caused by an evil agent called the devil,
over whom they have no control. God himself (Himself? Herself?) was
no match for the devil. How can any mere mortal take action in the
face of a fact such as that?

Education in the future must help students to become aware
of and to use for their own and the general welfare their own inner
resources. Students need help in looking inward to find the resources
for making meanings, decisions, choices, and judgments as a basis for
behavior, rather than for looking outward at some authority, either
benign or benevolent, to whom responsibility for human consequences

has been delegated by default. Education can move in this direction in a variety of ways, some of them less fructifying than others, depending on how rigidly mechanical they are as systems that impose (external authority again) the limits of the system on those whom it is ostensibly intended to liberate.

One of the most promising directions for education to move in, because it complements the sense of our propositions for substantive affective education, may sound rather flaky upon first hearing. The degree of flakiness you find in it may just be an index of how limited your own thinking and feelings are. In any case, I must mention it, at least, because it seems to be meeting the pragmatic criteria I have suggested as the basis for deciding whether something is worth learning. It helps its students, here and now, and in the short term, rather than at some indeterminate point in the future. What we have in mind (ready now? hold on!) is transcendental meditation and the science of creative intellect.

Does that sound flaky to you? Hold on again! Its principal advocate and teacher is Maharishi Mahesh Yogi.

Before you crumple under the weight of your own incredulity, you'd better check at least two pieces dealing with the use of Transcendental Meditation (TM) and Science of Creative Intelligence (SCI) in education. Both appeared in the December 1972 issue of the *Phi Delta Kappan*. The first, by Paul Levine, is "Transcendental Meditation and the Science of Creative Intelligence," and the second, by Francis Driscoll, is "TM as a Secondary School Subject." Levine is chief scientist of the Astrophysics Research Corporation in Los Angeles, California, and Driscoll is superintendent of schools in Eastchester, New York. Here is part of what Levine says:

> [The basic question being asked by those concerned about society today is] What should be the objectives of human activity? . . . If we adopt the common-sense position that the principal objective of *any* activity is to promote the fulfillment of the individuals engaged in and influenced by that activity, then the real goal of education is seen to encompass nothing less than the *fulfillment* of the student.
>
> In the sense we are using it here, fulfillment implies the actualization of the full potentialities for growth latent in the individual. Therefore, the measure of any educational system is first the breadth of its implicit *vision* of the range of these potentialities and second its *effectiveness* in providing every student with a practical means for achieving such full development. If a crisis is felt to exist in education, then it may logically be asked whether the fault lies in too narrow a vision of the possibilities and, in consequence, too restricted an armamentarium for achievement. . . .
>
> The concept of creative intelligence arises from an examination of the structure of purposeful change in nature. No matter where we look, new

forms and relationships are continually being created from lesser developed states. This evolution appears to be orderly, that is, governed by intelligible laws. The intelligence displayed by nature in this process may be called creative intelligence. . . . (p. 231)

Fulfillment, for example, comes to mean full expression in an individual's life of the creative intelligence inherent in his nature. Lack of fulfillment (which we may call suffering) in this view is ascribed to some restriction of the flow of creative intelligence from its source at the core of one's being to the level of conscious awareness from which one perceives and acts. A practical consequence of this approach is the intriguing possibility that human problems can be attacked at a common fundamental level—without specific regard to the nature of the problem—much in the same way that a gardener simultaneously attends to deficiencies in the development of the many separate leaves of a plant by simply watering the root. . . . (p. 232)

In a broader view of SCI, stresses are viewed as impediments to the spontaneous flow of creative intelligence from the inner being to the level of conscious awareness from which one perceives and acts. An integral component of fulfillment, therefore, becomes the progressive physiological refinement of the nervous system in the direction of a reduced accumulation of stress. Indeed, SCI associates such refinement with a "growth in consciousness" and delineates the remarkable potentialities of a fully stress-free, fully normalized nervous system. The attainment of higher states of consciousness, long thought to be incompatible with an active life, now is said to be within the reach of anyone through TM, and experimental evidence of this possibility seems to be one of the common cumulative effects of the practice.

The implications of all of this for education are quite exciting. At the most superficial level, the level of the problems, reduction of drug abuse among students and of social tension in the classroom is a likely concomitant of a widespread introduction of TM into the schools. The improved attitudes and behavior which generally are among the more immediate of TM's effects offer a chance for achieving affective goals without sacrificing performance goals. Indeed, preliminary reports of increased learning ability and reading speed with TM would seem to indicate that affective dispositions and cognitive resources grow hand in hand. Students at ease inside can be expected to respond more spontaneously and creatively to a learning environment . . . (p. 234)

At the risk of being repetitious, I must emphasize that the richest environment for learning the attitudes and abilities necessary for coping with reality lies outside the school: It is, as Alfred North Whitehead noted long ago, life itself.

Having said that, I will quote, briefly, from Driscoll's companion article:

The policy of offering TM to our students and adult citizens has continued and, so far as I can see now, will not be dropped. Our schools are open during all school vacation periods for programs of interest to the community. Consequently, it is standard practice for the Students' International Meditation Society to conduct lectures in our facilities throughout the year.

Reflecting upon our modest success, we feel that it is attributable to the great potential for student welfare that the practice of transcendental meditation offers. Another vital factor in the success of our program was the well thought out, comprehensive community and parent information program carried out in the autumn and early winter of 1971 before we introduced TM to the student population.

Finally, we believe that transcendental meditation has been of direct and positive help to students in our secondary school who have begun to meditate. Students, parents, and teachers report similar findings. Scholastic grades improve, relationships with family, teachers, and peers are better, and, very significantly drug abuse disappears or does not begin. (p. 237)

Although it is not my intention to appear critical of Mr. Driscoll (far from it, I admire the administrative skill and the educational vision that he demonstrated in making TM accessible to the students, and I am grateful for the opportunity to use his leadership as an illustration of the point I am making), I must say that it is a tribute to the potentcy of TM that it produced such immediate and apparent results even when classified as a secondary school subject.

It just seems to me that using TM for the purpose of raising levels of achievement in a conventional school setting is like using a sledgehammer to drive a thumbtack. Its power to achieve the purposes of affective education that I have suggested seems much too great to be confined to such small purpose. The value of TM as a means of effectively dealing with such critical problems as drug experimentation and dependency cannot be overstated. Its implicit value in dealing with other critical problems—such as anachronistic attitudes between and among human groups manifested in violence consequent to racial, or religious, or political definitions that emphasize primitive tribal differences rather than the commonality of human aspiration and feeling—remains to be realized.

My awareness of the abstract nature of my attempt to suggest possible futures for education must be mentioned, if only in passing. Any attempt to be more specific than the reference to the Levine and Driscoll articles seemed to be impossible in a brief treatment. All I have tried to suggest here is that the future might include a two-phase opportunity for redefining the role of schools in our society in an attempt to reduce the size of the gap between education and reality.

The first phase would redefine schools to permit utilization of electronic information/teaching systems in order to eliminate limits upon access to whatever portions of the cognitive domain students need or wish to get at.

The second phase would turn the "catastrophe" of putting present schools and teachers out of the business (of covering content) into an opportunity, by redefining their role. Schools would be primarily concerned with the affective domain, for the purpose of helping students to feel better about themselves as the basic stage in the process of becoming confident, competent, growing, learning, contributing human beings.

This role, the pious rhetoric of present schools notwithstanding, is incompatible with that of covering content and the accompanying rituals that constrain and standardize content, testing, grading, and student movement—physically, emotionally, intellectually, and cosmetically.

The second phase of redefinition will probably require the accomplishment of a good part of the first. Let us hope that the economic resources cannot be found to permit us to defer or avoid the first phase of redefinition. We cannot afford to find the money to do that. The ultimate price, our survival as a society in which the quality of life is such that we all value and enjoy it, is one we cannot pay.

Fred T. Wilhelms

Fred T. Wilhelms

In 1973 Dr. Wilhelms retired from the position of executive secretary of the Association for Supervision and Curriculum Development, an organization that grew significantly both in size and in scope during his tenure with it. Prior to his ASCD work, he was a professor and chairman of the Division of Education and Psychology at San Francisco State College and, for five years, headed an experimental study of teacher education for the National Institute of Mental Health.

tomorrow's assignment

I believe that the keynote of tomorrow's education will be the higher potentiation of the individual human being. I believe this for two reasons. First, in these turbulent times, the press upon the individual personality and character has grown so painfully distortive that action is imperative. Second, we are newly equipped with insights and resources to make the action possible. In fact, our new equipment is so good that we need not settle for a mere salvage or maintenance operation; we can plan toward the general release and development of personal human powers at a level never before considered possible.

THE ACIDS OF OUR TIMES

I do not wish this next to sound pessimistic (although it probably will). My basic assumption is most optimistic: that we stand at the opening of a great renaissance, from which persons and cultures may finally emerge at a level transcending anything that has gone before. But births are usually painful, and so are rebirths. A renaissance, like any revolution, is not achieved without enormous, shattering impacts upon all the established order. Tornadoes of turbulence are inevitable, and doubt and fear and groping replace any sure sense of direction. In our case the timing is such that our youth are the most involved of all.

If we had cared to look, it should hardly have been unforeseeable that profound conflict and change within human beings would have to appear at about this point in time. For many causative factors have been at work. This is not the place for detailed analysis of all of them. But a few stand out so starkly that we cannot turn our eyes away from them.

One is our great technology: It has brought us health and wealth and convenience unprecedented. Yet it has also altered the whole nature and conception of productive work so profoundly that one of the great foundations of human life (approximated by the term *work ethic*) is being seriously eroded. Its ever accelerating growth has exploited resources so that, as the scholarly Committee of Rome has put it, "All growth projections end in collapse," and a report in Britain's *Ecologist* sees unrestricted expansion leading to the "breakdown of society and the life support systems of this planet—possibly by the end of this century and certainly within the lifetime of our children." It is killing the earth in multiple ways, subtle and gross, for which the old smokestack-oriented word *pollution* is wholly inadequate. And it has produced the nuclear bomb and all the lesser bombs of Vietnam.

Another element is the population explosion: Already it has nearly filled the world with people, and in many lands the probable future is so gruesome that few are brave enough to look at it. Along the way it has produced mass societies and mass institutions that can crush individuality and threaten personal meaning.

It was never to be dreamed that the acids of such change would not etch their marks upon the inwardness of the human spirit—and they have. A new way of life is in the making. It is all too tempting to visualize it in terms of further technological embellishments, but very little of it will be that. To be sure, the great survival problems must be solved, with the help of technology, and radical adjustments must be made to resource scarcity and world contamination. Yet the essential newness will lie within. For the way of life we have known was based upon sets of beliefs, values, customs, relationships, and ways of seeing things—the entirety of what Charles Reich calls a "consciousness." And it is right there that the birth pains of a renaissance hurt.

It is hard to see clearly from the center of a whirlwind, or to get a true sense of direction with things flying every which way. But already, among many of our younger people especially, one can see significant symptoms.

Revulsion against the subhuman repetitiousness of factory labor.

Determination to stay out of the rat race of single-minded careerism.

Widespread anomie; feelings of being lost in a vast, impersonal machine hostile to personal identity.

Revulsion against materialism; austerity as to "things," especially showy status stuff.

Criticism of virtually all institutions, even of institutionalism itself.

Rejection of future orientation in favor of living now.

Rage against all forms of injustice and oppression, including racism but also class discrimination and the cruelties of war.

New emphasis on the affective side of life, with tendencies to reject the more coolly cognitive.

Search for new ways of relating, person to person, group to group.

Emphasis on personal authenticity, coupled with a struggle to break through to a new openness of communication.

Hunger for love, with visions of an all-loving world.

Search among religions and philosophies for a dimly envisioned better way of life; a kind of desperate groping for answers, accompanied by much faddistic scurrying from one solution to another.

Enormous dedication to preserving and restoring the environment.

Search for a new politics, representing probably a determination to take charge and build a new society in which persons will be paramount.

One could go on and on. It is a mixed bag; it ranges from a passive dropping out to a forceful activism; from something close to sheer panic to a driving vision. Taken all in all, it is the natural response in a time of crumblings and uncertainties moving slowly (we hope) toward new formulations.

For those in education, the salient point is that we are in a time of severe pressures on the young people we teach. Their generation is little blessed with old certainties, little privileged to grow up naturally into an accepted order of things. It faces *within its lifetime* the simultaneous climaxing of problems so devastating that survival is the question.

It scarcely matters, then, whether we see youth's response as a great quest for a new morality or as a mere loss of morals. The educational question in either case is: What can we do to help? For we cannot sit forever on the sidelines, to cheer or to whimper. We must move in.

I regret that this approach to the theme of higher human potentiation—by way of the dire factors that make it imperative to build for inner qualities that can stand the acids of our time—may give the whole enterprise a gloomy cast. I could have come in by way of an entirely different—and solidly optimistic—argument: that *we ought to do it because we can.*

We have the resources. We have resources such as no educators before us ever had. And we have insights they never had. If we do not yet possess a full-blown know-how, we have enough to start on, and we can work through to the rest. Development of this side of the equation will be worked out through the rest of the chapter.

CURRICULUM FOR HUMAN POTENTIATION

Simply by virtue of being human, a young human being represents enormous potentialities. The gathering evidence, much of it rather recent, indicates that in all dimensions the potentials are far beyond anything envisioned in the conventional wisdom. (The evidence is not all so new. The American experiment in democracy, for example, has surely given the lie to Old World assumptions of limitations inherent in ordinary people. And brief flashes from history—from Periclean Athens, for instance, or Renaissance Florence—illuminate the way people bloom when the climate is healthy.) To turn such potentials into realities is the function of the whole society as well as of the whole school.

In school terms, the task cannot be delegated to any one body of instruction. Anything approaching full actualization can come only out of the total instructional program plus an overall healthful climate.

A Climate for Growth

The first essential nutrient of human growth is the unconditional high regard of those who are important to the individual. Without love in his home, a child can hardly develop that basic trust which is the cornerstone of a healthy personality. Without a warm, sunny climate of affection, respect, and acceptance at school, there is bound to be some shriveling. (I have deliberately changed words as between home and school. I consider it ill-advised for schools to take on the obligation of loving every child—unless the word means something very different from the feeling of a parent; I think it produces little but guilt feelings in good teachers who know that they cannot literally love every child in their classes. The more modest objectives will be hard enough to achieve, especially because they apply as much to the feed-back a child receives from his peers as to that which he receives from his teachers.) The criterion of warmth and personal support is absolutely the first criterion of a climate for growth.

But it is not the only criterion. To the soft climate implied by affection must be added brisk and rugged elements of challenge. I assume that we wish to participate in the growth of persons with a certain boldness and inner toughness of fiber; persons with the nerve to stand on their own feet, take risks, and weather through failures. One of the salient ailments of adults in our society, as well as of children, is a sense of powerlessness, of inability to take charge of their own life space. I cannot conceive of a person learning a sense of autonomy and power and command in an environment that is wholly protective.

Therefore, the climate of the school must provide a constantly growing freedom and self-responsibility, accompanied by constantly growing challenge against hurdles that are generally possible but not necessarily easy. It must provide encouragement for bold risk-taking. If the challenges are accepted and the risks are taken, there will be many failures; with respect to these the school must provide the sure security that it is all right to have failures, that they will not entail any loss of positive regard. But this should be rather matter-of-fact, without excessive mollycoddling. The business of personal autonomy can be tough and rugged, and it needs to be learned that way. A child's basic experience should be a pattern of success experiences, against growing challenge and responsibility. But this is meaningless if success is always guaranteed and failure is always smothered in sweetness. A youngster needs rich opportunities to explore freely, to find himself and define his edges, to prove what he is and what he can do.

We have a very long way to go, to achieve anything even approaching a genuine participatory democracy in schools. Over many generations, school people have come to see minute directiveness and control as the norm. The advances we have made have mostly been in the direction of softening things—doing the directing more kindly.

The ideal of autonomy, with its corollaries of risk and roughness, only frightens most schoolmen into hiding behind a convenient fiction of student immaturity. But the bottleneck is not in the students.

I could go on at length with a recipe for a climate for individuality. That is not my purpose here. I only want to point out that there are some essentials that must pervade a school's whole atmosphere, or all the other gains will be in some degree cancelled out. And let me emphasize that these are essential *in the classroom*—in all formal instruction—as well as in the informal aspects of school life. (I add this because discussions of school climate often seem to lay the whole load on school activities, student government, and the guidance program.) An occasional hour of autonomy in the student council will not offset daily tyranny in men's physical education. If we mean to build for personal power with sensitivity, ruggedness with gentleness, bold action with ethical reflectiveness, the load is on the entire school.

Now, having said all this, I hope I may be permitted to concentrate wholly upon the human-growth-assistance which will have to be built right into the instructional program itself. My thesis will be that we can and must *choose and use subject matter to help each youngster toward his optimal self-actualization.*

I am not going to attempt a catalogue of all the opportunities to do this in all the subject fields, though all must be involved and it would not be hard to lay out some assignments. Physical education, for example, holds enormous opportunities to help a young person come to terms with one aspect of himself and to set standards for himself. The sciences hold a nearly unparalleled capacity to help a youngster learn to venture intellectually, to free his mind for untrammeled inquiry, and to live with the uncertainties and ambiguities that inevitably result from such daring. One could go on with examples from every worthwhile field. But I have arbitrarily chosen to probe only a few areas of educational endeavor to illustrate their potentials.

Finally, I remind the reader that my search here is exclusively for means of reaching toward full human potentiation. If this seems a cavalier attitude toward the systematic organization of knowledge and skill, I can only reply that there are already more than enough educators working that side of the street.

Early Childhood and the School

The period from about three to about age six offers unique opportunities. I advocate massive investment in this area, and I suspect that a major thrust is about to develop. I do not say this as it might be said by some neurotically anxious parent who wants his child to make impressive leaps right away—or by one of those excellence-hypnotized academicians of the early sixties who thought everybody ought to be pushed into learning faster what he was going to learn anyway in a year or two. In fact my fear (and it is a serious one) about the schools' institutionalizing programs for small children is that they will hurry into academic stuff. My own priorities for the use of this magnificent opportunity will probably seem odd to many people.

1. We can use this period to give all children a good *physical* start. Complete dental care will be essential. Full medical diagnosis and follow-up will be built-in. The various preventive programs appropriate to the age group will be set in motion. (Some of this needs to be started earlier, and, for the poor, at least, the schools may well become the administrative center for that, too.) Basic nutrition can be attended to, with the schools providing some part of it, but also with a strong, cooperative program of parent education. It is simply nonsense, in a society as rich as ours, for any children to start on the road to malnutrition, bad teeth, and preventable sickliness—and that nonsense will not be tolerated much longer.

Beyond this, at this impressionable age better than at any later time, the schools can teach sound health practices to the point of habituation. Furthermore, they can develop a curriculum of vigorous and creative physical activities that will bring children along toward sturdiness, and also toward better coordination and use of their bodies. This is no small thing. Full human potentiation has need for a sound physical base—and for the confidence and self-esteem that go with it.

2. We can tone up the senses. Human beings need to learn to notice what is relevant and significant. One of the great inhibitors of full human potentiation is what I have learned to identify (largely through introspection into my own shortcomings) as the *slob reaction*. It is a flaccidness of sensory response coupled with a slovenly lack of alertness. It is part of what enables us to drift vaguely through the innumerable woods of life, scarcely knowing or caring whether we are among oak or beech.

There is evidence that in every sensory modality children can learn a new acuity, a fresh liveliness. It is almost as if they could be given sensory booster shots: to hear more discerningly, to see more precisely and more vividly, to taste and to smell with greater discrimination, to use the sense of touch with heightened awareness. Along with basic acuity can come a cultivated ability to make finer and finer discriminations: "This stone is smoother," "That green has more yellow in it." Along with this, too, can come a developing ability to group things by their similarities and differences, which the late Hilda Taba thought to be so basic to clear thinking.

But perhaps that is intellectualizing too much, at this stage. What I have in mind is illustrated better by a laboratory-school primary group I once met wandering about the campus. I asked a little girl what they were doing. "We're smelling spring," she said, beaming. I had no doubt whatever that some of those apartment-bred youngsters opened up a new sensory awareness that day. And, in a more general way, I believe that zestful "playing with" impressions, images, sights, sounds, smells, and the endlessly varying feels of things—and talking about it, putting names to it—can create a sensitive openness to stimulation that is almost like an increment to intelligence.

Undoubtedly all this will have to be handled differently for different children. Some come from a rather bleak world and need enrichment; some from an environment so tortured with a mishmash of disorganized noise that they have to learn to hear one pure tone.

3. We can learn to build vocabulary and put together language. There are a great many children who need to be talked with and talked with and talked with—while they have fresh experiences of rich variety and tie physical action to verbalism. They need to know the names of things. They need to practice putting ideas together coherently. A little simple logic can be built in: "If I do this, then that will happen." Fluency is a primary objective, without too much stress on correctness. But a nascent precision is also important. Without derogation of the various nonstandard dialects—which deserve more respect than they have been given—there is still great need for language which will hold a fine edge, both in school and in our technical economic society. The early years of childhood are apparently unique in their capacity for language growth.

4. We can invigorate the brain. Perhaps we have already described this, in the sections above. Certainly we can raise the IQ, in the sense that IQ stands for ability to do school work. But, after long and reasonably searching study of the evidence, I conclude that more than this is at stake. From abundant animal experimentation, we know that a richer environment leads, for example, to a heavier cortex as well as to demonstrably better problem-solving ability. We know that barren environments lead to atrophy. Not all such experiments can be replicated with human beings. But I have a hunch that if they could be, the differential effects in people would be found to be far greater than those in animals—simply because the human brain is more flexible and its potential growth greater. I am personally certain that the attempt to exploit this possibility deserves an enormous investment.

To be sure, this is not wholly a matter for early childhood education. Few things seem sillier to me than to say that a child's intelligence is already almost fully formed before he has even entered Piaget's stage of formal operations. Adolescence opens up whole new horizons and modes of thought; and, if intelligence can be created, it can be created at age thirteen as well as at age three. Nevertheless, early childhood education does have the one unique advantage of bringing the child to his formal academic schooling able to handle it.

Career Education

One terrible blight stunts human growth more often than anything else I know: call it *inadequate expectation*. It strikes especially the poor, but not only the poor; it is deadliest among the depressed minority groups, but not confined to them. It is a withering thing, sapping vitality and energy, and leaving only apathy and hopelessness.

The problem lies in the image of what life can be. That is growing all through childhood; for many it is a happy, contented thing, rather heedless, with few questions asked; but in all too many it is drab and grim, with little to spark a new hope and determination. Then comes adolescence, with its sudden eye-opening; newly self-conscious, the youngster looks around him and looks ahead. What he succeeds in seeing will make all the difference.

A few are lucky. They are challenged by exciting visions of what they can be and do. Even *their* knowledge of possible alternatives may be grossly limited, but they have enough to release their energy for the rugged climb. Many others have only lackluster notions of a future; not necessarily unhappy, they just plug along with no real drive. But there are many others who are simply turned off. They see nothing out there worth trying for; they may know vaguely of superior opportunities, but they identify them with other people—hopelessly beyond their reach. And then they turn off in their schoolwork—and in their private lives as well—and their situation really does become hopeless.

This, I think, is the nub of the problem for career education. It is not essentially a problem of vocational training; a good program of that will be very useful to many; but, at bottom, the difference between the winners and the losers does not lie on that axis. It is much more an inward thing.

What can the schools do? The problem is not an easy one. The prospects of life *are* harsher for the children of the poor, and especially for the minority-group poor. They need the greatest energy and vision to break out, and they have been the most drained. And yet I am confident that the schools can make a great difference.

The Consumer Side

Consumer education must be the cornerstone of any real program of career education. It is commonly identified with competence in buymanship and money management, but its reach goes far beyond. However, such competence is not to be sneered at. Low-income families have the smallest margin for errors, and yet they are often the least thoughtful in their use of money. They are the group most consistently victimized by all sorts of gyps and frauds and outrageous credit terms. It is notorious that even for the ordinary staples of life—their groceries and meat, for instance—they are charged the highest prices and get the lowest quality. In the somewhat longer-range matters of using insurance wisely and husbanding their savings, they tend to be weak indeed.

This does not mean that they are the only ones who need competence in buying and managing. Any family can increase its real income by a fourth or more by using its resources well. And every school ought to have a planned K-12 program of consumer education that reaches all its students, with a thoroughly practical, hardheaded message.

But, in terms of the sober problem described a little earlier, I am interested especially in some other potentials of consumer education. My ultimate concern is with the *quality of the youngster's wanting*. It is perfectly easy, starting over and over again with immediate, earthy matters of shopping and buying, to slide over into the larger questions of what is worth buying in the first place. All but the most pampered children know that choices must be made; that money is hard to come by, and there is rarely enough to go around. They quickly see the point that the way one uses his money is a projection of the kind of life he means to live.

Then it is easy to start looking at alternatives. To begin with, young people generally assume whatever expenditure pattern they are used to as "given." They know little of any other life style. But full and free interaction and artistic teaching using many media can soon wedge open their narrow view of what is possible. This need not and should not lead to any Hollywood version of plush living; it should be thoroughly realistic. But some grace notes are possible at almost any income level. And, frankly, I choose to use consumer education to raise the level of aspiration—the youngster's mental standard of living—even if not every detail is immediately achievable.

Put it another way: I want each youngster to feel good about the possibilities inherent in his life. I even want him a bit excited about them. It is good if his mental standards have such pull for him that working toward them will be a pleasure. I do not mean this on a merely hedonistic basis, to be wholly represented by the acquisition of more things. What is needed is a thoughtful assessment of life values. With a few highly intelligent students this can be approached in terms of abstract ideas. But with the great majority of students it can be got at far more powerfully through consideration of the real and ordinary choices people make.

Nothing sucks the spirit and vigor out of a man or woman as badly as a feeling that life is inevitably dull and limited. In our opportunity-rich society, it is not necessary for schools to let this blight affect the young. The school does not need to promise them a rose garden. It need not—and cannot—disguise the fact that high effort will be needed. But neither does it need to act as if effort is futile.

The Producer Side

A nearly absolute requisite of the fulfilled life is the ability and inclination—and opportunity—to do well some kind of productive work. Knowing this, we have sought to provide vocational preparation. By and large, the junior colleges and colleges do pretty well at this, and the graduate schools are almost wholly vocational. But when we come back to the public schools, we find a pretty pinched-out version of vocational training. The comprehensive high school traditionally offers training in a narrow band of middle-middle jobs for middle-middle students, typified by auto mechanics for the boys and secretarial training for the girls. This much goes on fairly successfully. But rarely does a high school energize its less-than-collegiate students toward the burgeoning subprofessional, technical lines. Even more rarely does it provide the "low group" with anything much more than condemnation to the horrible general curriculum. A sweeping overhaul and expansion of vocational preparation is long overdue.

And yet the real problem lies deeper. To repeat: The difference between the winners and the losers seldom lies in the dosage of vocational education they have had. The real problem lies in the young men and women who simply see no challenging place for themselves in the world of production. Again, this blight infects most often and most deeply the children of the poor, and worst of all the depressed minority groups who have been shut out from the better jobs so long that they see no hope.

We need a vast program, starting low in the grades and intensified in the junior high school, to advertise the real opportunities that exist. Most children—especially those from meager homes—know little about the possibilities available to them. What little they do know of the better opportunities they tend to identify with other people—with some special group superior to themselves or born with silver spoons in their mouths. They know, from their parents and friends, only a handful of occupations, none with much pull.

Given the media we have at our command, it should not be hard to institute a massive "wake-up service." We could help every youngster get acquainted with what is out there for him, what it will require of him, and how to get to it. At the same time we could help every young person see what he has to offer. It is usually *enough*. Schools, with their academic pretensions, tend to make all but the few who suit them feel cheap and lacking. Some teachers and some schools almost forbid many youngsters to aspire. But, after all, it does not require any great genius to be a happily successful carpenter or electrician—or even an authentically good teacher or dentist. Far more of our children have such potential than most schools—strangely—are willing to admit. Virtually all have the capacity to do some worthwhile, respected work, and do it well.

We need ways of helping young people see this, of helping them dare to aspire. Undoubtedly, if we succeed, we shall create some frustration as some young men and women set themselves higher goals than their developed abilities will attain. But far more lives are blighted by needless hopelessness and low ambition than by reaching too high. Schools and teachers need to develop the nerve to look a tough world in the eye—and then infect their students with it. Self-fulfillment does not lie in drifting down the handiest path of least resistance.

Effective Politicization

Our society and the whole world are in crisis. We face multiple problems with such potential for catastrophe that continuance in anything like the present mode is in question. Along with its many benefits, our technology has generated a congeries of problems that have to be solved—and quickly—or we will be on the rocks. Yet they are problems which defy solution by anything less than intelligent, concerted, and Herculean effort, if indeed they can be solved at all: pollution, resource depletion, population explosion, urban decay, internecine hostility, the possibility of nuclear annihilation. Even if these problems are solved, the postsolution society will be deeply different from the one we have.

It is intolerable that in the face of such disaster our social studies should continue to drone on through their academic trivia (and that our sciences should concentrate on remaining "pure"). To me it is as plain as the nose on my face that we must demand a social studies designed *to go straight to the major survival problems of our day and to equip each youth to help solve them and raise our society to a new level.* That curriculum reform has to be one of the imperatives of tomorrow's education.

But let us turn this problem around and look at it from the standpoint of the individual student, with a view to his full personal potentiation. Right now he is likely to be disillusioned about our established institutions, almost to the point of cynicism. He does not believe that, operating as they do operate, they can solve the problems that have to be solved. He sees them as massive and impersonal, callous and indifferent, phony and self-serving. He does not believe that the individual has a chance against institutions.

Perhaps that last is the nub of it, the root of the *grand malaise* of our youthful subculture. The individual feels helpless. He sees things going to pot, and he despairs of being unable to do anything about it. Well, if that *is* the root problem, then the answer is to somehow restore his sense of mastery, to help him know that even if he is only one of millions, he can make his personal force felt. How can we do that? Not easily, for the establishment has many of the qualities of a glacier—and wistful fakery will be worse than nothing. But there are three things we can do.

First, we can help young people learn to sense and identify contemporary problems and opportunities quickly and with some precision, to analyze their elements, costs, and effects, and to search out their most promising solutions. The element of awareness is tremendously important. Many of the worst problems of our time could have been headed off rather easily and at little cost if the mass of people had become concerned about them as soon as the more sensitive observers did. The typical lag has been enormously costly and tragic, and with the present speed of events it is simply unsupportable.

Here is a nice problem in curriculum. How could people have been brought to see, in advance, that letting public transportation systems decay while we chased our own tails trying to provide enough highways and parking and fuel for mass automobilism would inevitably be self-defeating? Can young people be sensitized to see the problems no larger than a man's hand today that are going to be tomorrow's whirlwind? It might be worth trying. It has certainly never been tried on any large scale so far.

The studied analysis of insistent problems, with their causes, effects, and the opportunities embodied in their solutions, is even more immediately important. Here the developed techniques of the schools are in better shape; we are already pretty good at analyzing the fall of Rome. Two changes are in order. First, we must steel ourselves to devote large blocks of time. The average educator may be stunned by the idea of months of concentrated work on pollution or a year (in the right setting) on the problems of the city, even though he cheerfully invests years in teaching a foreign language to students who will patently never use it. That attitude will have to give way. Second, the study of contemporary affairs must be a much gutsier, more realistic thing than the namby-pamby, superficial stuff that usually passes for "Problems of Democracy."

There will have to blunt, hard-nosed consideration of vested interests (including one's own). Proposals will have to be costed out on a cost-effectiveness basis. Public inertia will have to be estimated, and ways of getting leverage on it calculated. So far as possible, there must be direct local involvement, firsthand study, and public advocacy. This strongly suggests concentrating most on the problems nearest home, with more of a general-intelligence approach to problems that center elsewhere. I doubt that schoolteachers, generally tender-minded, can generate the essential toughness of treatment unless they learn to involve many other persons as participants and instructors. For an honest facing up to problems and proposals will often get pretty hairy.

The second great thing we can do is to help each youngster hammer out for himself a system of social values: what he wants his society to be like; what his priorities are; what he is willing to sacrifice for the sake of what. This is not separate from the work I have just described, but it adds important dimensions.

For one thing, to talk of realism and tough-mindedness suggests a grim salvage job. That is needed all too often, but needed also is a shining vision of what is possible. Riddled as it is with problems, our modern society also has unprecedented opportunities—and possibilities beyond our immediate seeing. Idealistic adolescents have a terrible need for vision. And, in a way hard to describe, that vision itself can be put into reasonably specific form.

To this must be added *commitment*. If we are on the verge of sinking into the slough, it is going to take sweaty work to pull us out. Even if we are at the edge of a new Periclean age—and we may be—it is going to take work to get all that marble up on the acropolis. Fortunately young people, properly taught, will revel in this rather than be dismayed. They are not middle-aged and tired. A promise of nothing but blood and sweat and toil and tears will not put them off if they believe in the cause. But nice-Nelly schools have a long way to go to learn to generate—or even to handle—the fierce commitment of which youth is capable.

The third job the schools can do is the big one: to teach youth how to make their force felt; how to get results. Here we break mostly new ground—and the sod is tough. A few students have learned in, say, the student council, some mild lessons about the processes by which things get done in a genuinely democratic way. A few budding journalists have learned to affect public opinion. But, by and large, the social studies pass by on the other side.

Out on the street, in recent years, a good many young people have experimented with the direct application of pressure and force, sometimes illegally and violently. Here and there they made quick gains; but if they won some battles, they lost some campaigns, and most of them are now convinced they must work within the system. I am sure we do not wish to take their work as complete models—or leave the job to the street corner in any case. But they have shown us what energy is available. Can we help them to use it productively?

I believe we need a direct, functional study of how opinion is formed and action is generated. It deserves far more attention than the study of structures, which is the essence of typical civics. Probably it can be learned to some extent in a theoretical way, but that will have to be hitched constantly to participation in action; action within the school, but also out in the community. Social science can no more be learned without a laboratory than physical science can. The opportunities for functional practice are abundant enough, if we search for them.

But I think we shall also have to break out of the framework of the social studies to a more personal development. Young people can and should be taught the flexible, ingenious use of democratic group process. (In this context I mean *small* group process.) They can be taught the techniques, from buzz sessions to sociodrama and role-playing to other approaches. They can learn to hear one another, to share ideas, to disagree effectively, and then to build upon disagreement without mere weak compromise. In short, they can learn the ways of effective decision making.

A little deeper than this, they can also learn to feel and understand the dynamics of a group. They can become sensitized to the forces and motives that are operating. They can learn to support individuals and produce greater individual strength even as they develop group effectiveness. This is essential; group processes which sacrifice individualism are in the long run self-defeating and damaging manipulation.

Finally, each young person can be helped to understand himself better—what his own hidden motivations are, how he affects others, and so on. I am not entirely enchanted by all that I hear or read about the many varieties of sensitivity training. Yet I am convinced that there is something there—something fundamentally important. In school, because of the long time we have, it need not have any of the form of the often brutal weekend marathon or the two-week T-group. It could be long, slow, gentle, nonintrusive, and free of prying and overexposure. In fact, it could go on most successfully in a friendly, naturally supportive atmosphere where honesty and self-revelation are easy and natural.

No doubt it will strike many readers as odd that I should conceptualize major ingredients of effective politicization in such personal terms. But, as I see it, a paramount objective is to replace the young citizen's feeling of ineffectual helplessness with the earned confidence that he can make himself count. I do not think we will achieve that by urging him to write to his congressman at the end of every chapter. I believe we can do it if we get him into the act and then teach him how to act with effect, on the basis of sound examination of the facts and ideas and values, with due consideration of all the choices before us.

The Examined Life

The ultimate purpose of education—and perhaps of all life—is the fulfilled person. In these days when many of our finest youth are living lives of not-very-quiet desperation, that goal needs a fresh translation into education.

Just how much the schools can achieve, against the headwinds of a sleazy society, is impossible to know. At least it would be good to have the nerve to try. Schools have generally settled for providing instrumental knowledge and skill (little of which generally turned out to have real instrumental value). In the older tradition schools did concern themselves with character, as described by the copybook maxims regarding honor, honesty, and so on—epitomized by the scouts' oath. Those virtues are not to be sneered at, and I suspect that the teaching had considerable effect.

But I think we are ready now for a more sophisticated approach to personality structure and formation. The great modern psychologists and philosophers have built almost a new model of humanity—and, oddly enough, enabled us to read the older intuitive geniuses with new comprehension. (At least for me, the Biblical emphasis on inner peace means more after I read Carl Rogers; Socrates' "Know thyself" took new meaning from Lawrence Kubie.)

The problem of definition of goals remains exceptionally difficult. If we were able to generate within young people whatever characteristics we wanted to, what would they be? If I simply free-associate, I come up with a more-or-less random listing like this:

Magnanimity ("size")

Self-insight (with self-acceptance)

Freedom to frolic; playfulness and joy

Being in touch with one's inner impulse life; trusting it; honoring it

Self-trust, the feeling of being "enough"

Authenticity; to be oneself under all circumstances

Affectionateness; a generalized ability to love and be loved

Sensitivity: to others, to beauty

Commitment: to live by one's own standards, and do something about them; to be given to something bigger than oneself

Toughness of fiber; not to collapse when the going gets rough

Ability to stand—even enjoy—uncertainty and ambiguity

Freedom of mind and spirit; to explore, with nerve

Openness in communication; a real love of unblocked openness

Life-seekingness ("It takes life to love life")

Gentleness in strength; compassion

Peace; inside

High values; worked out personally and deliberately lived by

Reverence for life

Identification with the human condition; a sense of tragedy

I do not offer this as any scholarly compendium. (I really did free-associate it just now.) I expose it simply to show that what some of us now assume to be seminal and fundamental in a human being is miles apart from a similar list anyone would have been likely to jot down a generation or two ago. Without defending the particular items, I believe that today's insights are far superior—and that it is time to be using them in school.

I believe it is time for the school to be setting aside major blocks of time and effort, under no subject-matter rubric, *for the deliberate purpose of helping each young person as much as we can in his personal becoming.* I predict that the movement toward a unified humanities program, which has been springing up spontaneously in hundreds of centers out of the intuitions of good teachers close to young people, will become the most important curriculum development of our time.

It really cannot be otherwise. Our young people are in distress. Old values are shifting under their feet. They have little of certainty to go by. Everything is up for private decision—far more than any young person can stand. They are groping and experimenting—and risking far too much of themselves. They need our help.

And we have the resources to help them. Even though we must fight to stay free of being subject-matter-bound, we can guess ahead to the great wells of resources we can tap.

On the intuitive side
Literature
Art and architecture
Music
The high religions

From all times and places, including emphatically the present; the great treasure house of man's aspirations and struggles, his conflicts and his dreams, his insights into life and purpose.

On the scholarly side
History
Psychology
Philosophy
Cultural anthropology

The great modern disciplines in the study of man.

On the experiential side
Whatever seminal contacts with the real world we can devise to engender growth as persons.

Given our long imprisonment in subject-matter standards, it will be very hard not to use these simply to "teach more about" literature or psychology or anthropology. We will have to shovel away a vast midden heap of habits of teaching the great works and all that, before we get to the base ground of inquiring first into young people's needs and then searching for whatever speaks authentically to those needs—authentically in the youngster's own response.

It could be done. Just barely, maybe; and, to begin with, only by a few teachers with special gifts. Certainly it would be the greatest test of our professional sophistication of anything we have ever attempted. But it has a great deal going for it: The young people themselves are anxious as never before to dig into the great questions of life and purpose and personal significance. Their parents are so worried that they would welcome a direct approach to value formation and the setting of goals. And an increasing number of young teachers, themselves the product of the modern turmoil, have an intuitive affinity for such work.

We could open up a situation in which concerned young people could go directly at the big questions. We could make the school environment so supportive and warm that complete honesty would be possible. We could work toward genuine communication, using it and teaching it at the same time. We could develop a laboratory of humane sensitivity. We could supply background resources from many areas, finding what fits each youth. We could develop a mode of teaching—a virtually brand new mode—which would give full play to the affective side and permit untrammeled thought and discussion.

If we swing it, I have no doubt that we could produce young men and women of unprecedented inner strength, people at home with themselves, sure of their own significance, and growingly committed to their own developed personal purposes. Healthy, self-actualizing people such as have been rare in the history of this earth.

EIPLOGUE

I suppose this will turn out to be a maverick among the chapters of this book. Certainly I have not discussed the whole "future of education." I have restricted myself to the curriculum, and even in that area, only opened a small window here and there. Among the blind men groping about the elephant, I may have been the one who found only the tail!

But I have written out of a profound conviction that the greatest weakness of the school is a curriculum accumulated out of generations of looking only at criteria of content. The only true criteria are criteria of purpose. Two purposes seem to me to stand out as so imperative in our crisis that I am willing to sacrifice to them whatever must be sacrificed of cherished academic embellishments:

> To go straight to the great social problems of our day, and equip each young person to help solve them and take our society to a new ground.
>
> To go straight to the full potentiation of each young person, helping him as much as we can in his own personal becoming.

All the rest is ancillary.